## Additional praise for *The Analytics Revolution:*

"I have known Bill for many years and I admire him for his very pragmatic and straight forward approach to operationalizing analytics. Two decades of real-life, hands-on experience set Bill apart and define him as one of the top leaders in the analytics space!"

**Elpida Ormanidou, Vice President, Global People Analytics, Walmart**

"Franks has created another masterpiece of pragmatic insight and direction, taking the standard of practice and leaping it forward. While data scientists and data managers will appreciate the business value Franks offers, anyone who wants to advance data-driven decisioning and operational analytics needs to read this guide to reaching the next level of the analytics-based business. "

**Jeff Tanner, author of *Analytics and Dynamic Customer Strategy* and Director, Baylor's Innovative Business Collaboratory**

"As recently as a few years ago, many organizations, departments, and people remained dubious about Big Data and questioned whether analytics mattered at all. Today, those who haven't crossed the chasm are squandering massive opportunities. They appear outdated and hidebound. But where to begin? While no one book can possibly answer every question about making Big Data happen, *The Analytics Revolution* provides an excellent framework. I heartily recommend it."

**Phil Simon, keynote speaker and award-winning author of *The Visual Organization* and *Too Big to Ignore***

"This is a comprehensive and much-needed guidebook to successfully implementing operational analytics, automating decisions, and driving data analysis deep into business processes. There is no better guide than Bill Franks to this timely subject, fast becoming a critical strategic differentiator in the era of big data. "

**Gil Press, contributor to Forbes.com**

"The book offers an excellent perspective on what a business leader must do and consider to be successful with analytics. The way decisions are made at firms, by operational processes and even by customers is changing - all driven by analytics! This revolutionary change in decision-making will be a new norm in business. I highly recommend this book as a great guide on what to do and expect with operationalizing analytics!"

**Russell Walker, Clinical Associate Professor,**
**Managerial Economics and Decision Sciences,**
**Northwestern University Kellogg**
**School of Management**

"If you're in the thick of the Big Data movement at your organization (and who isn't?), then you must read this book. Through his unique storytelling ability, Bill Franks delivers entertaining and insightful examples of how firms around the globe capitalize on their data stores through operational analytics. In particular, there is a keen focus on how to assign value to smart use of data, something that has been missing in many conversations involving Big Data. Franks follows up his succinct analysis presented in *Taming The Big Data Tidal Wave* by providing a surfboard for those who want to optimize their ride on the wave, and provides his vision for the future of a data driven world."

**Linda Burtch, Managing Director,**
**Burtch Works Executive Recruiting**

"One our key learnings at Kaggle is that big data is about more than building advanced algorithms. Bill has written an important book about what's involved in putting analytics into practice."

**Anthony Goldbloom, Founder & CEO, Kaggle**

# The Analytics Revolution

## HOW TO IMPROVE YOUR BUSINESS BY MAKING ANALYTICS OPERATIONAL IN THE BIG DATA ERA

Bill Franks

For general information on our other products and services or for technical
support, please contact our Customer Care Department within the United States at
(800) 762-2974, outside the United States at (317) 572-3993 or fax (317) 572-4002.

Wiley publishes in a variety of print and electronic formats and by print-on-demand.
Some material included with standard print versions of this book may not be
included in e-books or in print-on-demand. If this book refers to media such as a
CD or DVD that is not included in the version you purchased, you may download
this material at http://booksupport.wiley.com. For more information about Wiley
products, visit www.wiley.com.

*Library of Congress Cataloging-in-Publication Data:*

Franks, Bill, 1968-
 The analytics revolution : how to improve your business by making analytics
operational in the big data era/Bill Franks.
    pages cm
 Includes index.
    ISBN 978-1-118-87367-0 (cloth); 978-1-118-97675-3 (ebk); 978-1-118-97676-0 (ebk)
 1. Business intelligence. 2. Big data. I. Title.
 HD38.7.F733 2014
 658.4'013–dc23

2014022308

Printed in the United States of America
10 9 8 7 6 5 4 3

*This book is dedicated to Stacie, Jesse, and Danielle.*

# Contents

# Foreword

If you have followed the topics of business intelligence, analytics, and big data over the last decade or two, you may have wondered what is coming next. After all, the initial flurry of excitement about big data is beginning to subside, and analytics of all kinds have become an important part of business, but a familiar one by now.

What's next is in this book. Bill Franks refers to it as "operational analytics," but it could also be called such terms as "production analytics," "real-time analytics," or "decision automation." As these terms suggest, the nature of how analytics are performed is changing rapidly. It's not the analytics themselves that are changing so much. As Franks notes, operational analytics are mostly the same analytics we've done for decades, even centuries. What has changed is the context in which they are carried out.

You can read the details in the book, and you should. I will say here that instead of the back-office, slow, batch analytics of the past, operational analytics are being done much more rapidly and continuously. They are being integrated with business processes and systems, rather than being done separately. I've called this trend "Analytics 3.0," as you will read in his first chapter, but Bill's term "operational analytics" is certainly more descriptive. And he gives a lot more detail about how this world works than I ever did.

This movement is long overdue, after 50 years of separation between analytics and the operations of businesses. The separation created a number of problems. Decision-makers often requested analytics and data to support their decisions, but didn't actually use them. They probably wanted to appear more rational and analytical than they actually were. Quantitative analysts, who should have been at the front and center of business decisions and actions, were generally at significant remove from them (as Franks notes from his own experience in Chapter 8). Everything with analytics took far longer than it needed to. Analytics were still useful in this context, but not nearly as useful as they might have been.

Given all these problems with traditional analytics, it is perhaps testimony to the power of the field that organizations still plan to embed and institutionalize them in their business activities, rather than leaving them optional and tacked-on. The work on operational analytics suggests that analytics can no longer be marginalized because of the way they are undertaken. Analytics need to inform decisions both strategic and tactical, and they need to be done at the pace, time, and location of business operations. As the pace of data flow has quickened within companies, so must the pace of analytics and decision-making be accelerated.

If you weren't wondering what's coming next, you're probably wondering whether this book is yet another one on big data. The answer is no—in part because Franks already wrote an excellent one on that topic, *Taming the Big Data Tidal Wave*. It's not a big data book in another sense, because it addresses the use of all sizes and types of data. In fact, this book might be described as the first *post*-big data book. Franks takes for granted that organizations will use their small, structured data assets as well as their large, less-structured data assets. Why would anyone do otherwise? It seems obvious that data can be useful no matter what its size or structure. Unfortunately, since small data came before big data, few if any other books have had "all data" as their focus, and have few have counseled that your technology environment and analytical activities should be tailored to the various types of data you will be managing and analyzing.

This is also one of the first books that focuses on the "analytics of things" topic. There are many books now on the "Internet of Things" (IoT); a quick search on Amazon today yielded more than a dozen, even though that term is relatively new. But much less has been said about the way to produce value from sensor data, which is to analyze it and mine it for insights and anomalies. Many of Franks' examples of operational analytics involve the IoT, and he discusses how analytics can be used to deal with the vast streams of data those sensors produce.

Despite the fact that Bill is the Chief Analytics Officer for Teradata, he is quite neutral about technologies and vendors. Chapter 5 in this book, for example, includes a very even-handed discussion about the relative merits of Hadoop and enterprise data warehouses based on relational technology. I think Bill is correct in that the vast majority of organizations will employ a variety of technologies to store and analyze data. Nothing ever seems to go away; new technologies augment the old ones, and the amount of data grows at a sufficient pace to require them all.

The book addresses a wide range of topics, from technology to privacy to people topics. It's all here in highly useful and digestible form. It's not Franks' style to make wild-eyed predictions or pronouncements; instead you get calm, straightforward discourse about the way things are with operational analytics in 2014.

The word "revolution" in the title is apt. This move to operational analytics is revolutionary in a variety of ways that are covered in the book. Embedded, real-time analytics raise a lot of questions about how organizations will work in the future. When computers are making most of the decisions, what happens to the people who were previously making them? How can humans monitor and improve the approach to decision-making when it is essentially invisible? Franks points out that when decisions are made in real time with little or no human intervention, it has to be a really good set of analytics and decision rules, or you can lose a lot of money very quickly. As luck would have it, I am working on a book myself that will delve deeply into the human aspects of operational analytics!

So jump into this book and into a previously unknown world where many important decisions are made through operational analytics. You have nothing to lose but your indecision and your office in the back!

Thomas H. Davenport, President's Distinguished
Professor of IT and Management, Babson College;
Co-Founder and Research Director, The International
Institute for Analytics

# Preface

Like manufacturing in the 1800s, the field of analytics needs to go through its own industrial revolution. Analytics processes today are usually created in an artisanal fashion with a lot of care and customization. That's okay in many cases, and the artisanal approach often still is appropriate. However, we must also push analytics forward to another level of scale and impact. The industrial revolution took manufacturing processes from an artisanal practice to a modern technological marvel that is able to manufacture quality items at massive scale. The same type of revolution must happen with analytics.

Centuries ago, if a bowl was needed, then a visit to a potter was necessary. A potter can make a custom bowl to fit any need. The problem is that such an approach isn't scalable. The limited pool of potters can create only so many bowls in a day. Today most bowls are created on a large scale in manufacturing plants. Although it is still possible to purchase a custom bowl from a potter, it isn't cost effective to use that approach except for special situations. Besides cost considerations, people today also often prefer the consistency of a mass-manufactured product. However, even in today's world, bowls don't magically appear. Someone still has to come up with a design, build initial prototypes, create a mold, and validate that the mold will produce the right bowl time and time again. Only then is an assembly line turned on to manufacture the bowl at scale.

A similar process is required for operational analytics. Framing and designing each new analysis is still necessary. Building a prototype of the analysis and testing multiple iterations of it to make sure everything works correctly is still necessary. Only at that point can the analytics process be promoted to an operational process, turned on, and executed in an automated fashion. After being turned on, the performance of the analytics process must be monitored constantly just like a real assembly line is monitored.

Making analytics operational doesn't remove any of the steps historically required to build an analytics process. Rather, it takes the process further. Operational analytics deploys analytics at industrial scale just like traditional manufacturing processes enable bowls to be produced at scale.

Operational analytics is about embedding analytics within business processes and automating decisions so that thousands or millions of decisions every day are made by analytics processes without any human intervention. Whether those decisions directly touch customers or simply optimize an organization's actions behind the scenes, the impact can be substantial.

If an organization doesn't begin to move toward operational analytics, it will struggle as its competitors drive analytics deeper into their business processes. The myriad operational analytics opportunities available to businesses today are driven by increased data availability, increased analytics processing horsepower, and increased accessibility of robust analytics techniques.

Whether we realize it or not, operational analytics is already at work around us every day and impacting our lives. In many cases, these analytics are no longer hidden behind the scenes. Consumers today are often both aware of the analytics that are occurring and even expect it. Let's briefly look at some ways that operational analytics is now impacting our daily routine to set the stage for what is to come in the book:

- Airlines automatically reroute customers when a flight is delayed in order to limit travel disruption and raise customer satisfaction. The analytics take into account a lot of facts about each customer, other passengers, and the status of alternative flight options.
- When people visit their favorite websites, the sites make recommendations as to what else they might like based on what they've viewed, what search terms they use, and what details seem most important to them based on the patterns of their behavior. Often this includes taking into account every action up to the last click.
- When a customer service agent is contacted to help with an issue, the agent often understands the caller's history and is

guided by analytics to the best actions to resolve the issue. The recommended actions account for many factors about the customer and the product or service the customer is discussing.

- Social media sites are able to identify, and connect people with, long-lost friends or colleagues through analysis of extended social networks. Within seconds of linking to a friend, more recommendations are found.
- People can go into a store and instantly obtain credit based on an assessment of the current state of their creditworthiness, as determined by analysis of a wide range of historical credit history data.
- Banks and credit card issuers constantly use analysis to protect us from fraud. Behind the scenes, banks are constantly reviewing accounts for behavioral anomalies that indicate fraud and are able to quickly freeze an account until the purchases are verified with the customer.

These are just a few examples of where operational analytics impacts us daily, where we determine the analytics to be valuable, and where we have come to expect even more. Later, we also discuss a variety of examples where people are largely unaware of the analytics occurring around them.

Many of the technologies and architectures that supported traditional methods of developing and deploying analytics processes won't work for today's complex requirements. The classic systems and architectures, as well as historical analytics methods, have started to groan under the weight of the requirements of operational analytics. Companies must adapt and change the way they store and analyze data as well as how they deploy the results. That's going to necessitate changing not only infrastructure and analytics methodologies but corporate policies as well. If an organization tries to squeeze rapid, high-volume operational analytics into systems and processes that were created and architected to support only batch requirements, it will have a very difficult time.

We can expect to see continued disruption of business models and competitive environments as the analytics arms race continues. Twenty years ago, many organizations used little or no analytics. Today, most organizations use a fair amount of analytics. Having data that was weeks old and analytics processes that were executed infrequently in a batch environment used to be good enough. That is no longer true as the leaders in the analytics realm make analytics operational.

Five to ten years from now, virtually no business will remain untouched by this trend. Resistance is futile. Your organization needs to implement operational analytics, and this book will help you get started. Watch for the continuing transformation of businesses in the coming years as analytics continue to become truly a critical, operational component of a business rather than simply a nice add-on. This book focuses on how this evolution has come to pass and what is required to understand and implement operational analytics in your organization.

Sit back, get comfortable, and let's go!

## Who Should Read This Book?

This book is intended to provide readers with a working knowledge of what operational analytics is, what an organization needs to know, and how an organization must act in order to succeed with operational analytics. The book comes from a strategic and conceptual level, not a technical and tactical level.

Although this book is accessible to anyone regardless of background, those who will find it most interesting are the executives and managers whose roles will touch operational analytics. Professionals involved in creating operational analytics processes will also find the book to be valuable.

If you read my book *Taming the Big Data Tidal Wave* (John Wiley & Sons, 2012) and you liked it, you'll like this one too. Although the subject matter is different, I have followed the same general tone and structure. While most of the focus is on totally new topics, sometimes this book builds on the themes from my earlier book. At the same time, the content of this book can stand alone, and familiarity with *Taming the Big Data Tidal Wave* is not a prerequisite.

## Who Should *Not* Read This Book?

This book is a business book; it is not a technical book. Readers looking for deep technical details, mathematical formulas, or examples of code will not find what they are looking for and should consider a different book.

This book avoids specific product, service, and platform recommendations. Instead, it focuses on product classes and general architectures so that readers will know what to look for when they search for products and services. Readers looking for specific recommendations that include company and product names won't find those here.

Last, this book does presume some working knowledge of the analytics space. Those looking for a review of fundamental analytics concepts won't find it here. Instead of taking time to define every term, I assume that common terms and approaches are already understood.

## What's in This Book?

This book consists of nine chapters divided into three parts. The first part of the book sets the stage by describing the market trends driving operational analytics, defining the topic, and providing examples to illustrate the concepts being discussed. The second part of the book covers how an organization can prepare for operational analytics by outlining how to make the business case, what infrastructure to consider, and how to govern operational analytics processes. The last part of the book discusses the analytics required, the people and teams that create and support the analytics, and the culture required to be successful. Each part and chapter is described in more detail next.

### Part One: The Revolution Has Begun

Part One focuses on the trends that are leading us toward operational analytics and provides examples of how operational analytics is already a part of our lives. It covers high-level themes that set the stage for the more detailed discussions that follow later in the book.

First, we define operational analytics and discuss how analytics approaches, methods, and processes have evolved to the point that they can support operational analytics. Next, we discuss how to cut through the hype around big data and focus on what is truly important for businesses to know as they incorporate big data into operational analytics. Last, we walk through a range of illustrative examples that showcase operational analytics in action.

### Chapter 1: Understanding Operational Analytics

Operational analytics can sometimes entail upgrading a batch analysis process to run in an embedded, automated, real-time fashion.

Often, however, operational analytics involves different types of analytics being applied in a different way. Increasingly, with the advent of big data, different sources of data are also utilized. The reason for the differences is in large part because operational decisions are different from many of the traditional decisions addressed through analytics. This necessitates changing how analytics processes are built, what methods are used, and how analytics professionals do their jobs.

This chapter defines what operational analytics is and how it is different from analytics of the past. How the development of analytics processes has evolved to enable support of operational analytics is also explained. Some perspectives on how analytics is changing the way companies do business are also provided.

### Chapter 2: More Data . . . More Data . . . Big Data!

It is hard to recall a topic that received so much hype as broadly and as quickly as big data. While barely known just a few years ago, big data is one of the most discussed topics in business today. As might be expected with such a meteoric rise, confusion and misinformation about big data are rampant today. This is leading many organizations to start down paths that they should not start down. The failures that result from these misguided actions will be painful and costly. Luckily, with a little work and some education, the average company is perfectly capable of avoiding the most egregious hype points and starting down sensible paths that make economic sense.

This chapter discusses many of the hype points and misunderstandings about big data. It not only points out the flaws in the common interpretations but provides some alternative views and approaches that are more realistic and rational. Big data will play a large role in operational analytics so it is important to understand how it fits.

### Chapter 3: Operational Analytics in Action

The concept of making analytics operational isn't new. However, it was rarely achieved in practice in the past. The fact is that companies could get away with less, and so they did. As technology has advanced and businesses have become more sophisticated, however, operational analytics is becoming an inevitable requirement. It just won't be possible to compete in the future without analytics being at the heart of a wide range of daily decisions and actions.

This chapter presents a variety of real-world examples of operational analytics. It illustrates how operational analytics can support decisions of many types and also shows how operational analytics can range from very simple to incredibly complex.

### Part Two: Laying the Foundation

Part Two helps readers understand how to put in place a foundation that can support operational analytics. A solid foundation is a critical prerequisite to success.

First, we discuss how to make the business case for investment in operational analytics. Nothing of substance can happen until the decision to invest is made. Next, we discuss how to create and utilize the right analytics infrastructure. The landscape today is more complex and more difficult to navigate than ever before. Last, we discuss governance and privacy issues that need to be addressed. When analytics is embedded and automated to the extent that operational analytics is, strong governance in place from the start is required.

### Chapter 4: Want Budget? Build the Business Case!

An early step in the pursuit of operational analytics is justifying the expense and effort that will be required to be successful. There are new tools, new data sources, and new skills required, and big data has only made the situation more complex. Many organizations won't be comfortable with the fact that there are more unknowns than usual and more perceived risk as well. Persuading an organization to take action will require significant effort and solid justification.

This chapter explores the factors that must be accounted for as a case for investment is built. The factors to be considered include technologies, services to implement and maintain the technologies, the work to create the analytics processes, and the effort to embed the analytics processes and make them operational. Only by accounting for the entire range of costs can the best investment decisions be made. Focusing on just a few line items will lead organizations astray.

### Chapter 5: Creating an Analytic Platform

As the use of analytics has exploded, the market has been flooded with products intended to facilitate the analytics. Although this is a good thing, it also leads to confusion and makes it necessary to weed through myriad options in order to choose what is right for any given organization's problems. Some technologies will be applicable almost universally, while others will be applicable only when circumstances are just right. Every organization will need to find the right mix of technologies for its needs.

This chapter discusses the technology landscape as of early 2014. The most important technologies are discussed, as well as when to apply them. Focus is on how to use a mix of technologies to create an analytics platform that will provide the required performance. Most important, guidelines on how to connect the different technologies together into a single, cohesive, unified analytics environment are provided.

### Chapter 6: Governance and Privacy

Operational analytics directly take action without human intervention. Care must be taken to ensure that appropriate governance is in place to minimize the risk of an unexpected problem causing serious damage. Different types of governance are required for the discovery and development process than are required for the deployment process. Special care also needs to be taken with privacy, given the sensitive nature of much of the data utilized today.

This chapter discusses the governance concepts required for both the discovery and deployment processes. It outlines how to effectively enable innovation and experimentation while still allowing for a safe and secure deployment. Specific attention also is given to privacy issues.

### Part Three: Making Analytics Operational

Part Three focuses on what it takes to put operational analytics into action. Once the foundation discussed in Part Two is in place, that foundation must be utilized effectively in order to realize its potential.

In Part Three, we cover important concepts related to the analytics approaches required to successfully evolve into operational analytics. We also cover how to staff and organize analytics teams for success. Last, we address the cultural issues that must be considered as an organization readies itself for the changes operational analytics will force. One of the hardest parts of making analytics operational is overcoming fear of change and getting people to embrace new approaches.

## Chapter 7: The Analytics

The centerpiece of operational analytics is, of course, the analytics themselves. But what do they look like? Although operational analytics have many similarities to traditional analytics, there are also differences between the two. Succeeding in the world of operational analytics and big data requires some new approaches. There is the need to leverage new techniques and new data, there are new types of problems to address, and there are new requirements for measuring success.

This chapter delves into the analytics requirements behind operational analytics. It discusses some of the techniques and methodologies that will be required and how some of the classic lessons from the past still apply. Last, the chapter covers how to effectively measure the success of an operational analytics process and monitor its performance.

## Chapter 8: The Analytics Organization

No matter the strategy chosen for analytics, somebody has to make it happen. Thus, an important part of making analytics operational is to have the right team in place. Having the right team is more than just hiring smart people with the skills to cover all aspects of operational analytics. The team must be structured and organized effectively as well. Also critical is putting in place effective incentives and empowering the team to do what is needed by giving it the authority, responsibility, and mind-set to succeed.

This chapter outlines how to charter and empower an organization that will succeed in driving operational analytics with big data. It outlines how to structure an analytics organization and who should be on the team. It discusses what the team's approach should look like and what type of incentives should be in place. It also suggests some behaviors and attitudes that will help the team to be as productive as possible.

## Chapter 9: The Analytics Culture

One of the most difficult challenges in moving toward operational analytics is the process of changing corporate culture. Unfortunately, this effort is often underestimated. Different attitudes and policies are required when a company becomes driven by analytics at the operational level. Analytics must be trusted, embraced, and demanded by everyone at every level of the organization. The cultural transformation can take longer and be more frustrating than the technological and analytics process transformations. When dealing with human emotions and personalities rather than facts and figures, things can get messy.

This chapter covers important changes to mind-set that must occur within an organization to succeed with operational analytics. It also discusses ways to utilize people's emotions and personalities to advantage as new analytics processes are deployed. Finally, it discusses how an organization can facilitate success while handling the inevitable failures that occur from time to time.

### Conclusion: Join the Revolution!

This final chapter is a short recap of the key messages from the book along with calls to action.

# Acknowledgments

I owe a big thanks to the members of my book review team, who each volunteered to review all or part of the book and provide input as I developed it. The team included (in alphabetical order) Ellen Boerger, Chahnse Bourommavong, Sheck Cho, Bill Franks (not me, but my dad!), Sarah Gates, Dan Graham, Richard Hackathorn, Bryan Jones, Jack Levis, Bob Sievert, Jeff Tanner, John Thuma, and Scott VanValkenburg. Your terrific input helped me make the book much better than it was before your input. I also owe thanks to all of the individuals and companies that provided me with the knowledge, experience, and examples that enabled me to write this book.

# PART I

# THE REVOLUTION HAS BEGUN

# Understanding Operational Analytics

Yes, the revolution has begun. Operational analytics are leading the charge in the industrial revolution of analytics and are already starting to push the boundaries of what companies do with analytics. Operational analytics will, over time, vastly increase the number of analytics processes that must be built and the speed with which those analytics must execute. As we'll discuss later, new concepts such as decision time and time to insight will become primary drivers of how to invest and where to focus effort.

Operational analytics require a disciplined and organized approach across an organization and a lot of technological, process, and cultural change as well. People are not initially comfortable turning over many day-to-day decisions to machines and analytics processes. However, time will prove that if organizations build the right operational analytics, the results will be well worth the effort.

Yes, the revolution has begun! Before that statement can be understood, it is necessary to explain exactly what it means. This chapter lays the groundwork that the rest of the book builds on. We define what operational analytics are. We also discuss some market trends that are supporting the push for operational analytics. Last, we reinforce several important themes that are worth remembering as an organization moves toward operational analytics.

## Defining Operational Analytics

This book is about operational analytics. But what *are* operational analytics? We need to define the term if it is to be the focus of this book. After first doing that, this section walks through what differentiates operational analytics from traditional analytics and makes operational analytics unique.

### What Are Operational Analytics?

The term "operational analytics" describes a situation where analytics[1] have become an inherent part of the individual decisions made and the individual actions taken within a business. Operational analytics don't support big or strategic decisions but rather the many small and tactical decisions that happen from moment to moment every day. More important, when an analytics process is operationalized, the process actually drives what happens directly. An operational analytics process does not simply recommend an action but directly causes an action to take place. The prior facts are the heart of what defines operational analytics. By directly driving decisions and actions without human intervention, operational analytics takes analytics integration and impact to a whole new level.

Most traditional analytics processes generate results that inform a decision or feed into a decision process. However, a person usually interjects human judgment into that decision process and then approves the action. When analytics are operationalized, an analytics process is run and actions are taken immediately as a result of that analysis. There is no human intervention at the point of decision or action.

Of course, it takes human intervention to decide that an operational analytics process is needed and to build the process. However, once the process is turned on, the process accesses data, performs analysis, makes decisions, and then actually causes actions to occur. The process may be executed thousands or millions of times per day. Once people within an organization realize that they're able to have analytics embedded at this level, they often want more. The result is demand for ever more analytics and an ever higher level of sophistication. Having automated operational analytics in place also leads to the need for careful monitoring of the processes. We cover that topic in Chapter 6.

## Get Prescriptive!

A defining feature of operational analytics is to go beyond being descriptive or even predictive. Operational analytics are prescriptive. This means that operational analytics are embedded within a business process to directly make decisions and cause actions to happen based on algorithms . . . all without human intervention.

There has been a lot of focus over the last decade on the shift from descriptive analytics to predictive analytics. Within a classic business intelligence environment, the focus is on summarizing what happened from a descriptive perspective. This might entail determining how many sales each region had, how many deliveries were on time, or other important metrics. With predictive analytics, in contrast, the goal is to predict what will happen in the future. How can on-time delivery rates be influenced moving forward? Which customers are most likely to respond to an upcoming marketing offer? Operational analytics take things a step further and make analytics prescriptive. An operational analytics process starts by identifying what actions will influence delivery times or increase response rates and then makes the analytics prescriptive by automatically causing the actions to occur. Table 1.1 summarizes these differences.

### Differentiating Operational Analytics

Differentiating operational analytics from an operational application of analytics is very important. At first that distinction might sound like a semantic game, but I assure you it's not. After we go through some examples, the distinction will be very clear.

Analytics have been applied to operational problems for many years. That's going to continue to be true, and the operational applications of analytics will remain important. Operational analytics take things further than past efforts, however. It would be ideal if a term

**Table 1.1  Descriptive versus Predictive versus Prescriptive Analytics**

| | |
|---|---|
| Descriptive analytics | Summarize and describe what happened in the past |
| Predictive analytics | Predict what will happen in the future |
| Prescriptive analytics | Determine actions to take to make the future happen |

existed that cleanly separated operational analytics from operational applications of traditional analytics, but I do not know of one. That is unfortunate because the similarity of the phrases can cause confusion, and the phrases certainly sound awkward when spoken together. When I was leading a discussion on this topic at a conference, I had an attendee jokingly suggest that I coin the term "Franks-izing" analytics, which is clearly too self-serving even if it wasn't a joke. So, I'll focus on the distinction between the two approaches rather than the labels applied to them.

The distinction between an operational application of analytics and operational analytics makes it easy to see why operational analytics are both important and complex. Operational analytics processes are often as sophisticated as any analytics process an organization has built before, but the process has to be automated, scaled massively, and executed lightning quick. There's a lot of power in such a process, but there's also a lot of complexity and hard work. Let's look at some examples that will further clarify the distinction.

One important differentiator is that with operational analytics, the analytics are executed in what might be called "decision time" in an automated and embedded fashion. Decision time means an analysis is executed at the speed required to enable a decision. In some cases, decision time is real time (or very close to it). In other cases, decision time can involve minutes, hours, or even days of latency. Knowing the decision time is critical to success because an analytics process has to be available and executed within that window in order to be used for the decision.

Historically, many organizations have customized websites by identifying key things about customers' buying habits and then allocating specific offers or customizations to be shown when each customer returns. Web customization has been proven very powerful and is almost ubiquitous today. Processing what is known about a customer tonight to precompute and make ready customizations for the customer to see in the morning is an operational application of analytics. Precomputing customizations is not an example of operational analytics. Precomputing customizations before a customer visits the site is simply applying traditional batch analytics in an operational environment.

Operational analytics require customizing a customer's next page after the "next" button is clicked and prior to serving the

## Don't Just Apply Analytics to Operations

Analytics processes have been applied to operational problems for many years. However, operational analytics go beyond using the results of a traditional batch analytics process for operational purposes. Operational analytics become embedded and are executed in decision time for each individual decision.

next page. The process must use not only the customer's historical information but also information up to and including what the customer has just done while on the website. Altering how a web page is presented in that short time between clicks is operational analytics. Note that this analysis isn't happening for just one customer but for all customers visiting the site, which leads to millions of microdecisions being made based on the analytics. Even if the customers do not perceive the difference between the batch and operational approaches when navigating the site, there is a real difference underneath the hood.

Another example of the distinction, which we dive into more deeply later in the book, comes from the manufacturing space. Engine sensor data is allowing manufacturers to derive much better maintenance schedules. Having detailed information on how a car, truck, airplane, or tractor engine is operating provides many insights into patterns that lead to failure over time. Developing an improved maintenance schedule using sensor data is an operational application of analytics.

Operational analytics based on engine sensor data is much more immediate and personalized than the prior example. Operational analytics are involved when an engine is operating and the sensor information coming from that engine is being analyzed in real time. If a pattern is identified that is known to lead imminently to a problem, an intervention is made either to avoid the problem or to fix it. When a driver gets a proactive alert that something is starting to go wrong with an engine right now, that's operational analytics.

If an organization hasn't yet figured out how to succeed with traditional batch analytics processes, it will not be able to make analytics operational. An organization must have foundational analytics capabilities in place before it can scale them up. The first focus must be on developing solid analytics that are effective in batch mode.

## There Are No Shortcuts

Without a mastery of traditional batch analytics, an organization can't proceed to operational analytics. Operational analytics build on a strong foundation.

That process can be made operational only after it is proved that the data and skills an organization has can be used to build a strong analytics process. If you want your organization to get to the next level, you must first ensure a strong analytics foundation is in place. Without that foundation, operational analytics are going to remain a dream.

### Cornerstones That Make Operational Analytics Unique

We just discussed how operational analytics are different from traditional analytics in some important ways. Let's summarize the differences by describing four cornerstones that define what makes operational analytics different from traditional analytics.

**Cornerstone 1: Operational analytics are embedded and automated.** To understand why this is different from traditional approaches remember that organizations traditionally ran analytics in an offline fashion and then shipped the results elsewhere to be taken into account for decisions. A human was involved not only in building the analytics process but in executing the process on an ongoing basis. An operational analytics process is executed within operational systems in an embedded and automated fashion.

**Cornerstone 2: Operational analytics are prescriptive.** Operational analytics go beyond descriptive analytics or even predictive analytics to actually prescribe an action. The process is not just predicting the next best offer to give to a customer when she comes back. Rather, the analytics process actually prescribes that offer to happen by directing the appropriate systems to deliver the offer.

**Cornerstone 3: Operational analytics make decisions.** The processes are not only prescribing or recommending decisions but also actually are making the decisions and then driving the actions that result from those decisions. This is very different from traditional analytics, where an analysis produces a recommendation that someone then must accept or reject. A human looks at the results of traditional analytics and makes the final decisions prior to letting the analytics drive action.

**Cornerstone 4: Operational analytics are executed in decision time,** which is real time in many cases, and not in a batch mode. In some cases, the analytics are applied to an incoming stream of data as opposed to a repository of data. Operational analytics don't have the luxury of waiting for the next batch window. They have to be executed right away to make a decision and then take action.

---

### Cornerstones of Operational Analytics

Operational analytics are embedded, automated decision-making processes that prescribe and cause actions to occur in decision time. Once an operational analytics process is approved and turned on, the process will make thousands or millions of decisions automatically.

---

Finding a new insight through analytics is terrific. As various insights are discovered within data, a big challenge is figuring out how to best get those insights implemented operationally. Determining how to take a new insight and develop a process that can replicate that insight, at scale, in near real time, and then feed a decision is very difficult. People are still going to be critical when implementing operational analytics. Somebody has to design, build, configure, and monitor operational analytics processes. The computers will not figure out what decisions to make on their own.

An important point worth stating again is that operational analytics are a new level of evolution for analytics processes. Organizations cannot skip straight into operational analytics if they don't have mastery of traditional batch processes first. As we discuss in Chapter 6, care must be taken to diligently test operational analytics processes prior to turning them on since automating bad decisions can cause a lot of damage. If millions of small decisions are going to be made, it is important to make sure they will be made with a high level of quality.

## Welcome to Analytics 3.0

The evolution of analytics over time can be seen in the Analytics 3.0 framework created by the International Institute for Analytics (IIA) and its research director, Tom Davenport.[2] I am on the faculty of the IIA and was lucky enough to be involved in some of the early conversations when the Analytics 3.0 framework was being developed. Let's next walk through what the Analytics 3.0 concept is all about because it helps put the evolution of operational analytics into a broader perspective. Learning what has changed in the world of analytics over the years makes it easier to understand why operational analytics are ready to become mainstream.

### Analytics 1.0: Traditional Analytics

The Analytics 1.0 era spanned everything organizations were doing with respect to analytics for many years. I refer to the Analytics 1.0 era in the past tense because organizations need to put it in the rearview mirror if they haven't done so already. The Analytics 1.0 era, as depicted in Figure 1.1, was very heavy on descriptive statistics and reporting, with a sprinkling of predictive analytics. Prescriptive analytics were not part of the equation at all. When it came to data in the Analytics 1.0 world, it was almost exclusively internally sourced and well structured. This data included all of the transactional data organizations capture, information within enterprise resource planning (ERP) systems, and so forth. While that data was considered incredibly large and difficult to work with at the time, by today's standards, it is relatively small and easy to work with. The data was gathered and stored by an information technology (IT) organization before anyone could use it. Unfortunately, in the Analytics 1.0 era, it took IT quite a while to make the data available for analysis. This limited the breadth and depth of analytics that were possible as well as the impact.

To make matters worse, once the data was available to the analytics professionals who wanted to analyze it, a lot of additional data preparation was required before analyzing it. That is because the way data is stored in corporate systems is rarely the format required for an analysis. Building an analytics process required a variety of

• Primarily descriptive
  analytics and reporting

• Internally sourced,
  relatively small,
  structured data

• "Backroom" teams
  of analysts

• Internal decision support

**Figure 1.1    Analytics 1.0: Traditional Analytics**
*Source:* The International Institute for Analytics.

transformations, aggregations, and combining of different data sources. That added even more time after IT made the data available before results could be generated. Therefore, the majority of time spent in the Analytics 1.0 era went into just trying to get data as opposed to doing analysis.

From a cultural perspective, the analytics professionals creating analytics processes were relegated to the backroom. In most cases, they were separated from both business and IT and were considered mad scientists who sometimes came up with interesting insights. Analytics professionals were not a core part of any team but their own. We'll talk about that more in Chapter 8. Almost all of the analytics processes created aided internally facing decisions. Customers or users of a product would rarely if ever have been explicitly aware of the analytics occurring behind the scenes.

### Organizations Must Move Past the Analytics 1.0 Era

The Analytics 1.0 era was very useful for many years. However, it is necessary to include additional capabilities and different approaches that go beyond Analytics 1.0 in today's business environment. Put Analytics 1.0 in the past.

Traditional technologies, such as business intelligence and reporting tools, were used to create wide ranges of reports, dashboards, and alerts. However, even simple reports were difficult to create. Creating a report required someone from a centralized business intelligence team to gather requirements from a user, configure a report, and then enable it to be viewed. The process was lengthy and formal, and very few users were able to create their own reports. There were pockets of predictive analytics present, but for the most part the Analytics 1.0 era was about descriptive analytics and reporting.

The irony is that there wasn't necessarily demand to make reports and analytics available faster because businesses couldn't react much more quickly anyway. Early in my career, when building models to support a direct mail campaign, we'd use data that was three to four weeks old to determine which households should get each piece of mail. The list that we generated was then sent to a mail house a couple of weeks ahead of when pieces were going to be printed and mailed. After the pieces were printed and dropped in the mail, they would take up to another week to get to a customer's mailbox. That means that we had at least six, and sometimes eight or ten, weeks of latency between our analysis and when it could impact our customers and our business. Executing the analytics processes faster wouldn't have helped because the mailings were on a fixed monthly schedule and the lists had to be created on a regular schedule. It is easy to see why a lot of analytics processes didn't reach their full potential within such an environment.

### Analytics 2.0: Big Data Analytics

In the early 2000s, the Analytics 2.0 era began to emerge and guide us into the world of big data.[3] Big data is in many ways new. It encompasses data that is often more complex than, larger in volume than, and not necessarily as structured as the data used in the Analytics 1.0 era. Big data can include anything from documents, to photos, to videos, to sensor data. A lot of big data used for analysis, such as social media data, is also external to an organization. Though externally created, data can still be very valuable.

In the era of Analytics 2.0 today, as seen in Figure 1.2, we also find that new analytics techniques and new computational capabilities are necessary in order to handle big data and the variety of

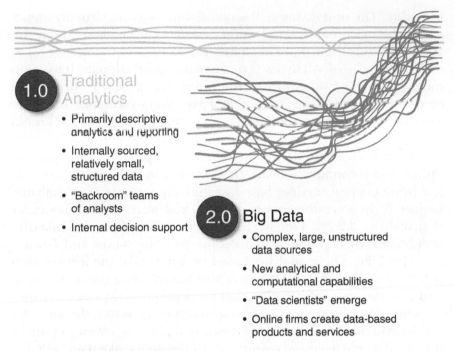

**1.0 Traditional Analytics**
- Primarily descriptive analytics and reporting
- Internally sourced, relatively small, structured data
- "Backroom" teams of analysts
- Internal decision support

**2.0 Big Data**
- Complex, large, unstructured data sources
- New analytical and computational capabilities
- "Data scientists" emerge
- Online firms create data-based products and services

**Figure 1.2    Analytics 2.0: The Big Data Era**
*Source:* The International Institute for Analytics.

analytics processes that are required. Technologies such as Hadoop (which we'll discuss later) have gone from obscurity to being well known, and analytics processes have been updated to account for such new technologies. A major focus in the Analytics 2.0 era is finding the cheapest way to collect and store data in its raw format and then worrying later about figuring out how to make use of it.

One strong trend has been the recent rise of the term "data science" to describe how analytics professionals analyze big data and the term "data scientist" to describe the analytics professionals doing the analysis. A primary difference between data scientists and traditional analytics professionals is the choice of tools and platforms used for analytics. Traditional analytics professionals in large organizations tend to use tools like SAS and SQL to analyze data from a relational database environment. Data scientists tend to use tools like R and Python to analyze data in a Hadoop environment. However, those differences are tactical and largely a matter of semantics. Anyone strong in one of those environments can easily transition to the other. The underlying skill sets and mind-sets are virtually identical across these analytics professionals even if the labels are different. We discuss this topic more in Chapter 8.

In the era of Analytics 2.0, analytics professionals have now moved up in organizations to the point that if they're not a part of the decision-making team, they have direct influence on those who are. Analytics professionals are certainly no longer backroom resources thoroughly separated from the business community.

As we discuss later in this chapter, many organizations, especially online and e-commerce firms, have started to develop moneymaking products and services based exclusively on data and analytics. Online firms were the first to do this and were the first to enter the Analytics 2.0 era. One of the best-known examples is LinkedIn, which developed products like People You May Know and Groups You May Like. These analytics-based products take the information collected as part of administering and maintaining users' accounts and generate new information that users will in many cases pay for.

One counterintuitive fact about Analytics 2.0 is that the analytics produced are often not very sophisticated. This is driven in part by the fact that the scale and complexity of the data make it a challenge to get the data into a format that enables analysis. It also has to do with the data sources being early on the maturity curve and the lack of maturity in the analytics tool sets being utilized to analyze the data. For all the hype, the Analytics 2.0 era still has a huge dose of reporting and descriptive analytics and only relatively small doses of predictive or prescriptive analytics.

## Analytics 2.0 Alone Isn't Enough

The Analytics 2.0 era brings big data and novel analytics opportunities to the forefront. However, it doesn't make sense to have distinct people, data, and tools focusing only on the analysis of big data. Analytics processes must encompass all data and all analytics requirements. That's why Analytics 2.0 isn't the end point.

One misunderstanding that happens in the Analytics 2.0 era results from the fact that many analytics professionals who enter the era of Analytics 2.0 did not pass through the era of Analytics 1.0. Many Analytics 2.0 professionals have a computer science background and gained entry into analytics via the technology side of the house rather than the analytics side. Sometimes people new to analytics in the Analytics 2.0 era aren't aware of everything that happened in innovative large businesses during the Analytics 1.0 era. Such professionals may believe that all of the analytics concepts and methods they are using are brand new. Sometimes that's true, but most often it isn't. Let's look at an example that illustrates this point.

I saw a young man give a great talk at a conference. I won't disclose his name or company because my point isn't to cause embarrassment but to shine light on a common flaw in logic. The presenter discussed all the reasons he and his team were creating various analytics processes for his company's e-commerce site. His logic and methods were solid. The company was doing all the right things, such as affinity analysis and collaborative filtering, to identify what additional products customers might be interested in based on what they had previously bought or browsed. This kind of analysis is something that traditional retailers have been doing for many years.

The presenter's mistake was when he said that the affinity analysis was not possible before big data and some new technologies came along. He truly believed that applying these common algorithms was breaking new ground because he had no exposure to what had been happening over the years within the traditional retail industry. While it is certainly not true that affinity analysis is new, the fact is that it was new to him (and others like him). He simply hadn't been exposed to what had been going on in the past. With all the hype around big data, it is easy to assume that nothing of interest was happening in the past if you don't know better from experience. Unfortunately, such lack of knowledge can lead to a lot of time spent re-creating solutions that already exist, which is not an efficient use of time.

Much can be gained in the Analytics 2.0 era by learning from and borrowing from the Analytics 1.0 era. To maximize success, it is critical that an organization combines the best of the Analytics 1.0 era and the Analytics 2.0 era and then pushes forward from there. That leads us to the Analytics 3.0 era.

### Analytics 3.0: Unified Analytics for Maximum Impact

The Analytics 3.0 era focuses on evolving, not replacing, what was learned in the Analytics 1.0 and Analytics 2.0 eras. Just as the

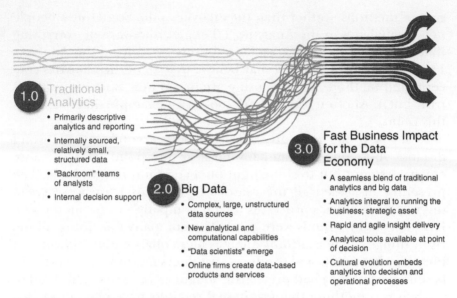

**Figure 1.3    Analytics 3.0: Fast Business Impact for the Data Economy**

*Source:* The International Institute for Analytics.

Analytics 2.0 era didn't replace the Analytics 1.0 era, the Analytics 3.0 era does not replace the others. The Analytics 3.0 era combines everything learned in each of the prior eras into one overall framework, as can be seen in Figure 1.3. It's about combining traditional analytics on traditional data with big data analytics on big data. As organizations started using big data, they found that it's not possible to have big data analytics as a completely separate function. Big data is just more data on which more analytics need to be done; it has to be integrated with everything else. The Analytics 3.0 era marks the arrival of this new, integrated, and evolved analytics paradigm. As of early 2014, we are just starting to see the leaders, both online and traditional firms, enter the Analytics 3.0 era. Operational analytics are a natural outgrowth of this trend.

One concept that the Analytics 3.0 era places renewed focus on is the importance of the discovery process. A discovery process is aimed at rapidly finding new insights in data and identifying actions, products, and services that might be derived from the insights. Fully realizing the potential of the discovery process requires a substantial cultural evolution for many organizations. Analytics must be embraced as a core part of an enterprise's strategy. The increased status of analytics must be driven and mandated from the top. It also is necessary to change the way analytics platforms and processes are built. We discuss the discovery process and the changes it requires in detail later in the book.

The variety and novelty of the data types and sources available is one of the big challenges of the Analytics 3.0 era, but these new data types and sources also lead to a huge variety of new and novel analytics. New analytics approaches will be one of the defining characteristics of the Analytics 3.0 era. The power of the data and the scalability of processing will finally move organizations toward widespread use of predictive and prescriptive analytics. While there will always be a need for descriptive analytics and reporting, during the Analytics 3.0 era, organizations will finally start to realize the dream of having analytics embedded and operational. Analytics will be embedded not just in centralized, large-scale corporate systems but also within operational applications that are deployed to end users, such as within mobile devices, ATMs, and kiosks.

## Evolve into Analytics 3.0

The Analytics 3.0 era represents the latest evolution of analytics. It combines the best of the Analytics 1.0 and Analytics 2.0 eras and then evolves analytics further.

The new architectures that are required for Analytics 3.0 will add complexity to an organization. Analytics 3.0 makes it necessary to have not just parallel processing in a relational database environment but also parallel file processing in an environment such as Hadoop. It may also be necessary to mix in some in-memory environments, some graphics processing units, and more. All of this is discussed in Chapter 5.

Perhaps the most exciting aspect of the Analytics 3.0 era to me, given my background as an analytics professional, is that analytics professionals will finally be part of a formal organization that's valued as a strategic part of how business is done. These teams will be led by a chief analytics officer or, at minimum, a vice president level, analytics professional who oversees all corporate analytics. A chief data officer will also become much more common. We'll discuss these roles more in Chapter 8. The Analytics 3.0 era is a particularly exciting new world for analytics professionals.

### Operationalizing Analytics with Analytics 3.0

Let's consider an analysis that many large banks and telecommunications companies are applying today. The analysis identifies actions associated with a customer closing his or her account and is a way to illustrate how operational analytics processes works in the Analytics 3.0 era. Note that while predicting attrition, or churn, is not new, what is new are some of the expanded analytics and applications of churn analysis being utilized today.

As part of the churn analysis process, it is necessary to collect data on any action that might be tied to the closing of an account. This will include both traditional and big data sources, such as balance history, complaints, requests through various channels for a fee reversal, balance changes over time, social media statements, and more.

Over time, churn analysis has evolved to look for certain patterns of action that in combination are much more dangerous than each individually. This is often called path analysis. In other words, it might not be a big deal to turn down a fee reversal request when a customer asks for it while looking at the account online and seeing the fee for the first time. However, if the customer calls customer service to ask for a fee reversal again and follows the call up with a branch visit, turning the customer down may substantially increase the risk of him or her closing the account.

Building an analytics process to pinpoint important paths of action involves some complex work. A customer might reach out to a bank at any time through any channel, whether a call center, a branch, a live chat on the web, or an e-mail. The bank must know exactly what else has already transpired so that the correct action can be taken. Creating an operational analytics process requires updating the recommended action for each customer after every interaction. Once an inquiry is made about a fee reversal and it's known that the request was accepted or rejected, that new information has to immediately feed into a recomputation of what the correct response will be during the next interaction with him or her. Not creating an operational analytics process in this case can cause trouble. Let's see why.

## It Is Easy to Be Too Late

Operational analytics enable an organization to make the best decision possible at any moment. Using analytics that are based on data that is outdated by even a few minutes can lead to suboptimal, if not dead wrong, decisions.

What if a bank executes analytics only in batch overnight when I have requested a fee reversal? The bank would know I asked for a fee reversal via e-mail that day and that my request was rejected. The analytics determine that the rejection does not increase the risk I will close my account, so the recommendation is that the bank should reject an additional fee reversal request from me. That recommendation is loaded into the system and made ready for the next day.

The next day I call while I'm in the car and I ask again for the fee reversal. My request is rejected, as planned and appropriate. However, because I am now very annoyed, I decide to walk into the branch I am driving past and talk to the manager in person. This is where the problems start. The batch analysis won't be run again until that evening so neither the branch manager nor the system will realize that I just called and was turned down again. The recommendation to reject further fee reversal requests will still be active. It won't be until later that evening that the analytics will identify that my branch request should be granted to retain my business. The risk of losing my account greatly increased based on my last interaction, but the branch manager didn't know it because the analytics weren't run. This is a classic example of an operational application of traditional analytics, and it is easy to see where that approach can go wrong.

With operational analytics, the system will update the data to reflect my phone call. Then the analytics process will be executed immediately for my account based on that new data. By the time I walk into the branch, the recommendation will be updated to suggest granting my request, the manager will reverse my fee, and I'll keep my account open. The original recommendation of rejecting my request made sense just minutes before I walked into the branch. However, my phone call to customer service totally changed what the appropriate response was. To succeed, the bank has to be able to collect all the data on all my interactions as they happen and then run the analytics process after each interaction to correctly identify what should happen next. That is how operational analytics work in the Analytics 3.0 era. My friend James Taylor, CEO of Decision Management Solutions and author of *Decision Management Systems: A Practical Guide to Using Business Rules and Predictive Analytics* (IBM Press, 2011) has written a lot about operational analytics. He says, "Organizations that want to thrive, not just survive, must transform themselves from top to bottom. Operational excellence is no longer optional and the path to excellence is an analytic one. Making every decision analytically and driving better decisions into all their operational processes should be in every executive's plan."

## How Analytics Are Changing Business

While analytics have become more pervasive, many people have not realized the extent to which analytics are now fundamentally changing business models. In this section, we cover a few important concepts and trends that must be understood. Your organization will quite possibly have to think bigger and more boldly about how analytics fits within its future.

### Analytics as the Goal, Not a By-Product

A big trend that is connected to operational analytics is that a large number of products now collect data. In many cases, the analytics executed against that data are actually a primary, if not *the* primary, purpose of the product. In other words, a physical product often is simply a mechanism for collecting data today. Let's dig deeper into what that statement means.

Historically speaking, companies have always developed new products, whether it was a toy, a calling plan, or a type of bank account. The goal was obviously to have that product succeed, but the success of the product didn't depend much on data or analytics. Companies would collect data over time about the sales performance of a product, who was buying it, and what defects or issues were commonly identified. This would lead to ideas on how to improve the product, but the data was a by-product of the efforts to sell the product rather an inherent property of the product.

What has changed today is that products are being released whose entire purpose is the data it's collecting and the analytics that it enables. The physical product itself is actually secondary and is nothing more than a channel for the collection and analysis of data. In some cases the value of the product to customers will be the analytics provided; in other cases customers get value another way while the company gets value from the analytics. When the analytics are for the benefit of customers, the product that can provide the most valuable data and analytics, rather than more traditional features, will beat the competition

### Who Cares about the Product? Check Out These Analytics!

One driver of operational analytics is the evolution of products that exist primarily to enable the collection and analysis of data. In some cases, physical products are really nothing more than collection tools for analytics processes.

Examples are starting to abound. A lot of the free services available on the web fall into this category. Consider free e-mail services. The companies providing free e-mail aren't giving people free e-mail service because they want to perform a community service. The companies give away free e-mail service because they can learn a lot about subscribers as they use the e-mail service. The provider has opportunities to serve advertisements based on users' behaviors, and it gets paid when they respond. In some cases, a free e-mail service actually reads through users' e-mail texts and analyzes it to generate offers. If you frequently e-mail your friends about sports, you can bet that you'll be getting a lot of offers focused on sports. In addition, the e-mail provider may sell its knowledge of your interest in sports to other organizations that are willing to pay to find sports fans. It all comes down to reading privacy policies very carefully before agreeing to them. We talk more about privacy issues in Chapter 6.

The marketplace also now has analytics processes that have been directly turned into products. One example is Netflix's well-known movie recommendation engine.[4] It uses the data collected from customers as they navigate the Netflix site to identify other movies that the customers might enjoy. The movie recommendation system is actually considered a formal product at Netflix. It has its own product managers who manage it just like any other product would be managed. Netflix looks for opportunities to add features and functions to the recommendation engine and to improve how it is presented to customers. One example is the introduction of the "Max" interface, which makes a game out of tuning recommendations for users.[5]

The recommendation engine is credited with being a huge factor in Netflix's success. But this product called a recommendation engine is really just analytics and the use of data. The engine is also a fully operational process that runs its algorithms and presents results to customers millions of times per day with no human intervention.

### Analytics Products Are Blurring Industry Lines

Let's now explore an interesting example that illustrates how products focused on analytics are starting to blur industry lines by discussing the new wave of personal fitness monitoring devices that are worn on a wrist or waist. While there are a number of products on the market from Nike, Jawbone, and FitBit, we focus here on Nike.[6]

If I went out, surveyed 100 people on the street, and asked them what Nike does, probably at least 98 to 99 percent would respond that Nike is a clothing manufacturer, a sportswear manufacturer, or something very similar. None of those statements is untrue. After all, to a large extent, that's what Nike has been known for over the years. However, some changes at Nike necessitate a reexamination of what industry the company actually is in. The same type of change is happening for many other businesses as well.

In 2012, Nike released a product called the FuelBand.[7] The FuelBand is a device that is worn on the wrist like a watch, and it measures things like the number of steps taken each day and several facts about sleep patterns. The device and other products like it are very popular. In fact, I have a similar device on my wrist as I write this. Let's examine what the FuelBand does to challenge Nike's industry classification and how it alters Nike's traditional business model.

Although most people still think of Nike as a clothing or sportswear manufacturer, the FuelBand breaks this assumption. To start with, the FuelBand is actually a piece of high-tech equipment complete with sensors, a transmitter, and more. Nike is now in the high-tech manufacturing business.

What's the first thing customers have to do after buying a FuelBand if they are going to make effective use of it? They must download software to their desktop, tablet, or mobile device. Nike's now in the software business.

## Is Your Company Still in the Industry It Used to Be In?

As traditional manufacturers suddenly find themselves embedding sensors, collecting data, and producing analytics for their customers, industry lines blur. Not only are new competencies needed, but the reason customers choose a product may have less to do with traditional selection criteria than with the data and analytics offered with the product.

And why do customers need the software? So their mobile device or computer can interact with the FuelBand and upload the data it collects to Nike. Nike is now in the data collection and storage business.

The reason for all of this activity is to enable Nike to provide analytics and trends about customers' sleeping and activity patterns. Nike is now in the analytics as a service business. It is even possible to argue that Nike is in the health business too if over time the company finds ways to correlate the data a FuelBand collects with health issues. By now you should get the point. As a result of the FuelBand, Nike has entered a lot of business lines that truly have nothing to do with fashion or clothing.

Perhaps the most important point is that the choice of buying a FuelBand or a similar competitive item really doesn't come down to how nice it looks or how fashionable it is. Those factors are important for traditional Nike items, but with a product like the FuelBand, it comes down to which device customers believe will collect the best data and which device will provide the best analytics. The data and analytics drive the purchase of the product. There may be a physical product involved, but what Nike is really selling, and what customers are really buying, is data and analytics.

Nike is transforming into a wearable technology and analytics consumer goods organization. Eventually, sensors will be found in shoes, gloves, shirts, and other Nike products. These products will work together to form a richer set of analytics for customers as well as for Nike.

This is an important and fundamental shift. We now have a physical product that isn't purchased based on the attributes of the physical product itself. Nike recognizes this, and it is pivoting its business to embrace products of this nature. To succeed with the product, Nike has had to start hiring web developers and high-tech electronics designers. It has had to hire analytics professionals to design the reports and analysis. It has had to hire IT people to build systems to store all the data. Products like the FuelBand require a lot of different skills from those that are required by traditional sportswear or clothing manufacturers.

I focused on a personal fitness product, but the same concept is playing out in other industries as well. Cars, airplanes, tractors, wind turbines, and trucks are all being embedded with sensors. Customers are beginning to use the data collected by those sensors for more and more purposes. As people decide which car model to buy, it may be a close race between two options. The final choice today could well depend on the data and analytics that are available from one automobile versus another.

There is opportunity and there is risk in this shift to having analytics and data become the focus of a product rather than the physical product itself. But we can't view business as we have in the past, given the state of the world today. Data and analytics are most likely going to change a lot of things about your business.

### Operational Analytics Will Be Transformative

Some industries will be fundamentally transformed by all of the new data and new analytics generated. This is especially true for industries that historically have severely lacked both. While there are many possible examples to focus on, we focus here on one industry that is ripe for change: the education industry.

We're still following a decades- or centuries-old model in education. We take children who just happen to be born around the same time and regardless of their background and skill level (with rare exceptions), we throw them all into a classroom together. Nine-year-olds in third grade are going to cover a certain curriculum regardless of how well or poorly they are doing in school. Instead of moving away from this model, the United States is migrating toward enforcing ever more rigid rules about what kids learn during each year of school.

But in the age of big data and analytics, why don't we allow self-paced learning? Wouldn't school be more engaging if teachers became enablers who are there to answer questions and help students when they're stuck rather than reciters of mandated material? As students proceed through lessons at their own pace, they can ask the teacher for guidance at any time. There are already organizations, such as Khan Academy and Coursera, working to enable this approach.[8] The way it works is that educational material is posted online for viewing. Then users watch the videos and take tests to verify that they have grasped the material.

Why can't we use data and analytics to allow students to learn at their own pace all the time? Why can't students learn material from different grade levels every day? To complete third grade, a student still will have to pass the entire third-grade curriculum, but why can't a student be at a fifth-grade level in science coursework while still completing some of the third-grade classes for his or her history requirements? If a student learns all the required material at his or her own pace and can pass the tests, why should anyone care what route he or she takes or when the student was born?

## Expect Analytics to Transform Business Models

Some industries have already embraced analytics and changed how business is done, but others still look much as they did decades ago. The farther behind an industry is, the greater the potential for disruptive (but positive!) change to be achieved through the use of operational analytics.

The key here is that data and analytics will enable this transition. It is possible to monitor exactly which instructional videos each student watches, exactly which exercises each student completes, and how the student performs on each and every exercise and test question. Which areas does a student need to revisit? It is easy to tell because the analytics generated from the exercises can identify not just that a student is struggling in calculus but that he or she is struggling on topics related to one specific underlying concept.

Since it is possible to quickly analyze every question a student has answered and identify the pattern that led to his or her performance on the test, the student can be guided to the right support material immediately. By collecting and analyzing data at a very detailed level, the operational analytics behind the scenes will help a student navigate the material in a way that provides freedom while still ensuring that all the necessary material is covered.

I recall being bored in many classes. In fact, I remember that due to an anomaly in the way my high school credits transferred to my college, I effectively had to sit through a class I had already taken. I spent an entire semester listening to a professor go through material I already knew and taking tests I could have passed on the first day. I had no opportunity to demonstrate that I did not need to sit through the entire semester. It didn't make any sense to me then, and it doesn't make any sense to me now. The use of operational analytics to track and analyze student performance and progress at a new level may lead to education being one of the industries most disrupted by data and analytics in the coming years.

## Putting Operational Analytics in Perspective

Operational analytics are an evolution that moves beyond historical analytics practices, but that doesn't mean that all the lessons from the past are irrelevant. One theme throughout this book is the consistency of many core principles over time. In this section, we look at several important themes that deserve consideration to keep operational analytics in perspective.

### Data Quality and Timeliness Are as Crucial as Ever

Data quality and timeliness have always been crucial to analytics processes. These issues are even more important as organizations make analytics operational. When a process uses data from just seconds ago to make a decision just a second from now, the data has to be both current and accurate. With an automated decision from an operational analytics process, there is virtually no opportunity to catch data errors.

I have a friend who works for a large logistics organization. I will refrain from naming his organization because my intent is not to single out one company; many organizations have the same issue. My friend was describing the pain his company goes through when trying to route drivers appropriately. He outlined a major problem his company faced with data quality when it comes to street map data.

Think about when you use a common map application or GPS device. Haven't you noticed that the directions often take you to slightly wrong places? For example, a hotel's address may officially be on Main Street, but the parking entrance is around the corner on Elm Street. Your mapping application will take you to the Main

Street location, and then you have to figure out how to get to the parking deck from there.

That slight error is simply annoying when you're trying to get to dinner or find a store. Losing a minute or two isn't a big deal to you that one time. However, it's absolutely devastating for a company that has thousands of drivers experiencing the same kind of misdirection repeatedly over the course of hundreds of stops each day. As a result, my friend's company has a large team of people dedicated to updating the company's mapping database with the most up-to-date information drivers report.

## Don't Skimp on Quality

Data quality has always been critical, but it is even more so in the world of operational analytics. The automated and rapid nature of the processes means that there is little opportunity to catch data issues. The data must be pristine.

The mapping data team takes into account everything. Team members note that a hotel parking entrance is really around the corner from the official entrance. If a hotel moves an entrance location due to traffic issues, the database is updated as soon as the entrance is opened. A typical mapping application navigates to the street in front of a home. What about a rural area where the house sits a half mile down a dirt driveway? That delivering something to the door is going to be an additional five minutes up and down that driveway is critical for the algorithms to know. If the logistics company doesn't have fully current and correct data, it will suffer millions of dollars in lost productivity. The analytics processes that optimize drivers' routes won't be accurate if the map data isn't, so the company puts the utmost focus on getting the data right.

It is very easy to imagine how having incorrect data can cause operational analytics to go off the rails. This point gets back to why an organization can't leapfrog over traditional analytics and move straight into operational analytics. A large part of operational analytics is still gathering the needed data and making sure it is of sufficient quality. Analytics has always been a garbage-in, garbage-out discipline. The difference when going operational is that there are fewer opportunities and less time to sanity check and validate that data looks okay before analytics are executed and actions are taken.

Data quality must meet a very high standard or else data errors will lead first to errors in the analysis and then to errors in the decisions that are made. By the time a data error is found, a lot of damage may already be done.

### Do Operational Analytics Stifle Creativity?

Some people question the relationship between analytics and creativity. When analytics permeates an organization, is creativity stifled? In other words, are we taking all of the creativity and all of the human factor out of business by letting automated computer algorithms take over more and more decisions?

I'd argue that quite the opposite is true. I believe that operational analytics enables creativity. The reason is that when automated decisions are being made, it's very easy to track the effectiveness of those decisions. Tracking the decisions lets an organization test what's working and what's not. Instead of leaving a productive and creative brainstorming session and then having to pick one or two specific paths to go down, analytics makes it possible to test many ideas and then move forward based on the results. Creativity is still used to come up with the options. However, it is possible to better quantify the potential of those creative ideas and lower risk through experimentation. This is something that websites do all the time.

> ### Get Your Creative Juices Flowing
>
> Let analytics free your creative spirit rather than repress it. As long as creative ideas can be tested through experiments and analytics, an organization will be able to try many more creative ideas than in the past.

On leading websites like eBay or Amazon, it is almost assured that somewhere on every page viewed, there's some sort of test being applied. The test could be something as simple as the color of the banner at the top, or whether there are two ads or three ads, or whether there is a longer or shorter product description. Users never know what part of the page is a test and what part is standard, and that's the point. Those responsible for the site are running little experiments all the time. Industry leaders can rapidly test any creative idea someone comes up with and can quickly determine if it's a winner while investing little cost and being exposed to virtually no risk.

Embracing analytics and making them operational can actually free up more time to be creative. Let the system take care of the rudimentary, day-to-day decisions by building sophisticated operational analytics processes. Employees can then sit back and think up other fascinating ideas to try. The collection and analysis of data can allow creativity and innovation to flow freely throughout an organization. It should in no way stifle it.

### Many Concepts behind Operational Analytics Aren't Really New

Let's close out the chapter with an example of how many of the classic, tried-and-true analytics principles apply to operational analytics. Many operational analytics aren't necessarily new conceptually, no matter how complex and crazy they may seem at first. Often operational analytics are simply the latest, most modern logical extension of long-held best practices. The speed, timeliness, and automated nature of operational analytics processes are new, but the fundamental analytics concepts themselves often are not at all new.

One of my favorite examples of old concepts being applied in new ways is web customization and keyword optimization. Those topics seem new because we didn't even have web pages 20 years ago, let alone the ability to customize those pages in hundreds of ways on an ongoing basis. However, the concepts behind web page layout and keyword optimization have been around for quite some time.

During a media interview, a journalist in Europe pointed out a fascinating illustration of this to me. The journalist discussed a man he knew who had been in the newspaper industry for decades. Back 20 or 25 years ago when the editors were preparing the daily paper, there were often debates over what stories should be on the top and bottom of a page as well as what the headlines should be. The journalist's friend would always be able to deliver good insight in terms of what the right article placements and the right titles should be based on his experience.

How did the man's experience help? Because he had personally tracked and collected data over time about what stories and what titles sold best in different geographies within their subscriber area. Some of the data was written down and a lot was just in his head.

Without realizing it, he was effectively performing both keyword optimization and page layout optimization. His logic, methods, and thought processes were virtually identical to what happens on the web today. He was working in a much more rudimentary fashion, of course, but he was in fact following the same basic principles. It is important to note that a lot of the analytics being done today is an extension of what was done in the past, albeit often in a much more sophisticated and analytical manner. The same is true with operational analytics.

## Wrap-Up

The most important lessons to take away from this chapter are:

- Operational analytics represent the industrial revolution of analytics. They go beyond applying traditional analytics to operational problems.
- For years, organizations have been moving beyond descriptive analytics and reporting and into predictive analytics. Operational analytics take it a step further by making analytics prescriptive.
- Operational analytics are embedded, automated decision-making processes that prescribe and cause actions to occur in decision time.
- It is not possible to succeed with operational analytics without a strong foundation in traditional analytics to build on.
- The Analytics 1.0 era represents the traditional approach to analytics. It was focused on batch analysis of internal, structured data.
- The Analytics 2.0 era represents the rise of big data. It includes new data types, new analytics methods, and the use of external data.
- The Analytics 3.0 era enables operational analytics. It evolves the best of the Analytics 1.0 and 2.0 eras toward a unified analytics approach.
- Increasingly, purchase decisions are driven as much by analytics as by the physical attributes of a product.
- Industry lines are being blurred as companies suddenly find themselves supporting high-tech sensors within their products and generating analytics based on the data.

- Given the automated and rapid decisions driven by operational analytics, data quality is as important as ever.
- Analytics can enable creativity rather than stifle it. The freedom to test new ideas on a small scale exists today.
- Many operational analytics are based on concepts that are not new but take the concepts to a new level.

## Notes

1. As stated in the Preface, we will not take space to define common terms like analytics. It is assumed that readers are familiar with basic core concepts.
2. For details on Analytics 3.0 including a free e-book, see http://iianalytics.com/a3/
3. For more information, see Bill Franks, *Taming the Big Data Tidal Wave* (Hoboken, NJ: John Wiley & Sons, 2012).
4. See Xavier Amatriain and Justin Basilico, "Netflix Recommendations: Beyond the 5 Stars (Part 1)," *Netflix Tech Blog*, April 6, 2012, at http://techblog.netflix.com/2012/04/netflix-recommendations-beyond-5-stars.html.
5. See Dawn C. Chmielewski, "Meet Max: The New Voice of Netflix Recommendations," *Los Angeles Times*, June 28, 2013, at http://articles.latimes.com/2013/jun/28/entertainment/la-et-ct-meet-max-new-voice-of-netflix-recommendations-20130627.
6. Based on my International Institute for Analytics blog, "Is Big Data Changing the Business You Are in without You Realizing It?" August 8, 2013, http://iianalytics.com/2013/08/is-big-data-changing-the-business-you-are-in-without-you-realizing-it/.
7. See http://www.nike.com/us/en_us/c/nikeplus-fuelband.
8. See https://www.coursera.org/ and https://www.khanacademy.org/.

# More Data . . . More Data . . . Big Data!

This chapter discusses what readers need to know about the important trend of big data if their organizations are to leverage big data to support operational analytics. As the years pass, organizations have always collected more and more data. However, the pace has accelerated in recent years. It's not just that data sources are getting bigger either. Often today, data also comes in new formats and contains information that requires different analysis methods. Big data is the label that has been applied to this trend that leads to the challenges of more data, from more sources, in different formats.

An organization must keep in perspective a number of concepts when starting to consider big data and how it will affect the organization's analytics processes. This chapter discusses a variety of the hype points surrounding big data that organizations sometimes get caught up in and some ways to prepare for big data and keep it in perspective. Big data isn't as scary as it first may seem. Understanding how big data fits into the picture is necessary in order to incorporate it successfully into operational analytics.

## Cutting through the Hype

There is no doubt that a massive amount of hype has been built around big data. Organizations must cut through that hype and focus on what is really important. This section covers several concepts that help to do that. The content in this section is not meant in any way to diminish the importance or value of big data but rather to bring it back into the realm of reality. Developing realistic expectations should be the first step in the process of working with big data.

### What's the Definition of Big Data? Who Cares!

One of the first questions I am often asked when I meet with a customer is "How do you define big data, Bill?" People seem preoccupied with defining big data.[1] To see this firsthand, visit some of the LinkedIn groups devoted to big data. Each group will have the question of how to define big data, in some form or another, repeated over the past few years. One discussion thread I was involved in had dozens, if not hundreds, of responses to the question "What's the definition of big data?" That is extreme in a forum where a post is usually lucky to get a couple of responses. As the discussion went on, people were trying to outdo each other with one more nuance that may or may not fit into the definition of big data. It seemed silly and overly academic to me.

People are much too concerned about defining big data. In fact, I always like to propose what may be the shortest definition of big data anywhere. My preferred definition is a contrarian one that has only two words, but I believe it to be the most relevant definition of big data: "Who cares!" That may sound extreme at first. Why in the world would I say that? Let me explain.

If an organization's main concern is solving a business problem by implementing new operational analytics, it doesn't need to worry about the definition of big data. Here's why. The process that should be followed, and that organizations should have been following over the years, is simple. When you have a problem to solve, you should look around and ask this question: "What data, if collected, organized, and used within an analytics process, would improve the answers that we are able to generate to address our problem?" Once the necessary data is identified, at that point it is necessary to figure out how to collect, organize, and incorporate it into the analysis. But here's the key point. That first question of "Does this data have value for my business?" has absolutely nothing to do with the definition of the data. It could be big data, small data, or a bunch of spreadsheets.

By the time an organization is at the moment of realizing that it must make use of something that resembles big data, it is too late to worry about definitions; the data is needed. Perhaps the data is not well structured and there is a lot of it. It might just fit the

### Definitions Don't Matter, Results Do

Even if everyone agreed on a single definition of big data, it wouldn't add any value to solving a business problem. While defining big data is an interesting academic exercise, knowing that a given data source is officially big data (or not) doesn't do any good. If you need to analyze a data source, you'll have to find a way to make use of it regardless of the label you put on it

famous "Volume, Variety, Velocity" framework that industry analyst firm Gartner helped to coin.[2] Knowing that the data fits the Three Vs framework doesn't help because at the point the data is needed, there is no choice but to figure out how to make use of it, and the fact that it may be big data is really irrelevant. I also always like to propose that the most important, but often overlooked, V related to big data is Value.[3] The only reason to worry about the other characteristics is because it is believed that there is value in the data and that it is worth going to the effort to collect and analyze it.

Don't misunderstand what I am saying. If an organization is dealing with data that fits the typical definitions of big data, then that will certainly influence the tools and techniques the organization must use to incorporate big data into its analytics processes. The important distinction here is that the choice of tools and techniques is a tactical implementation issue. The strategic question initially is simply "Is the information this data contains important?" Once that question is answered, an organization must do what it takes to put the data to work.

Don't get overburdened trying to understand what qualifies as big data and what doesn't. Just worry about incorporating the important data sources you've identified into your organization's analytics processes.

### Start from the Right Perspective

The preceding topic implies that it is important to start from the right perspective. An organization can't start collecting data and storing it with hopes that one day a use for the data will be found. As Figure 2.1 illustrates, organizations should start with a business problem first and then let that business problem lead to the right data. Make the effort and incur the costs to acquire and use a data source once there is a reason to do so. In the world of big data, it is very

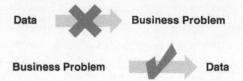

**Figure 2.1   Start from the Right Perspective**

easy to become overwhelmed by collecting every piece of data that can be found and worrying about how to drive value with it later. An organization can get so busy collecting data that it never gets around to doing anything with it.

Starting with a business problem instead of the data sounds obvious, but I have seen many otherwise very smart, very careful organizations totally abandon this principle when it comes to big data. At first I was very much puzzled by this trend, but then I realized what is going on. There is such hype around big data as I write this in early 2014 that no one wants to be left out. Every board of directors is asking every chief executive officer, "What are you doing with big data?" Every CEO is asking every chief information officer and chief marketing officer and chief financial officer, "What are you doing with big data?" And each of those executives then asks his or her respective team, "What are you doing with big data?"

### Don't Be Pressured into Being Shortsighted

Don't give in to the pressure to show you're doing something, anything at all, with big data. You should build systems and capture a lot of data only to support validated business opportunities. Many smart organizations have rushed into big data due to the hype and are at risk of learning some very visible and expensive lessons.

The only answer nobody wants to give is "Nothing yet" or "We are planning to do something but we're first going through the diligence of figuring out how to do it right." Because of the hype, those are not acceptable answers. As a result, organizations are rushing headlong into big data. In some cases, organizations are starting very large, expensive big data initiatives without having a solid plan for how to make use of the investments. They're simply buying a bunch of storage and collecting a bunch of data and hoping that they'll figure it out as they go.

Here's the biggest problem with that approach: It gets you past this year's conversation just fine. You'll get the pat on the back for being on top of the big data trend and for "doing something." However, what's going to happen 12 or 18 months down the road when the same person comes back and asks, "I see you applied a lot of resources to that big data project. What do we have to show for it?" If you didn't know up front what you were going to do with the data, you're probably going to have a hard time showing fast value on the back end. I'd hate to be the person who has to respond "Well, we jumped into big data aggressively as requested, but as yet we have nothing to show for it."

Make sure your organization is disciplined as it gets into big data. Take a little extra time to start with a real business issue and develop a plan. Identify some specific analytics that can be built with the data. It won't take much extra time, but it will make the probability of success much higher. Don't get pressured by all the hype to abandon basic principles.

### Is There a Big Data Bubble?

Amid all the hype around big data, the question often arises as to whether there's a big data bubble.[4] Industry analysis firm Gartner put forth an official opinion in January 2013 that claimed big data was past the peak of the hype cycle and heading for the trough of disillusionment.[5] A journalist called me after reading the Gartner article and asked if I thought big data was heading for a fall and a bubble was about to burst. I thought about the question and gave an answer that at first will seem self-contradictory but will make sense after I explain it. My answer was that in some ways, yes, there *is* a big data bubble. But in even more important ways, no, there's not. These views are summarized in the text and in Table 2.1.

I do believe there's a big data bubble that's going to burst from one perspective. The problem stems from unrealistic expectations

**Table 2.1    Is There a Big Data Bubble?**

| In These Ways, Yes | In These Ways, No |
| --- | --- |
| Unrealistic expectations | New information always adds power to analytics |
| Belief in easy buttons | Big data does yield value with effort |
| Money thrown at companies in the space | Real success stories exist |

in the marketplace. Many people seem to believe that they can get into big data cheaply and easily and that there's an "auto-magical" button that they can press to get all of the answers to their questions delivered. That's always been a ridiculous assumption for any analytics endeavor. It's still ridiculous in the world of big data.

There is no easy button for big data! It will take time and effort to build analytics processes with big data just as it always has with any type of data. It likely will take even more time initially since big data is new. There will certainly be some very visible big data failures in the marketplace as a result of those wrong assumptions. I have seen some failures already starting to happen. To the extent that those initial failures help burst the hype bubble of unrealistic expectations, they will be good for everyone. This is because it is absolutely possible to succeed with big data and to make it operational. However, organizations must get into big data with realistic expectations in terms of cost, timing, and effort.

### There Is No Easy Button for Big Data

It is absolutely true that expectations are out of line regarding what it will take to succeed with big data. In that sense, we have a bubble. However, the impacts of big data, and its analysis, eventually will far surpass the hype-filled claims of today. The Internet bubble didn't stop the potential of the Internet, and neither will a big data bubble stop the potential of big data.

Now let's turn our attention to the ways in which there is not a big data bubble about to burst. Often people think that a bubble bursting means that an underlying premise was bogus to begin with. You can be sure that big data is not a bogus premise. Big data is going to have a very large impact on our future. I'll use an analogy to demonstrate why.

Think back to the Internet bubble in 1999 and 2000. There was a huge bubble for Internet companies, and a lot of people lost a lot of money. But there's an important point to understand. Go back and find news stories from late 1999 or 2000 at the very peak of the Internet hype. Then look at what the articles claimed regarding how the Internet would change our personal lives and how we do business. I'm confident that you'll find that the Internet has already exceeded even the wildest dreams of that era.

You see, the Internet bubble had nothing to do with the Internet being bogus or not holding all the promise (and more) that was being hyped at the time. Rather, the Internet bubble was about people thinking it would be too cheap, too fast, and too easy to realize those benefits. During the Internet bubble, a company could get funding as long as the founders threw an "I" or an "e" in front of the company's name. This sounds a lot like big data today to me. If I had started a company in 2013 and claimed that it was a cloud-based, big data, machine learning, analytics-as-a-service company, I probably would have rounded up some cash pretty quickly.

There will be market consolidation and there will be business failures in the big data space in the next few years. There will also be disillusionment as companies that dove in too quickly without realistic expectations realize their error. However, five to ten years down the road, big data will have had all of the impacts it has been purported to enable and much more. The impact from operational analytics based on big data is going to exceed anything being discussed today. Despite the cautions at the beginning of this section, organizations should not sit on the sidelines with big data. In fact, your organization absolutely must get into big data. Just do it intelligently and rationally.

## Preparing for Big Data

Once an organization has set realistic expectations about big data, how does it prepare? What are some of the most important concepts to consider when developing a big data strategy? This section focuses on themes to help an organization prepare for big data after moving past the hype.

### The Big Data Tidal Wave Is Here

There is no doubt that a tidal wave of data has come our way and that every organization is going to have to tame the wave in order to succeed. This was the theme of my book *Taming the Big Data Tidal Wave*.[6] The reason I chose that title for the book is that the sea is a very good analogy for data. Imagine waves crashing on the shore. If you sit on an inner tube right where the wave crashes, you'll learn that even a wave not much above your waist has the power to flip you over backward. If you start sitting under really big waves, you can be injured by letting them crash upon you. So it is with data. Data, as it gains in volume, can become overwhelming and hard to handle. If you just let the wave of data hit you, it will simply knock you around and you won't accomplish anything with it.

What you must do is to figure out how to ride the wave, whether it is a wave in the ocean or a wave of data. When it comes to surfing in the ocean, we have surfboards. For someone who doesn't know anything about surfing, it is easy to think that a surfboard is a surfboard and that surfing is surfing. But that's not true. Visit a surf shop and look around. There are many different types of surfboards. There are long boards and short boards. There are different shapes. Some have fins and some don't. The reason surfers choose one board over the others has to do with what kind of wave they will ride, how skilled they are, and if they want to go for speed or want to do tricks.

Similarly, when it comes to data and analytics, outsiders often assume that all that is required is to just grab data, store it, and then analyze it with a tool. But anyone who understands analytics realizes there are many different types of tools and many different types of platforms that can give access to the data and allow it to be analyzed. Big data can certainly necessitate adding a few new tools into the mix, just as a surfer might need to add multiple boards over time. Just as there are more similarities in how to use two different surfboards than there are differences, so there are more similarities than differences when it comes to using different analytics tools and platforms for different types of data and analytics.

### You're Ready to Surf the Wave of Big Data

If an organization has strong people on staff who have been able to help the organization make effective use of data in the past, those people are fully able to help with big data even though it will take some effort. Just as a professional surfer can surf anywhere with any surfboard, analytics professionals can analyze any data with any tool or platform.

When an organization gets to the point of adding tools for big data, it will need people who know how to use the tools. If you give me the best surfboard to surf the best waves, I'll fall right off because I don't know how to surf. Expert surfers, however, will be fine if they are given a new surfboard on a new beach with a different size and shape of wave than they are used to. They may be a little wobbly at first, but within a few hours they'll be up and surfing just as strongly as they ever have. That's because the new board on the new beach for the new wave is an incremental change. It's not a quantum leap that can't be overcome. Similarly, expert analytics professionals already have the underlying skills to handle big data and simply need to tune their skills slightly for the new data and analysis requirements. Just as a surfer can adapt to any board on any beach, analytics professionals can adapt to any type of analysis for any type of data because it's an incremental change. It's not a huge quantum leap that they can't overcome.

### New Information Is What Makes Big Data So Powerful

What is it that makes big data so powerful and exciting? Why have I predicted that big data will have huge impacts? It is because of the *new information* that big data can provide.[7] Big data sources often provide information to an organization that is novel in one or both of two dimensions. First, big data is often at a level of detail not seen before. Second, big data also often provides information that was not available before.

Let's consider how automobile manufacturers now use big data for predictive maintenance purposes. For many years, as cars broke down, an auto manufacturer would do its best to figure out why the cars had broken down and then work back to what may have caused the problem. Today, embedded sensors are providing intensive data during the development and testing of engines as well as from engines that have been sold once the car is released. Leveraging the sensor data, auto manufacturers can now often identify troublesome patterns before the damage is done and a car breaks down. This is called predictive maintenance.

With engine sensor data, it is now possible to identify early warnings of trouble. Does a certain part heat up before a failure? Does the battery lose a bit of voltage prior to a common electrical problem? Do some parts break in pairs or in sets rather than individually? The answers to these questions would never have been known before since there was no data available to provide the answers. Today the data is available, and it is being analyzed in detail.

The power of the sensor data in this case isn't just that it is more data. It is that the data contains entirely new information not available previously. If a problem is predicted before it happens, there is often time to get the issue fixed proactively before a break down occurs. This can result in higher customer satisfaction and lower warranty costs since cars are spending less time in the shop and it is usually cheaper to avoid a problem than to perform repairs after a problem has occurred.

Traditionally, analytics professionals spent a lot of time fine-tuning existing models using a given set of data sources. Over time, analytics professionals try to incorporate the newest and latest modeling methodologies and to add new metrics derived from the data. This leads to incremental gains in the power of the models, and those efforts are worthwhile.

## New Information Beats New Algorithms Almost Every Time

The reason organizations need to pursue big data aggressively is because of the totally new information it often provides. Tweaking existing analytics processes using existing data is worthwhile. However, adding new information has the potential to yield tremendous gains. Always prioritize testing new information over testing new methodologies or new metrics based on old information.

It is possible, however, to greatly increase the power of a given analytics process with one simple change. Organizations should deviate from the traditional tuning approach as soon as new information relevant to a problem is found. New information can be so powerful that once it is found, analytics professionals should stop worrying about improving existing models with existing information. Instead, they should focus immediately on incorporating and testing that new information.

Even a fairly simplistic use of new information can have impacts on the performance of an analytics process that go far beyond what's possible by tuning the process using existing information. Incorporate new information into a process as soon as possible, even if it can be done only roughly at first. After that is done, then return to tuning and improving the analytics incrementally. New information will beat new algorithms and new metrics based on existing information almost every time.

### Seek New Questions to Ask

As an organization changes the breadth of data and tools it is using, it must make a point to look for new questions to ask as well as new ways to ask old questions. Often, when people find a new data source,

- Add additional value to existing analytics processes
- Identify new ways to solve existing problems
- Identify entirely different problems to solve

Figure 2.2    Three Ways to Drive Value with Big Data

they immediately think about how it can add additional power to existing solutions of old problems. But there are two other angles that need to be considered, as shown in Figure 2.2.

First, look for entirely new and different questions that can be addressed with the new information. This is a seemingly obvious suggestion, but it is easy for people to get into a rut and simply apply the data to the usual questions. An organization must put emphasis on looking for new opportunities with data. Second, look for new and better ways to address old questions. Do this by examining problems considered solved and thinking about whether the problems could be approached from a completely different direction through the incorporation of the new data. It just might improve the power of the insights generated.[8] One helpful framework for pursuing these activities in the context of customer data is the concept of a dynamic customer strategy, as proposed by Jeff Tanner in the book *Dynamic Customer Strategy: Big Profits from Big Data*.[9] That book can be a further reference for readers interested in the topic. Asking new questions is a straightforward concept, so let's focus on an example of revisiting old questions in new ways using big data. In the healthcare industry, clinical trials are the gold standard. A clinical trial has the ultimate test and control structure through what is called a double-blind methodology. In a double-blind clinical trial, neither the patients nor the doctors know who's getting what treatments. It's a tightly controlled atmosphere, and it makes it possible to very precisely pinpoint the positive and negative effects of the treatment or drug being tested. However, after hundreds of millions of dollars and years of effort, a clinical trial will have 2,000 to 3,000 participants if it is lucky. That's not a lot of sample size. This means that while a clinical trial can very precisely measure the things researchers know they want to measure up front, there's not enough data to test for a broad range of unexpected impacts.

What does this lack of sample lead to? Situations like those that occurred a few years ago, when multiple drugs from a class of painkillers known as COX-2 inhibitors, which includes the drugs Vioxx and Celebrex, ran into trouble. Researchers found that these drugs had an association with heart trouble that was two to four times the normal rate of heart trouble.[10] The issue wasn't identified in the original clinical trial, and it took several years after the products went on the market before the problem was identified.

## Take a Fresh Look at Problems Considered Solved

When new data with new information is identified, be sure to revisit old problems. Often a problem that is considered solved might be solved in a much more robust fashion by using the new information and approaching the problem from a different direction.

Let's flash forward to today. Can we enhance clinical trials with big data even outside a controlled environment? In the near future, detailed electronic medical records will be the norm. Once a drug is released, it will be possible to monitor trends within the thousands, hundreds of thousands, or millions of people who start using that drug. It will be possible to analyze every combination of ailment that people have as they use the drug as well as every combination of other drugs and treatments that are taken alongside the drug. There will be people using the drug for things it wasn't supposed to be used for and with other drugs it wasn't supposed to be used with. These are specifically the things that would not be assessed in a clinical trial.

Using electronic medical histories, it will be possible to mine for unexpected positive and negative effects of a drug (while protecting patient privacy, of course). Granted, the data won't be from a fully controlled environment like a clinical trial. However, might it be possible to identify that something is happening, like the heart issues with Vioxx, much, much earlier? Further controlled studies may be required to validate the findings from the medical records, but researchers will know where to look much faster. It is not about uncontrolled medical data ever replacing clinical trials, but about researchers' ability to identify unexpected positive and negative effects of new drugs and treatments can rise immensely through the use of the uncontrolled data. All that is required is thinking about how to solve problems differently . . . even if they are already considered solved today.

## Data Retention Is No Longer a Binary Decision

Big data necessitates a change to policies related to what data organizations collect, how they store it, and how long they store it. Until recently, it was too expensive to waste resources on anything but the most critical data. If data was important enough to collect, it was important enough to keep for a very long time, if not forever. With a lot of big data sources, we must move from a binary decision of "to collect or not to collect" and also from storing what is collected forever. A multiple-tier decision is necessary.

First, is it necessary to collect any part of a data source or not? Second, how much of the source should be collected and for how long should it be kept? Only a small portion of a big data source might be captured, and that portion may be stored for only a short time before deletion. Determining the right approach requires assessing the value of the data both today and over time.

To illustrate data that isn't worth collecting, imagine that you have a highly connected house with sensors all throughout. Every room has its own thermostat constantly sending the current temperature back to the central system so that each room's temperature can be kept stable. The thermostats will generate data continuously as they communicate with the central system, but is there any value in that data? The data has value for a very specific tactical purpose, but it's hard to imagine why it would be worth capturing the data for the long term. Millisecond-level temperatures just don't matter beyond the basic purpose of updating the system. That's okay. If a power company, for example, tried to store all of this detailed data from all of the homes and buildings under its purview, its storage capacity would be overwhelmed while nothing of value was provided.

It is also possible to perform analytics to reduce the data. Data reduction is the process of identifying fields of data that can be either ignored or combined so that there are fewer metrics to work with but little information is lost. For example, it may be found that adjacent rooms in your house always stay within half a degree of each other. Instead of storing readings for each room, just store one of the room's readings and associate it with a zone of the house rather than a specific room. That will cut down on data storage requirements without degrading the quality of information available for analytics.

Let's look at a scenario where data is critical for only a period of time. Railroads have sensors along the tracks monitoring the speed

### Apply an Expiration Date to Data

One big paradigm shift that is underway is the idea of deleting data after a period of time (if it is collected and stored at all). It is necessary to assess the time value of data to an organization. Some data will expire almost immediately, while other data will expire over time. Only a small percentage of data will be kept for the long term as is the standard today.

of trains as they go by. What I didn't know until recently is that the wheel temperatures of the train cars are also monitored. If the load in a car gets unbalanced so that there's more weight on one side than the other, it will cause the car to start to lean. That lean puts more weight on one side, which adds friction, which will heat up the wheels. If wheels start heating beyond a certain point, it's an indicator of a serious imbalance and a potential derailment. The railroads monitor wheels in real time as a train moves along the track. If a set of wheels heats beyond guidelines, the train will be stopped and someone will be sent to inspect and fix the load. This saves the railroad a lot of money in the long run because a derailment is a catastrophic and costly, if not deadly, event.

Let's turn attention to the data collected on wheel temperature and the time frame in which it's important. Consider a long train traveling 2,000 miles over a period of many days. At regular intervals, perhaps every 30 seconds, another measure of each wheel's temperature is taken. It is critically important to collect that data and analyze it right away to ensure that nothing's going wrong.

Now fast-forward a few weeks. The train experienced no issues and arrived safely. All wheel readings are within a half degree of the expected temperature. There's really no point in keeping the readings at that point. It might make sense to keep a sampling of trips where everything was fine against which exceptions can be compared. The data surrounding the trips where there was a wheel temperature problem can be kept virtually forever along with a small sample of uneventful trips. The rest of the data doesn't add further value.

Of course, there is still data that will make sense to keep for a long time. Banks or brokerages have a relationship with customers that can last years or decades. These organizations will want to keep records of every deposit that each customer makes and every e-mail exchanged with each customer. That will help provide better service over time and provide legal protection as well. In this case, data that gets collected is still kept virtually forever just as was done traditionally.

The key takeaway is that organizations are going to have to get used to assessing the collection, storage, and retention of data in a different fashion. It's uncomfortable at first to think of letting data slip past and intentionally deleting data that is captured. It is necessary in today's big data era, however.

### The Internet of Things Is Coming

The concept of the Internet of Things (IOT) has been getting steadily more attention in 2013 and early 2014. The IOT refers to all of the "things" that will be online and communicating both with each other and with us. As sensors and communication technologies become cheaper and cheaper, more and more items will have the capability to assess surroundings and report information. We already see mundane items like refrigerators and clocks being connected to the Internet and regularly sending and receiving information.

The IOT has the potential to drive absolutely massive amounts of data. It may even outpace all of the other sources of big data. The interesting thing about much of the data generated by the IOT is that it is often very tactical. Any given communication is very short and may contain only simplistic information. For example, a clock may receive a time update from a trusted external source and then pass that information on to other clocks within a house over a home network. In aggregate, this produces a large amount of data, but much of it has very low, very tactical, very short term value.

Many of the examples outlined in this book could be considered a part of the IOT. Once sensor data is involved, it is usually fair to assume the realm of the IOT has been entered. Both businesses and consumers will benefit from all of these devices talking to each other. As more and more of your possessions are able to communicate, new possibilities open up:

- Your home will learn your preferences for lighting, heating, and more and then automatically make adjustments for you.
- Items like light bulbs and air fresheners will be able to warn you when they will soon need replacing.

- Grocery lists will be created automatically based on what you've consumed and what has passed its expiration date.
- Video and audio content will follow you seamlessly from room to room, removing the need for you to turn anything on or off.
- Sensors on or near your body will monitor and report sleep patterns, calorie usage, body temperature, and all sorts of other facts.

---

### Our Things May Become the Biggest Source of Personal Data

The Internet of Things is arriving quickly. Soon many of our possessions, both big and small, will contain sensors and will communicate. The amount of data our things generate will eclipse whatever data we personally collect today. Personal image and video storage will look small compared to the combined volume of all the messages sent by all of our things over time.

---

While the IOT may drive some of the biggest volumes of data, it will likely be filtered much more aggressively than most data. In fact, what we decide to keep may be fairly manageable. We'll let all of our things communicate freely on an ongoing basis and only capture critical pieces of those communications. We discuss this concept more in Chapter 6.

Soon the IOT will become a very hot and popular topic. It is impossible to do the topic justice with just this small introduction, but the topic can't be ignored. Similar to the big data phenomenon, books and articles on the IOT will soon abound. Readers who have interest should carefully monitor the progress of this trend. As many of the examples in this book illustrate, a lot of operational analytics will be driven by data that is sourced from all of the things around us. The IOT will become a component of virtually every organization's analytics strategies.

## Putting Big Data in Context

How does big data fit? Why is it special? Where will big data go from here? Questions like these are common and arise in most organizations. As with anything that is relatively new, there is confusion and disagreement on what big data is all about. This section explores themes and concepts that must be understood to put big data in the correct context. Placing big data within the correct context will make it much easier to succeed when applying it to operational analytics.

### It's Not So Much Big Data as It Is Different Data

As we discussed earlier in the chapter, what makes big data exciting is the new information it contains. As we also discussed earlier, many people think that what makes big data challenging is simply the fact that the volume of the data is so large. Volume is not really what makes many sources of big data stand out. What often is most challenging about big data is that the new information it contains is found within a different type or format of data and can require different analysis methodologies.

Most data historically collected for analysis in the business world was transactional or descriptive in nature and was well structured. This means that information was clearly identified and easy to read. For example, a column labeled Sales in a spreadsheet would contain dollar values. The less structured data that organizations had, such as written documents or images, was not considered for analysis purposes. With big data, organizations now come across new types and formats of data, many of which are not structured like traditional sources. Sensors spit out information in special formats. GPS data describes where people and things are in space. The strength of the relationships between people or organizations is often desired. These are fundamentally different types of data both in terms of format and in terms of how the data must be analyzed. We talk about the different types of analysis in Chapter 7.

### "Differentness" Can Be More Challenging than "Bigness"

While the "bigness" of big data gets the most focus, it is often the "differentness" of big data that really poses the challenge. There are many new sources of data in many new formats describing new types of information. Determining how to extract what is needed from the data can take more effort than determining how to scale the analytics processes.

Analyzing a social network and assessing the number and strength of connections between people requires entirely different methodologies from predicting sales, for example. This "differentness" of big data can actually be a much bigger challenge than the "bigness" of the data. Why can it be challenging? Let's look at an example.

Consider an organization looking to do text analysis for the first time. Even to analyze just a few thousand e-mails, it is necessary to acquire a text analysis tool, to set up and configure the tool, and to define the text analysis logic that the organization would like applied. It requires just as much time and effort to initially create a text analysis process to handle 10,000 e-mails as it does to create a process to handle 10 million or 100 million e-mails. The same logic just has to scale as more e-mails are processed. Due to the fact that text is a different type of data, it is necessary to go to a lot of preliminary setup work to get started even for a very small volume of text data.

Of course, when the text analysis process defined is executed, 10,000 e-mails will process more quickly than 100 million. While it is necessary to scale the process as more volume is added, the underlying analytics logic is the same. Figuring out how to handle the differentness of a source of big data is often step one. Once the differentness is handled, then it is possible to move on to figuring out how to handle the differentness at scale.

### Big Data Must Be Scaled across Multiple Dimensions

The big data challenge that gets the most attention is the problem of scale. Specifically, the usual focus is the amount of data and the amount of processing required. However, other dimensions of scale, as illustrated in Figures 2.3 and 2.4, are also required if an organization is to implement analytics at an enterprise level, and especially if it will make those analytics operational.

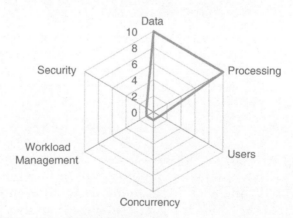

Figure 2.3    Scaling Big Data: Typical Focus Dimensions

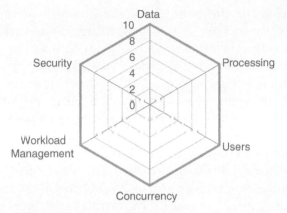

**Figure 2.4     Scaling Big Data: Necessary Focus Dimensions**

First, it is necessary to have scale in terms of the number and variety of users that access both the underlying data and the results of the analytics processes built on it. Tens or hundreds of thousands of employees might need to see various views of raw data and analysis results at any time. Enterprise platforms must be user friendly and also compatible with a wide range of tools and applications.

## Scale Isn't Just about Storage and Processing

Most of the focus when discussing big data's scale challenges is on storage and processing scalability. Often overlooked are other critical dimensions that also must scale, including the number of users, the level of concurrency, workload management, and security protocols. Without systems that scale across all of these dimensions, an organization won't succeed with operational analytics.

Second is a crucial need for scale in the dimension of concurrency. Concurrency refers to the number of users or applications that can access a given set of information at the same time. Concurrency at an enterprise level also means that as data is changing, users will receive consistent answers. As concurrency levels increase, the risks become quite large if a system isn't engineered to handle processing requests appropriately. For a large organization desiring to build operational analytics processes, it is necessary to have an environment where many different users and applications can interact with the same information simultaneously.

Third, there is the need for scalable workload management tools. With different user types submitting a wide variety of analysis requests with a layer of security on top, something must manage the workload. It is not a trivial task to balance many requests at once, and it is easy to forget this aspect of scalability. Creating a system that can effectively manage both very small, tactical requests and very large, strategic requests simultaneously is very difficult.

Last is the need to scale security protocols. An organization must be able to lock data down and control access as needed. Users must be allowed to see only those pieces of data that they are allowed to see. A large organization must have security built into its platforms in a robust fashion.

All of these dimensions of scale—data, processing, users, concurrency, workload management, and security—have to be present alongside each other from the start to succeed with operational analytics. Organizations that worry only about scaling the storage and processing dimensions will fail.

### Getting the Most Value from Big Data

One of the most common mistakes I've seen organizations make as they try to incorporate big data into their analytics processes is that they consider big data a completely separate and distinct problem. Many companies are setting up an internal organization to focus specifically and only on big data.[11] In fact, some organizations are going so far as to open new offices in Silicon Valley to handle their big data initiatives. That approach is asking for trouble because it is imperative that big data is simply another facet of an overarching data and analytics strategy. There should be a single, cohesive strategy to execute against that includes all data, big and small, as illustrated in Figures 2.5 and 2.6.

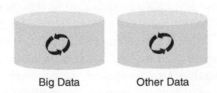

Big Data            Other Data

Figure 2.5    Big Data as Distinct Silo

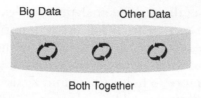

Figure 2.6   Integrated Big Data

Let's explore a historical parallel that shows why not having a single data and analytics strategy will be problematic. When e-commerce came of age, many retailers did not think about e-commerce as another facet of their retail strategies. Instead, many retailers handled e-commerce as though it was something totally new. As a result, many retailers established a separate division to handle their e-commerce activities. In some cases, this division was also a separate legal entity. Those separate entities set up their own supply chain processes, their own product hierarchies, their own pricing policies, and so forth.

Fast forward to today. These same retailers now desire a single view of their business. They want to have their e-commerce and traditional store environments not only within a unified view, but they want to provide a seamless experience for customers across channels as well. However, it is taking years and millions of dollars for retailers to reconcile what in some cases are completely incompatible hierarchies and systems.

## Develop an Overall Data and Analytics Strategy

You must make big data another facet of an overall data and analytics strategy. If you don't, you'll face the same type of problems retailers have faced as a result of not initially considering e-commerce another facet of their retail strategies.

Retailers 10 to 15 years ago correctly recognized that e-commerce would have new challenges. But they also should have recognized that e-commerce needed to fit within their overall retail strategy. Setting up their e-commerce business in a way that kept it integrated with the core business would have taken a little bit longer initially, but it would have saved a lot of time and money in the long run.

Make sure your organization doesn't make this same mistake with big data. Take the extra time up front to think through how big data will fit into your overall data and analytics strategy. This is important because no data source by itself will provide optimal value. Mixing various data sources together is the only way to maximize value. For example, it is necessary to mix sales data, web browsing data, demographic data, and more to fully understand a customer.

Once an organization establishes separate systems and processes for big data without thinking up front about the need for integration, it will just make it that much harder to derive the value needed on the back end. Companies need to work toward a unified analytics environment that allows people to perform any type of analysis against any type or volume of data at any time. We discuss in much more detail how to make this a reality later in the book. Readers wishing to take a deep dive into getting the most value from big data as it relates to marketing should consider reading *Big Data Marketing: Engage Your Customers More Effectively and Drive Value*, written by my colleague Lisa Arthur.[12]

### Back to the Future

A highly hyped concept around big data is the supposedly new world of nonrelational tool sets that are not based on a relational database and do not use SQL as the primary interface. SQL stands for Structured Query Language, and it has been called "the language of business" for years. Nonrelational tool sets do not leverage SQL exclusively, if at all. The premise behind the nonrelational movement is that there is need for additional languages since SQL has in many companies been virtually the sole language of business. After all, why shouldn't businesses be multilingual? They should be. Furthermore, they should have been all along.

Let's get right to the fatal flaw in the hype. The fact is that nonrelational analytics is not a new concept. When I started in my analytics career, relational databases did not yet exist in the business world. There literally was no SQL. Therefore, everything we did to generate analytics was based on nonrelational methods. In my case, I usually leveraged tools from SAS. To people like me, SQL is actually the new kid on the block. Over time, we analytics professionals realized that SQL is a better way to go for certain kinds of problems and processing. There have also always been certain kinds of processing that analytics professionals have executed outside of an SQL environment.

With big data, what's really happening is that organizations have rediscovered the value of processing outside of an SQL context when it makes sense. As it happens, using nonrelational options makes sense much more often with many big data sources than with many traditional data sources. Many companies went too far and tried to fit all processing into an SQL paradigm. That was a mistake; organizations do need to incorporate other options into the mix. Just keep in mind that nonrelational options have always been available. It isn't that there was no need for nonrelational processing during the first decade of the 21st century. Rather, companies moved too far toward SQL. We can expect that SQL will remain the dominant approach for analyzing data in the future and that nonrelational analysis will be focused on specific needs.

### The Huge Big Data Flip-Flop

After years of predictions that SQL was going to die, nonrelational platforms are now scrambling to implement SQL interfaces. Although this represents a huge flip-flop, it also reflects the reality of business needs.

Organizations should embrace the use of nonrelational tool sets where it is appropriate but can't for a minute think that doing so negates the need for SQL right alongside them. It is very easy to swing too far in the other direction, and many are at risk of doing just that today. In fact, for several years, many people advocated the death of SQL. In a case of massive opinion flip-flop, there is now a large movement to enable SQL-like functionality on a wide variety of nonrelational platforms, such as Hadoop. Once again, we're going back to the future. We talk more about this trend and how to leverage the right kind of processing in Chapters 5 and 6.

### Big Data Is Going through a Maturity Curve

A lot of people talk to me about how big data feels overwhelming to them. There are so many new data sources and so many new things to do with the data that many organizations are just not sure how to begin and how to handle it all. Before despairing, consider the fact that big data is going through the same maturity curve that any new data source goes through.[13] The reality is that the first time a new data source becomes available, it is always challenging. People aren't sure exactly how to best use the new data, what metrics to create from it, what data quality issues will be found, and so forth. However, over time, the handling of that data source becomes standardized.

Many years ago when I first started analyzing retail point-of-sale (POS) data, my team and I weren't sure how to best use the data to analyze customer behavior and drive better business results. We weren't even thinking yet about how to make analytics operational with the data. We had a lot of theories and ideas, but which of them would work hadn't yet been proven. We certainly hadn't standardized how we would input, prepare, and analyze the data. Over time, those analyzing POS data regularly did standardize all of those aspects. Today, POS data is considered easy to deal with, and it is applied to a wide range of problems.

### Don't Despair

New data sources are always intimidating when we first start to analyze them. Over time, our understanding matures and we become comfortable with the data. The same maturation process will happen with big data. It seems worse than usual with big data because we have so many new sources to deal with at once.

Organizations must go through the same process outlined in Figure 2.7 with each new big data source. The fundamental difference with big data is that, in the past, one truly new and unique data source might be made available to an organization every few years. With big data, an organization may be faced with multiple new data sources all at once.

Analytics professionals today can be tasked with trying simultaneously to analyze social media interactions, customer service interactions, web behavior, information from sensors, and more. This data may have to be leveraged together all at once within a single analytics process. In such a case, multiple new data sources

- The quality of the data is not understood
- The best methods to store and process the data are not identified
- The most valuable metrics to create from the data are not known
- The ability of the data to address business problems has not been proven
- How the data overlaps and is distinct from other data has not been assessed

Figure 2.7    Challenges with Any New Data Source

going through the maturity curve all are being applied together. That is much more challenging than having a single new data source to worry about. Making matters worse, as we discussed previously, is the necessity to think not just about how to handle each data source by itself but how to connect them together.

Don't lose sight of the fact that working with new data is always difficult and always intimidating at first. There are always bumps in the road to get past. Inevitably, how to incorporate and analyze the data becomes largely standardized and everything is just fine. Then it is time to move onto the next new data source. That's exactly what is going to happen, and is already happening, with big data.

### Big Data Is a Global Phenomenon

A final big data trend worth discussing is how consistent the views and maturity of big data are around the world.[14] It is true that some organizations are farther ahead or farther behind in the adoption and maturity cycles. However, I've gone to several continents and I've talked to banks, insurance companies, retailers, government agencies, and more. What I've found is that everyone across the globe is struggling with almost the exact same issues. There are always local market considerations with respect to customs and regulations, but the fundamental business issues tend to be very consistent. Moreover, most people think that other industries and other parts of the world are well ahead of their own organization, even though often that really isn't true.

Math, statistics, analytics, and data don't really speak a specific language or belong to a specific culture; rather, they are universal in nature. A trend graph in China looks exactly the same as a trend graph in Spain and relays similar information. An average will be computed in India the same way as in Germany. A transaction record in Japan will have the same information as a transaction record in Brazil. The claim that big data is something that's a unique problem for an industry within a country is not true except in extremely rare instances.

Consider forming relationships with peers from a business just like yours elsewhere in the world. With social media today, it is easy to do. The other organization is probably struggling with the same problems your organization is. It isn't possible to get into

**Your Organization May Not Be as Far Behind as It Thinks It Is**

Companies around the world are all facing very similar issues with big data. No matter where in the world you go, organizations often perceive that they are behind other industries as well as those in their own industry in other regions of the world. Although everyone thinks the others are ahead, in many cases the differences are much smaller than perceived.

a meaningful discussion with a direct competitor about how your organization analyzes data. However, it is quite possible to talk to somebody halfway around the world who poses no competitive threat. By sharing information and lessons learned, both organizations can benefit.

Whatever pains your organization is going through with big data, you can be sure that many others are going through the same pains as well. Over time, the solutions to those pain points will be found and the solutions will become widely known and implemented. Incorporating big data into operational analytics will become much easier and more commonplace. An organization doesn't necessarily have to be the first in the world to tackle something, but it shouldn't wait till the problem is fully solved either. At that point, the effort is nothing more than playing catch-up. Being the company following everyone else is not a winning approach.

## Wrap-Up

The most important lessons to take away from this chapter are:

- Don't worry about how to define big data. Worry about what data, whether big or small, is needed for your analytics. Definitions don't matter; results do!
- Always start with specific business problems. Don't implement big data technology just to claim you are doing something with big data.
- Despite excessive hype and unrealistic short-term expectations, big data is here to stay. Just as the Internet bubble didn't mean the Internet wasn't a huge opportunity, the big data bubble doesn't mean that big data isn't a huge opportunity.

- What makes big data so exciting is the new information it provides. New information will beat out new algorithms almost every time.
- Don't just use big data to improve existing analytics processes. Also look for ways that big data can solve old problems from a new perspective or can solve entirely new problems.
- Expect the hype around the Internet of Things to rise rapidly in the coming years, but also expect to rethink data retention policies in order to handle new floods of data that have lower value.
- The "differentness" of big data compared to traditional data can lead to more challenges than the "bigness" of big data.
- Big data requires scale, but not just of processing and storage. Scalability is also needed for the dimensions of users, concurrency, workload management, and security.
- Big data must be made a component of an overall data and analytics strategy. Big data can't be tackled effectively by itself.
- After years of predictions that SQL was going to die, non-relational platforms are now scrambling to implement SQL interfaces. Although this represents a huge flip-flop, it also reflects the reality of business needs.
- Big data seems overwhelming today, but it is going through the same maturity curve as other data sources. Big data feels worse due to the number of new data sources coming at us all at once.
- Around the world and across industries, most organizations perceive they are well behind with big data. In reality, few organizations are very far ahead today, which means few are far behind either.

## Notes

1. Based on my blog for the International Institute for Analytics from June 14, 2012, titled "What's the Definition of Big Data? Who Cares?" See http://iianalytics .com/2012/06/whats-the-definition-big-data-who-cares/.
2. See "Gartner IT Glossary" at www.gartner.com/it-glossary/big-data/. Also see Svetlana Sicular, "Gartner's Big Data Definition Consists of Three Parts, Not to Be Confused with Three 'V's," *Forbes*, March 27, 2013, at www.forbes.com/sites/ gartnergroup/2013/03/27/gartners-big-data-definition-consists-of-three-parts-not-to-be-confused-with-three-vs/.
3. See my article "Defining Big Data: The Missing 'V,'" *IT Briefcase*, August 2, 2012, at www.itbriefcase.net/defining-big-data-the-missing-v.

 4. Based on my blog for the International Institute for Analytics from December 12, 2012, "Will the Big Data Bubble Burst in 2013?" See http://iianalytics.com/2012/12/will-the-big-data-bubble-burst-in-2013/.
 5. See Svetlana Sicular, "Big Data Is Falling into the Trough of Disillusionment," Gartner, January 22, 2013, at http://blogs.gartner.com/svetlana-sicular/big-data-is-falling-into-the-trough-of-disillusionment/
 6. Bill Franks, *Taming the Big Data Tidal Wave* (Hoboken, NJ: John Wiley & Sons, 2012).
 7. Based on my blog for the International Institute for Analytics from January 11, 2013, titled "Driving Analytic Value from New Data." See http://iianalytics.com/2013/01/driving-analytic-value-from-new-data/. Also covered in my book *Taming the Big Data Tidal Wave.*
 8. Based on my blog for the International Institute for Analytics from March 14, 2013, titled "Think Differently to Maximize Value from Big Data Analytics." See http://iianalytics.com/2013/03/think-differently-to-maximize-value-from-big-data-analytics/.
 9. Jeff Tanner, *Dynamic Customer Strategy: Big Profits from Big Data* (Hoboken, NJ: John Wiley & Sons, 2014).
10. See "Pfizer Study Finds that Celebrex May Increase the Risk of Heart Attack," August 10, 2010, at www.drugrecalls.com/celebrex.html.
11. Based on my blog for the International Institute for Analytics from August 9, 2012, titled "A Strategic Mistake with Big Data." See http://iianalytics.com/2012/08/a-strategic-mistake-with-big-data/. Also covered in my book *Taming the Big Data Tidal Wave.*
12. Lisa Arthur, *Big Data Marketing: Engage Your Customers More Effectively and Drive Value* (Hoboken, NJ: John Wiley & Sons, 2013).
13. Based on my blog for the International Institute for Analytics from July 11, 2013, titled "Big Data Analytics Doesn't Have to Be the Wild West." See http://iianalytics.com/2013/07/big-data-analytics-doesnt-have-to-be-the-wild-west/.
14. Based on my blog for the International Institute for Analytics from February 14, 2013, titled "The Global Nature of Big Data and Analytics." See http://iianalytics.com/2013/02/the-global-nature-of-big-data-and-analytics/.

CHAPTER

# 3

# Operational Analytics In Action

In this chapter, we turn our attention to a variety of examples of operational analytics in action. The examples make it clear that, in the future, an organization's focus won't simply be on more of the same old analytics but rather on different analytics that are being applied in new ways. The analytics that organizations have been implementing for years are now becoming table stakes in more and more industries and settings. Organizations will find it necessary to expand beyond traditional batch analytics in order to succeed in the future. In other words, they'll have to start making analytics operational.

One of the most important shifts that operational analytics help an organization to make is to enable it to become highly proactive in its actions. In some cases, the analytics are quite sophisticated. In other cases, the analytics are very basic. The examples in this chapter cover the entire range. However, the common thread is that operational analytics help an organization to be proactive rather than reactive. Instead of responding as issues arise, operational analytics usually aim to avoid problems altogether. Where it isn't possible to avoid problems, operational analytics aim to deal with problems that arise quickly and automatically.

Let's now explore a number of examples, some basic and some fancy, to illustrate operational analytics in action. The examples are ordered loosely by subject area and the level of sophistication of the analysis involved. Readers will notice that many of the examples involve sensors, which ties to the concept of the Internet of Things

(IOT) discussed in Chapter 2. A large percentage of operational analytics will be tied to the IOT.

## Improving Customer Experiences

One of the areas where consumers will notice the changes brought on by operational analytics the most is in their day-to-day interactions with organizations. For many years, organizations have strived to provide more deeply personalized products, marketing, and services to their customers. Operational analytics enable progress in the area of customization and personalization to continue to evolve. The following examples provide a glimpse into the potential.

### Providing Magical Moments

Let's turn our attention to the Walt Disney Company. Disney has been very sophisticated in its analysis of guest behavior for a long time. The company aims to understand the patterns and preferences that its guests exhibit so that an improved experience can be delivered. One of the areas where Disney has applied a lot of resources is research on the movement of crowds through Disney parks and how those crowds impact guests' experience.

Historically, based on the data available, Disney was forced to primarily see a crowd as a blob that was a singular item. In other words, a crowd was a single blob that was studied as a single group of people moving around. During the morning, a park might be more crowded on one side, and as the day goes on, the crowd shifts to the other side, for example. However, Disney's implementation of MagicBands is revolutionizing its approach to both guest experience and crowd management.[1] MagicBand data can generate both operational and traditional analytics to help improve the Disney experience.

MagicBands are wristbands with an embedded radio-frequency identification (RFID) sensor. Disney is using this technology to change the experience that guests have at a Disney park. To begin with, it will no longer be necessary to carry around a ticket and a credit card. The MagicBand is a guest's ticket and lets the guest buy things at any of the stores or restaurants in the park. The MagicBand also lets guests acquire Fast Passes for rides. A Fast Pass allows guests to come back at a later time and enjoy a ride then rather than waiting in line for an extended period.

MagicBands do something more than making park transactions easier, however. They allow Disney to study park traffic at a much more granular level. Instead of seeing a crowd as a single blob moving through the park, Disney is able to see guests as individuals exhibiting unique behavior within the crowd as the crowd moves through the park. This enables Disney to identify the different ways that people traverse the park. Some guests prefer to go on a ride or two and then take a break, have a snack, and rest before proceeding to another ride. Other guests push themselves to progress through the park without stopping. Disney can use this information to drive traffic patterns and distribute the population better through its parks. For example, guests can be alerted if there is a lower crowd level in another area of the park than their current location. Or guests can be enticed to extend their break with a discounted snack when ride lines are long. The analysis of crowds can also extend outside the realm of operational analytics, but that is a topic for another time.

Disney is also able to alter how it interacts with guests both before and during their visits as a result of the information provided by the MagicBands. By enabling guests to sign up for a Fast Pass using the band, Disney enables guests to spend less time standing in line. That will entice guests to spend more money since they'll have more time to eat and shop. By analyzing and managing how guests migrate through the park, Disney can aim to not only improve guest experience but drive additional revenues as well. Guests might not even notice these changes explicitly; all they'll notice is that their experience is terrific because they are not wasting another hour in line. Instead, they are free to have a snack or buy another souvenir before returning to the ride. It's good for everyone.

### More Analytics Equals a Better Experience

As organizations capture more and more details about how we interact with them, our experience can be even further customized. By running operational analytics processes that continually take into account our latest actions, organizations can both personalize and improve our experience.

If guests are willing to enable the functionality of the Magic-Bands, employees can know who guests are as they walk up to a cash register or a character. This is easy to do with devices that read the unique identifier from each MagicBand. The example that follows has privacy implications (which we talk about in more detail in Chapter 6); for now, let's just focus on the impact that MagicBands can have on guest experiences.

Imagine a young child visiting Disney for the first time. One of the greatest experiences as a child at Disney is to have a princess or Mickey Mouse come up and talk to you. With the new bands, as Mickey Mouse approaches a child, his handler will use a tablet to sense the child's band and bring up information on the screen. For example, the handler will see: "This is John Smith. He's from Atlanta, Georgia, and he's here for his ninth birthday. He really likes gummy bears." Analysis can be done behind the scenes to determine what type of special offer to make based on what is known about the child and his or her family. The handler can whisper the details into Mickey's ear.

Now consider how magical it will be for the child when Mickey doesn't just come and say "Hi, how are you doing?" but says "Hi, John. It's great to see you here. You came a long way from Atlanta, and I'm so happy that you're celebrating your birthday with us. If you go to that candy store right over there, you can choose a pack of gummy bears as my birthday gift to you. Just tell them I sent you, and they'll hand you your candy with a smile!" If the child's family goes to the store, the cashier will see that the offer of free candy was extended and will quickly process the transaction. This personalization experience creates a completely different experience for that child and the family.

In this case, the analytics aren't very complex at all. However, an analytics process does need to determine who should get which offers, must ensure that multiple characters don't provide the same gift later in the day, and must ensure that the family doesn't try to acquire free gummy bears more than once. Updates to guest data must occur very quickly. These simple analytics performed on highly detailed data with rapid turnaround can greatly impact guest experiences.

### Enabling Consumer Transparency

Let's now explore an example of how sensors can directly serve customers. One product that's taken a classic service to a new level through the use of data and analytics is the SenseAware program from FedEx.[2] SenseAware is an offering that allows a device outfitted with sensors to be included with a package that is being shipped. The sensors track a variety of environmental factors, which we'll discuss in a moment. Given its cost, this isn't a product that customers will add when they're just shipping a document or small package. However, the product is compelling if there is a need to ship something that is very expensive and sensitive to its environment.

Consider items like fine art, high-end collectibles, or an expensive and perishable item. One of the riskiest parts of buying such items is the process of shipping them across the country or around the world so that the product arrives safely. Once placed in the package and activated, a SenseAware device constantly monitors multiple environmental metrics of interest. These metrics include location, temperature, humidity, and even the light exposure and barometric pressure of the package. Light exposure, for example, indicates if a box or crate has been opened. As soon as it is, light will stream in, and it will be registered by the light sensors.

All of this data then gets transmitted back to FedEx in real time so that customers can monitor what is happening with the shipment at any given moment. One exception to the real-time feed is when the SenseAware device is on an airplane. When in flight, the data gets cached due to regulations. Once the plane lands, the cached data is uploaded in bulk, and then the continuous updates begin again. Customers can check the latest data at any time.

This service provides valuable information. When you have something expensive and sensitive that you need to ship, wouldn't you love to be able to verify that the carrier can keep it at the right temperature and is handling it carefully throughout the journey? A carrier that doesn't offer this type of visibility will be at a severe disadvantage compared to a carrier that does.

The product is also good for FedEx of course, because if FedEx is accused of mishandling a package and causing damage, it can use the SenseAware data to help defend against the accusations by providing the sensor readings as evidence. The data can show whether, in fact, FedEx employees had control of the package at the time that the temperature and humidity rose to unacceptable levels. SenseAware is not relevant in all cases. However, when SenseAware is relevant, it is very, very relevant. The analytics in this case are fairly simplistic, but they're valuable.

## *Upgrading Customer Service*

Operational analytics can improve customer satisfaction while simultaneously lowering operational costs. One terrific example of this is how airlines reroute customers when flights are disrupted. In the old days, a late flight would land and dozens or hundreds of passengers would flow off the plane frustrated and stressed. The passengers would then swamp both the local agents and the phone lines. Available seats on alternate flights were allocated basically in a first-come, first-serve fashion. Whoever got to an agent first would get the seat on the next flight.

Today, the processes for handling these situations have gotten much more sophisticated. Once an airline recognizes that a flight will be delayed, it can identify which passengers will have an issue. For example, if my flight is delayed by an hour but my final destination is the termination point of the flight, then I don't need any adjustment. Similarly, if a flight is delayed 30 minutes, then passengers with two hours to connect to another flight do not need any adjustment either. The airline can identify who needs assistance and what alternatives are available. It can then prioritize which passengers get which alternatives based on ticket price, frequent flyer status, prior travel disruptions, and a variety of other factors. The analytics behind these decisions might also include complex models that predict how a given customer will respond to varying degrees of disruption.

The impact of disruptions cannot be removed entirely, but it can be minimized. Today, when passengers land late, they usually do not have to stand in line or make a call. They can quickly check with agents by the gate or check on their mobile device to see that they've been rerouted and taken care of. If a passenger does choose to talk to an agent, the process is much faster and friendlier because the agent is just confirming the details of the changes made rather than having to figure out what is required. The agent can also help identify additional alternatives if the alternative automatically offered didn't meet the passenger's needs.

The level of stress related to the disruption is greatly lowered for passengers (I can personally vouch for this!), and they can relax and eat some food while waiting for the new flight. The process also dramatically lowers the operational costs for the airline. The rerouting decisions are made quickly and automatically instead of requiring expensive people to inject themselves to make the itinerary changes. The rerouting decisions are made in a consistent fashion as well, since the algorithms follow the guidelines precisely. The airlines also lower the amount of interaction that agents have on the ground and over the phone, which saves more money.

The automated, operational rerouting analytics processes are a win all around for both passengers and the airlines. In this case, the analytics do have some sophistication in comparison to the prior examples. We end this section with an example where the analytics are very complex.

### Enhancing the Online Experience

There are situations where operational analytics already routinely incorporate a high level of complexity. Web personalization is one such situation. When people visited a website in the early days, they typically saw offers or customizations that were determined well in advance of their visit. While a site may have been personalized to a user, it was not personalized in real time. Typically, the owner of the site executed a batch analytics process that told the system to show certain offers or customizations to each customer when he or she returned to the site. If the analytics were executed overnight, no information about customers that was learned after the analytics process was run would be taken into account. Clearly, then, nothing about customers' current browsing sessions would be taken into account when customizing the web pages.

### The Basics Must Be in Place First

Most operational analytics processes start with fairly simple analytics that serve as a foundation to build on. Once a simple solution is successfully embedded and running, it is possible to increase the complexity of the analytics over time.

There are now many organizations executing web personalization at a whole new level by optimizing the customer experience in real time based on all customer data up to and including the last click made. Literally, the action customers take right now will influence what they see one second from now. That's a much higher level of sophistication than some of the earlier examples in this section.

Modern web personalization approaches involve complex optimization algorithms layered on top of a variety of statistical models and business rules.

To evolve to such a robust solution requires starting with simple personalization approaches to establish the operational processes that serve customized content. Then, after the basics are in place, it is possible to get fancy. Expect to see a lot of the simple examples discussed in this chapter become more and more sophisticated as time passes.

## Time Is of the Essence

The speed with which analytics processes must be executed is shrinking, and operational analytics must run at lightning speed. There are cases where seconds or even milliseconds really do matter. Let's look at two specific examples of operational analytics where speed is of the utmost importance.

### Security through Analytics

The International Air Transport Association (IATA) envisions a future where security lines at airports are monitored by very sophisticated and real-time analytics.[3] The IATA sees a world where airports have security tunnels that are a couple dozen yards long. The risk each passenger presents will be assessed prior to his or her arrival so that each passenger can be directed to the tunnel that contains the correct level of security checks for his or her computed risk profile. Passengers will walk through a tunnel while carrying their belongings just as if they were walking down a hallway. As they walk through the tunnel, a variety of scans and tests will be performed. Passengers won't even slow down as metal detection, explosives detection, and more are applied. After exiting the tunnel, passengers simply continue on their way unless an alarm is triggered. The IATA's vision will be a huge upgrade to the current method of having to stop, wait in a long line, and remove some of your clothes and belongings before taking a turn in a scanner under intense watch by security officers.

Think for a moment about what it will take to make the IATA's vision a reality. This proposed security protocol is all about data and analytics. There will be perhaps a ten-second window while passengers walk through a tunnel to identify and react to any risk. During that time, the tunnel's scanners and sensors must collect data on the presence of explosives, data on where prohibited items like water or animals might be within bags, data on what objects are weapons or could be used as a weapon, and more. After the data is collected, the vast majority of data analysis must be automated to determine if a threat is present or not. If a threat is detected, security agents have perhaps 20 or 30 seconds to intercept someone before the passenger is gone.

## Operational Analytics Will Drive Life-and-Death Decisions

Analytics already underpin many security decisions. In the future, it won't be a matter of "who" is scanning and patting down people in security lines but "what" is doing it. Most security scans will be automated through data and analytics.

All of the data collection and analysis will be happening in real time. The operational analytics processes that are run against the data will have seconds to make life-and-death decisions. Not only will the analytics be very complex, but they must be highly accurate. If the analysis misses a single bomb or gun, the consequences are severe. However, officers today have been known to miss weapons due to fatigue or lack of concentration. At least the automated algorithms will be able to run continuously without any drop in accuracy. If the IATA's vision is achieved, we'll be safer and at the same time have much easier and faster security procedures. That's operational analytics at its best.

### The Hundred-Million-Dollar Millisecond

I read a very interesting book called *Automate This: How Algorithms Came to Rule Our World* by Christopher Steiner.[4] The book discusses how computerized trading in the stock market has evolved. In case you aren't aware, computers are now running complex analytics algorithms that make buy-and-sell decisions in milliseconds. The algorithms then directly execute buy-and-sell orders to trade in and out of stocks within a blink of an eye. The goal is often to capture very slight price inefficiencies and then immediately close out the trade. Repeat these actions millions of times per day, and the profits add up even if a typical trade generates only a small profit. Trading stocks automatically through analytics in subsecond time increments is about as operational as it gets.

Computerized trading was hardly a factor just a few years ago, but today computerized trading accounts for well over half of all trading volume in the major markets.[5] With this type of operational analytics process comes both great responsibility and great risk. After all, computers are analyzing the latest data and immediately putting real money on the line. Great responsibility is needed to make sure that the trading algorithms are fully tested and monitored closely on an ongoing basis in case something unexpected starts to happen. The risk comes when something unexpected does happen and it isn't caught in time.

In the Flash Crash of 2010, a massive drop in the market occurred seemingly out of nowhere and for no reason. It was traced to a computerized trading program gone wrong.[6] By the time the problem was identified and steps were taken to mitigate the problem, a lot of real-life damage had been done. Clearly, the analytics processes behind the problematic trading programs had some issues.

---

### Milliseconds Sometimes Matter

It sounds crazy to invest hundreds of millions of dollars just to shave a few milliseconds off of data transmission. But at the speed at which computerized trading programs operate, it pays off. Automated algorithms now account for the majority of stock market trading and represent operational analytics in the extreme.

---

One of the challenges with operational analytics is accepting and dealing with unexpected issues. When an organization allows decisions to be proactively and automatically made by algorithms, things can (and will!) go wrong. It is important to remember, however, that things can (and will!) go wrong with any type of decision made via any method. When people choose to drive a car, they understand that every now and then they will get in an accident. Accidents are a risk of driving. People still drive because they assess that in the long term, they will get enough benefit from driving a car to outweigh the risks and costs of those intermittent accidents.

Similarly, negative incidents will happen with operational analytics. Every organization implementing operational analytics will have glitches and bugs at some point. However, in the long run, if an organization is implementing its processes correctly, the benefits gained will more than make up for those glitches. The glitches are simply the cost of doing business. A few isolated issues can't be allowed to derail the entire approach.

When examining the speed of analytics, it is interesting how extreme it can get. Steiner's book discussed investors putting up hundreds of millions of dollars to build a more direct routing of data transmission lines from New York to Chicago. Instead of following the traditional, public rights-of-way along roads and rail lines, private rights-of-way were acquired to create a more direct transmission route. If a new transmission path can shave just a fraction of the mileage off the current path of transmission between the cities, it will shave several milliseconds off the data transmission time. At the pace at which the trading algorithms operate, saved milliseconds actually translate into billions of dollars over time. This is because algorithms using the faster data feed are able receive, analyze, and act on information before the competition using the traditional communication lines has even received it. The investors were confident that investing hundreds of millions of dollars to save a few milliseconds would pay off.

## Making Us Safer

A wide variety of operational analytics aims to keep people, products, or property safe. By leveraging new data sources to create new operational analytics, it is possible to increase the safety of the world we live in. The next section looks at a few examples, including one from the government sector. Commercial entities aren't the only organizations that can gain from operational analytics. Governments can gain too.

### Avoiding Adverse Events

Automobiles are becoming more and more sophisticated. Today, mechanics need as much understanding of computer systems to service a car as understanding of mechanical systems. Several recent innovations are aimed at keeping drivers safe by avoiding adverse events.

Cruise control may soon be enhanced with automated crash avoidance analytics. If a car recognizes that a crash is imminent based on the computed speed differential of what is in front of the car and the car itself, the car will automatically hit the brakes even before the driver does so. In the case of driverless cars, which we discuss shortly, drivers aren't expected to hit the brakes at all. Very simple analytics also help cars detect people or things in the way when backing up.

Many cars now beep or otherwise alert drivers when something that can't be seen is in the way and also indicate how close the obstacle is. The analytics are incredibly simple but save lives given how often small children are killed by vehicles backing up.

Think to the example from Chapter 2 of how railroads use trackside sensors in real time to monitor the temperature of wheels of cars as they go by. If the system notices that the wheels of a car are getting too hot, the train is actually ordered to stop. A technician is then sent out to inspect the train car and make adjustments. It's far more cost effective for a railroad to stop a train and fix the problem before a derailment occurs than it is to recover from a derailment after it happens. Not only will a derailment cause serious delays, but it can also cause a lot of damage and even death. The use of sensor data in this fashion not only makes rail lines safer, but it also saves money. Although the algorithms used in this example are quite simple, they still are quite powerful.

### Ensuring Product Freshness

Let's move on to growers of fresh produce. After growers pick their produce, it is usually stored on pallets in a warehouse and then placed in transit. The temperature of the produce needs to remain in a certain range with a certain range of humidity at all times. What if one of the air conditioners or heaters goes out in a section of the warehouse? The warehouse manager can identify that very quickly as sensors start sounding alarms. Employees can immediately move the produce that is impacted to a better location. Equally important is the fact that the grower will know exactly which pallets of produce had an issue and can inspect them to make sure everything is okay.

In the old days, it might have been hours before someone realized that the back end of the warehouse was a little warmer than it should be. By that point, the impacted produce may have already been shipped. That would necessitate sending an alert to all stores that received produce from the warehouse that day to double-check their deliveries.

Today, the specific pallets impacted can be identified before anything leaves the warehouse. Much of the time, the analytics are just basic alerts that compare current sensor readings to established thresholds. Over time, algorithms will evolve that take into account the specific temperature and humidity variations experienced by a given pallet to predict the risk of spoilage issues. Heating up a few degrees for a few minutes usually isn't a big deal, but a pattern of slight anomalies over a few days could add up to trouble. More advanced analytics processes will certainly be developed to look for these deeper patterns.

### Government Can Get Operational Too

Operational analytics aren't just for private companies. Governments and nonprofits can benefit as well. Let's look at predictive policing, which is one of the more interesting examples of analytics applied to government functions. Predictive policing also utilizes both operational applications of traditional analytics and operational analytics.

Let's start by explaining what predictive policing is.[7] For a number of years, police departments and law enforcement agencies of all kinds have used analytics to become more efficient. Law enforcement agencies look for crime patterns associated with factors such as temperature, adverse weather, holidays, and special events. A city can increase or decrease the number of police in a given area at a point in time based on predictions of crime levels.[8] Using analytics in this fashion is an operational application of traditional analytics because the analytics are executed in batch and used to generate predictions for upcoming shifts or days.

What's interesting is that agencies are starting to take into account more up-to-date information to make adjustments much closer to real time. In other words, the analytics are becoming operational. For example, a local police department has predicted the crime patterns for this evening based on historical patterns and has deployed officers to reflect that. As the weather shifts in temperature or several parties are identified within a small area, the department can update those projections and reshuffle resources again if required. Updating plans based on the latest information is making the analytics operational.

### Where There Is Inefficiency, There Is Opportunity

Let's face it. Governments are not known for being efficient and streamlined. Due to the scale of many government operations and their known inefficiencies, government agencies have much to gain from effective use of operational analytics.

One important operational tactic police have started to use is monitoring social media channels. It turns out that, just like the rest of us, a lot of gang members are very active on social media. Law enforcement is able to identify when known gang members start to pick a fight online. By monitoring the chatter back and forth, it is possible to see when words start to escalate. A common cause of physical confrontations between gangs today is an argument and taunting on social media channels. Police can identify who's involved in something that appears to be escalating, go out and find them, and work to defuse the situation before it is too late. One neighborhood may have more trouble than usual brewing on social media while another is unusually quiet. As a result, officers can be sent where they are needed most.

## Increasing Operational Efficiency

One of the areas where operational analytics will have the largest impact is increasing the efficiency of business operations. This is especially true for business processes that traditionally had little or no analytics behind them. For large organizations, even 1 or 2 percent increases in efficiency can translate into many millions of dollars. Let's take a quick look at some very interesting examples, several of which focus on efficient energy generation and usage.

### Maximizing Power Capture

Windmills have been around for centuries. Today, they are more efficient than ever before, and some of the latest technology is amazing. Bill Ruh of General Electric (GE) and I both spoke at the Rock Stars of Big Data event in San Jose in late 2013. Bill described how GE now places sensors throughout the wind turbines it manufactures to track and assess all sorts of information on the turbines' operation and performance. The sensor data is analyzed, and changes to the wind turbine's operating settings are made continuously in near real time to optimize performance.

I was amazed to hear that wind turbines available today can respond to the variability of wind by changing the position and angle of the blades to provide smooth, predictable power generation. Changing the angle of the blades to better capture energy from the wind yields an extra percentage or two of output. One or two percent doesn't sound like much at first, but it translates into a huge amount of money over time, given the scale of wind farms. Bill explained that these new technologies have now solidified GE as a technology leader in the industry. Bill credits the company's gains in large part to the hardware innovation as well as the software differentiation of embedding operational analytics into the machines.

### Optimizing Power Generation

Large gas turbines and generators are also getting more sophisticated and utilizing operational analytics in order to maximize output and efficiency. At the Rock Stars of Big Data event, Bill Ruh also spoke about how analytics have been applied to power generation via gas turbines. Research has shown that under certain operating conditions, heating fuel before it is fed to the turbine will increase power output, while under other conditions, heating the fuel will decrease power output. GE has embedded sensors throughout its turbines to track operating conditions at a high level of detail. Operational analytics processes monitor the turbines' performance and proactively heat (or don't heat) the fuel that is fed into them so that efficiency is maximized for the current conditions. Once again, this leads to small improvements that may not sound like much, but over time they add up to huge dollar savings. For example, over the life of a combined cycle power plant, a 1 percent increase in efficiency can equate to $750 million.

### Little Improvements Will Add Up

Often, operational analytics enable only small improvements in efficiency. Any given process may yield gains of only 1 or 2 percent. However, such gains are very meaningful on a large scale, particularly when profit margins are tight. Chaining together a few processes with a small impact can lead to major impacts that provide a massive competitive advantage.

### Increasing Fuel Efficiency

We've already discussed a few ways that railroads are applying analytics, but let's look at one more. Train engineers traditionally tend to go as fast as possible as they guide trains on their journeys. Engineers would go as fast as they were safely able until they reach a stop point. At that point, they'd wait until they were clear to move again.

This is probably how you drive your car, if you think about it. Most of us accelerate quickly and drive at or above the speed limit until we come to the next traffic light, stop sign, or traffic jam. It should not be a surprise that this method is not an optimal one for fuel efficiency for either cars or trains.

Accelerating from a stop uses far more fuel than what is required to keep a car or train moving. Momentum is a powerful force! By integrating GPS technologies on the trains with up-to-date information on traffic patterns throughout the rail network, railroads have come up with a more fuel-efficient way to cover routes. Algorithms continually identify what speed a train should go so that it arrives at the next stop point at just the right time to move through without stopping. This means that the train may travel much slower than is possible on some stretches, which might seem odd at first. However, the fuel saved by not stopping and starting the train and interrupting its momentum makes a difference. And, in the end, the train arrives at the same time because it was moving more slowly only when it would have been stopped anyway.

As algorithms dictate speeds to optimize fuel efficiency, the gains are once again incremental. However, given the scale of rail operations and the amount of fuel consumed, the savings are substantial. It is important to note that using analytics to improve energy efficiency doesn't just benefit companies' bottom lines. The analytics benefit us all because burning less fuel is better for the environment.

### Improving Call Center Performance

Our last example illustrating improvements in operational efficiency goes in a totally different direction. Until this example was described to me, I had no idea that such things were happening today. Most people are aware that call centers now have software listening to every conversation from the moment it starts. The common statement "This call may be recorded for training and quality purposes" is your notice that the conversation you are about to have is not private.

Organizations have moved beyond simple transcription of conversations to actually analyzing what was said. Algorithms can now identify a lot about callers and their moods from how they speak. It is even possible to identify callers' accents based on what they say. Using information on each caller's accent, a call center can route callers to someone whose accent matches their own. Why would an organization make the effort to connect callers to a representative with a similar accent?

Research has shown that people trust strangers with a similar accent more than strangers with a different accent.[9] Matching customers with someone who sounds familiar increases the success rate of call center agents resolving callers' issues satisfactorily. The idea of matching accents makes sense if you think about it for a minute. It is easy to see how a conversation could go wrong between someone from Mobile, Alabama, and someone from Long Island, New York. The speaking styles and paces of people from those geographic areas are very different. Pairing a caller from Mobile with a representative from somewhere nearby in the southern United States intuitively seems less risky. So does connecting two people from New York. By matching a caller with a representative who sounds like they are from the caller's neighborhood, agent and caller are both more comfortable. Operational analytics are required to make that match.

## Improving Our Lives in the Future

Many of the examples we've covered so far in the chapter don't have a meaningful, daily, personal connection with us as individuals. Receiving better customer service or a better online experience is nice, but neither provides ongoing benefits to our day-to-day lives. Luckily, there are cases where operational analytics will have a large impact on our lives. Next we take a look at two examples where operational analytics, while still in their infancy, will soon impact the lives of you and your loved ones.

### Freeing Our Time

Driverless cars are already here.[10] You don't own one yet (and it may be a few years before you do), but the technology and analytics that support driverless cars exist. Are you surprised that I would mention analytics in the same sentence as driverless cars? You shouldn't be. The volume and variety of analytics that go into helping a car navigate streets safely without human guidance is impressive.

How does a driverless car determine what markings on the road are lane markers as opposed to old construction markings, a paint spill, or a puddle? It comes down to analytics. The car has to scan the road ahead, analyze the images in real time, and determine where to steer by identifying the components of the image that are most likely to be lane markings.

The car also has to continually determine if it must slow, accelerate, or stop. When stopping, it must compute how hard to hit the brakes based on the distance to the object it is approaching and the relative speed of the object. Those computations must be updated continually to account for any changes, such as a car in front slamming on the brakes or a deer suddenly running across the road. Driverless cars require numerous, often sophisticated analytics. At the same time, the analytics must be very robust, stable, and accurate. After all, lives are on the line.

### Analytics Don't Have to Be Visible to Have Impact

Some of the best experiences that analytics will provide us will be in situations where analytics aren't even on our minds. When operational analytics are done well, as with driverless cars, users don't have to be aware of what's going on under the hood. They can just enjoy the ride.

Many passengers riding in driverless cars won't realize how much the experience is driven by data and analytics. But that's part of the point. Operational analytics done well can permeate a process and an experience in a way that doesn't require people to be aware of the work being done under the hood (pun intended!).

### Keeping Us Healthy

We discussed the growing popularity of fitness bands in Chapter 1. The medical field is starting to be inundated with a wide range of new opportunities to change how we view our health and medical care. The intersection of medicine, the Internet of Things, and operational analytics has vast potential. The way we seek and receive medical care will look very different in a few years. Let's walk through a scenario that will be our reality in the near future. In fact, pieces of this scenario are already starting to happen on a small scale today.

Chronic diseases, such as diabetes, not only cause a lot of health and quality-of-life issues for those who suffer from them, but also cost a lot of money to treat. It is easy to test blood sugar levels with test sticks. However, today sensors are available that constantly monitor blood glucose levels, analyze the readings, and sound an alert when intervention is required.[11] This not only makes a diabetes patient safer, but it also avoids costly medical problems.

Patients are also starting to have the option to recover from major injuries or illnesses at home instead of in a healthcare facility. Various sensors can monitor vital signs, administer drugs, and more. Patients can be kept on track automatically without requiring a nurse or doctor to stop by just to deliver a shot or pill. Instead, medications can be administered automatically when the analysis of current data says it is appropriate.

When vital signs or blood readings drift into troublesome patterns, a doctor or nurse can call right away to check in. If necessary, a visit can be made in person to the patient's home. It is far cheaper to hire extra nurses and doctors than it is to build additional wings for new hospital beds. Hospitals can expand their reach without expanding their physical footprint. The idea of going back to in-home visits by medical professionals sounds expensive. However, when patients are stable and rarely need a visit, it can be far cheaper than an extended hospital stay. Plus, patients are more comfortable and recover more quickly in the comfort of their own homes.[12]

Many of the analytics that enable patients to stay at home will be basic comparisons of vital sign versus thresholds. In other cases, such as interpreting an electrocardiogram reading or brain wave pattern, the analytics will be more complex. Over the next few years, operational analytics will help to enable a new era of healthcare.

## Finding Unexpected Value in Data

Operational analytics, and the data required to enable them, can also facilitate inventive reuses of data. The reuse of the data supporting operational analytics can produce new revenue streams to help offset the cost of collecting and analyzing the data. The concept of reusing data is particularly relevant for the data used by many operational analytics processes. Note that some of the additional uses for data have nothing to do with operational analytics. However, the value that the operational analytics create is what enables the data to be collected in the first place.

In each of the three cases discussed next, a massive amount of data is captured initially for operational purposes but then becomes an asset that can generate revenue or save costs. Finding creative ways to reuse data and offset the costs of collecting it for operational analytics makes it is easier to justify making the investments that are required. Ensure that your organization looks for novel ways to monetize the data it collects by identifying data uses that were not part of the original operational requirements. This strategy ties to the theme of analytics becoming a product from Chapter 1.

### Leveraging Location Data for Traffic Updates

Both cellular providers and GPS providers have to collect data on where every customer is at any point in time in order to provide their core services. A cellular provider is aware of where its customers are, as phones connect to cell towers. A GPS device obviously can't do the analysis to tell users how to go from "here" to "there" unless it knows where "here" happens to be. The same data that's being collected to help these organizations deliver the services that customers have purchased has tremendous value for other purposes.

When you check the status of traffic on your mobile device, often that status is generated from the same location data collected to provide your core service. As service providers see customers moving along an interstate highway, they know what speed the customers are going. The providers see this information on a lot of customers at any point in time. While each customer's location data is collected initially to provide the committed base services, the data has value outside of that purpose.

Service providers take location and speed information and reuse it at an aggregate level to support traffic reporting systems. Rush-hour commuters are able to see the most current traffic conditions based on the input from thousands of fellow commuters. The neat thing is that none of those commuters had to do anything to provide that input other than to turn on their cell phones or GPS devices.

### Leveraging Sensor Data to Improve Crop Yields

We've already discussed the detailed sensor data being collected from cars, planes, and other similar equipment. Let's consider now the data being collected from modern tractors. As farmers run a tractor across their fields, sensors collect information on how the equipment is being used. How fast is the tractor moving across the field? How deep is the tiller being set? What temperature is it outside? And more. The initial uses of this data focus on operational issues, such as predictive maintenance analytics or warranty compliance analytics. However, there are some other exciting possibilities for this information.

## Value May Be Hiding in Plain Sight

Much of the data collected for operational analytics seems boring and tactical at first. However, it is often possible to find creative and unexpected ways to apply the data for other purposes that aren't boring or tactical at all.

As tractor manufacturers gain insight into exactly how farmers across the world use a given piece of equipment, it will be possible to identify practices that optimize yield. As farmers report their yields, the manufacturer can correlate those yields with a variety of farming practices. What if by making simple adjustments, it is possible to increase yields? Knowing this would be very valuable to farmers. For example, think how farmers would benefit from being alerted that yields would increase if they simply adjust the tillers up one-eighth of an inch. This is possible, however, only by combining operational equipment data across many farmers and using the data in a new way.

### Leveraging Compliance Data to Improve Sales

Manufacturers in the consumer packaged goods industry spend massive amounts of money each year on advertisements, coupons, and in-store displays. Given that in-store displays can be expensive, manufacturers want to ensure that the displays are installed properly and for the correct duration. To monitor compliance, it is possible to add sensors to the display cases so that manufacturers can validate the location of the display without sending a person to make a visual check. This saves a lot of money, and manufacturers can identify exactly when the display was put in place and how long it stayed there.

By correlating the location data with sales data, it is possible to get a much better view of promotional performance. Perhaps a certain location at the local grocer looks like a great spot, but it really isn't. Or perhaps the display was placed in the wrong spot or was removed a day early. The analytics that assess the effectiveness of the promotion can take this into account. When planning future promotions, manufacturers can target better placement of displays and negotiate what they pay for the promotion based on more precise measures of sales by location and time. Although the data is originally collected for compliance validation, it can be used to adjust promotional strategies.

### Create Strategic Analytics Too

We've discussed a lot of tactical applications of operational analytics. However, once the data is collected, there are many strategic, longer-term analytics that are enabled as well. For example, many organizations now use sensor data and analytics to determine patterns of failure across time. This is especially true for auto manufacturers, airline engine manufacturers, and manufacturers of heavy equipment, such as tractors and dump trucks.

The data collected is used for predictive maintenance. Remember that predictive maintenance is the practice of using analytics to identify maintenance issues before they happen and to proactively address problems before failure occurs. We touched briefly on this topic in Chapters 1 and 2, but let's dig deeper here and also look at how the data can be used strategically in addition to operationally.

We'll use aircraft as a way to illustrate the potential. An airline employee once told me confidentially that if a large commercial aircraft is taken out of service and an engine is removed from the plane for maintenance, the base cost is about $1 million dollars to the airline. That cost accounts for the loss of revenue from the plane being out of service and the time and effort required actually to dismantle and reassemble the engine. Therefore, airlines (or air forces) don't want to take an engine off any more than absolutely necessary. Analytics and data are transforming maintenance practices on both a short-term, operational level and a long-term, strategic level.

Traditionally, if an engine broke down, mechanics would look at the engine, ask what symptoms were noticed right before it broke down, and then examine the engine to identify what needed fixing. The mechanics would also attempt to determine what led to the problem.

Manufacturers today are able to use sensors to monitor in high detail how engines operate over time. As maintenance issues arise, the data is analyzed to find early warning indicators. Does friction build up on a certain part of the engine, along with a slight temperature increase, in the days or weeks ahead of a specific part failure? If so, analytics can look for a similar pattern arising in other engines and then raise an alert for a proactive maintenance intervention. This is the practice of predictive maintenance.

Predictive maintenance processes lead to a couple of benefits. First, they let manufacturers better understand the dynamics of how equipment is operating in the real world so that engineering adjustments can be made to improve the equipment in the future. Second, it allows manufacturers to identify breakdowns ahead of time. Manufacturers can get equipment serviced before there's a problem. Ideally, the service can occur within an already scheduled maintenance window so that impacts are minimized. Maintenance may also be less expensive than a repair because nothing has yet broken.

Note that there are operational analytics involved here as well as opportunities for operational applications of traditional analytics. Operational analytics are involved when an engine that is operating is being monitored for problems in real time. This is tactical. The strategic component comes into play when long-term maintenance plans are adjusted based on the analysis of the sensor data. Analytics can be used to establish better recommended maintenance schedules based on past performance. This is a strategic operational application of traditional analytics. A lot of performance history from many engines is analyzed in batch mode to develop updated maintenance guidelines.

Predictive maintenance analytics are lowering costs for manufacturers. The analytics are also improving safety for the consumer and improving the service level that manufacturers can provide to consumers. It's another example of a win all around. The organizations that are the best at figuring out how to do predictive maintenance and monitor the way that products are working will stand out from the crowd.

## Wrap-Up

The most important lessons to take away from this chapter are:

- Today, many examples of operational analytics in action involve fairly simple analytics. The level of sophistication will increase with time.
- Operational analytics can provide customers with an entirely new level of service and customization. Disney is at the forefront here.

- When events like flight disruptions occur, operational analytics can mitigate the impact on customers while saving time and cost for the airlines.
- Milliseconds can literally make the difference for some processes. Computerized stock traders invest huge sums of money to gain an advantage of just a few milliseconds for their analysis.
- By providing transparency, operational analytics can protect both an organization and its customers. The FedEx Sense-Aware product is an example.
- Operational analytics can make us safer by ensuring product quality via environmental sensor data and keeping our neighborhoods and the places we visit more secure via predictive policing.
- Government agencies have much to gain from effective use of operational analytics due to the scale and known inefficiencies of many government operations.
- Improving efficiency by even a small percentage can lead to huge gains. This is especially true in areas like energy, where GE has done a lot of work.
- When operational analytics are done well, as with driverless cars or health monitoring, users don't have to be aware of what's going on under the hood. They just have to enjoy how their lives are improved.
- Healthcare is already being transformed by data and analytics. Operational analytics will enable new care protocols that are both more effective and more comfortable.
- Always keep an eye out for new uses of data originally collected for operational purposes. Just as GPS location data can enable traffic applications, multiple uses often exist for other data as well.
- In addition to using a data source for tactical operational analytics, look for ways to use the data strategically as well.

## Notes

1. See "Unlock the Magic with Your MagicBand or Card" at https://disneyworld.disney.go.com/plan/my-disney-experience/bands-cards/.
2. See www.senseaware.com/
3. See "Smart Security," www.iata.org/whatwedo/security/Pages/smart-security.aspx
4. Christopher Steiner, *Automate This: How Algorithms Came to Rule Our World* (New York: Penguin, 2013).

5. See Steven Goldberg, "Could Computerized Trading Cause Another Market Crash?" Kiplinger, August 24, 2011, at www.kiplinger.com/article/investing/T041-C007-S001-could-computerized-trading-cause-another-market-cr.html

6. See Ben Rooney, "Trading Program Sparked May 'Flash Crash,'" CNNMoney, October 1, 2010, at http://money.cnn.com/2010/10/01/markets/SEC_CFTC_flash_crash/index.htm

7 For a nice introduction to this topic, see Zach Friend, "Predictive Policing: Using Technology to Reduce Crime," FBI Law Enforcement Bulletin, April 9, 2013, at www.fbi.gov/stats-services/publications/law-enforcement-bulletin/2013/April/predictive-policing-using-technology-to-reduce-crime

8. See "The Los Angeles Police Department Predicts and Fights Crime with Big Data," Big Data Startups, April 14, 2014, at www.bigdata-startups.com/BigData-startup/los-angeles-police-department-predicts-fights-crime-big-data/

9. See Susan Perry, "People Tend to Read a Lot into Voices, Including Accents," MINNPOST, July 22, 2013, at www.minnpost.com/second-opinion/2013/07/people-tend-read-lot-voices-including-accents

10. See Chunka Mui, "Fasten Your Seatbelts: Google's Driverless Car Is Worth Trillions (Part 1)," Forbes, January 22, 2013, at www.forbes.com/sites/chunkamui/2013/01/22/fasten-your-seatbelts-googles-driverless-car-is-worth-trillions/

11. See Medtronic MiniMed, 2014, at www.medtronicdiabetes.com/treatment-and-products/continuous-glucose-monitoring

12. See Deborah Rudacille, "Home Sweet Home Care," DOME 57, no. 3 (April 2006), at www.hopkinsmedicine.org/dome/0604/newsreport1.cfm

# PART

## II

# LAYING THE FOUNDATION

CHAPTER

4

# Want Budget? Build the Business Case!

As an organization evolves to operational analytics, various investments will be required. These investments include the people, tools, and technologies that must be put in place in order to implement operational analytics successfully. The process of making analytics operational will be neither cheap nor easy, but with the right discipline it can pay off. Of course, getting the agreement and approval for the investments required is no easier today than it ever was. Therefore, building a business case for operational analytics is critical.

In this chapter, we lay out concepts and frameworks to assist you in building the business case for operational analytics in your organization. Many of the concepts can be applied more broadly to investments in analytics. The good news is that if time and care are taken to develop a business case and ensure that it accounts for some of the unique aspects of analytics, you and your organization can be successful.

## Setting the Priorities

Before starting on a business case for operational analytics, it is necessary to lay out what investments the business case will address and how the business case will address them. As with anything, the direction and tone of a business case can be as important as the supporting facts and figures. In this section, we discuss how to start with the right perspective to give your business case the maximum chance to succeed. A few small adjustments to common practices can make a business case far more interesting and compelling and, therefore, make it more likely to be approved.

### Start with a Business Problem, Not Data or Technology

We discussed in Chapter 2 the need to identify a business problem before collecting data. Collecting data or purchasing technology without a clear plan is a losing strategy. It is also important not to build a business case for acquiring a new data source or purchasing a new tool or technology. Rather, a business case for analytics must solve real business problems that an organization faces. As luck would have it, acquiring that shiny new data source or software may be a key part of solving the identified problem. A strong business case doesn't abandon the data, tool, or technology acquisitions; it simply puts them in the right context.

The difference between a technology focus and a business focus is also the difference between justifying a cost and justifying an investment. In most organizations, it is far easier to get people interested in a business case that solves a specific set of business problems than it is to get them interested in a business case that solves a specific set of technical challenges. It is not clear to me why so many organizations sell acquiring data or technology instead of solving a problem. Let's explore two hypothetical discussions to illustrate the difference between these approaches.

In the first discussion, the vice president of information technology (IT) for a large utility walks into the executive committee meeting alone and says, "We need to collect sensor data from our smart grid infrastructure. It's going to cost several million dollars to do it. All of the business units we partner with have asked for it and are willing to partially fund it. We can cover all the costs of the data acquisition and storage with the funds the business units are offering plus a small incremental IT investment."

## Partner Up

Make the pitch for an investment in operational analytics as a joint effort between business and IT. Focus on solving a problem for the business, not covering costs for IT. The IT costs should just be a necessary piece of the bigger solution.

In the second discussion, the VP of IT walks into the meeting alongside a VP-level business partner. Together they say, "We're going to make our existing power capacity meet demand for an additional five years, which will enable us to delay several power plant projects.

We will do this by incenting customers to change their usage patterns so that we can lower peak demand levels by analyzing our smart grid sensor data. Of course, to acquire, store, and analyze that data will cost us several million dollars. Those costs will be more than offset by the tens of millions in savings that we've identified by postponing the new plants in addition to the many other analytics we've identified that will be possible once we have the smart grid data."

The first discussion is all about cost and data, is driven by IT, and is not very persuasive, even though the cost will be covered. The second discussion is driven by the business with IT support and is focused on the value of collecting new information instead of the cost. Which argument do you think your executives would find more persuasive?

### Focus on Returns, Not Costs

The previous examples illustrate two approaches to requesting funding. The primary difference is that one is trying simply to justify itself as cost neutral, while the other is attempting to drive huge value. Unfortunately, many technology- and analytics-related investment pitches put outsize focus on the costs and the attempt to offset those costs. It's better to make the costs simply a part of a high-impact solution, as outlined in Table 4.1.

The focus on costs came about, in part, because it used to be necessary to justify technology investments in this way. Historical technology investments often involved huge up-front costs that would be spread across a wide range of uses that generated various returns over time. For example, due to the massive scale of the investment required, a mainframe would never have been justified in the 1980s by just a handful of analytics requirements. Rather, it took a large set of enterprise-level requirements in total to justify a mainframe.

Today, however, tools and technologies are often inexpensive enough that it is possible to gain entry with a moderate investment. The benefits demonstrated by the initial analytics use cases and the

Table 4.1   Making a Case for Investment in Analytics

| Maximize Focus On | Minimize Focus On |
| --- | --- |
| Business problems solved | Tools or technologies required |
| Benefits and returns | Costs |
| Differentiators | Incremental improvements |

initial investment can be leveraged to get support for further investment later. Investment in analytics no longer has to be a massive, business-altering expense for an organization. With today's flexible cost structures, it's often possible to start on a far less grand scale, and often it is a straightforward cost-benefit analysis that's very achievable at a business unit level.

### Target Differentiators, Not Incremental Improvements

Exciting new ideas usually get more attention than improvements to existing ideas. That's also true with analytics. To the extent that new data and new analytics can be utilized to solve new problems, it will be easier to get attention for a business case. When addressing new problems using new data, often larger returns are possible than when simply tuning existing analytics processes to address existing problems. Often it is possible to outline a plan that enables short-term, incremental improvements as well as long-term differentiators at the same time. Such a situation is especially nice because it promises fast, visible progress while chasing the larger long-term benefits. That's a win on two dimensions at once.

One of the best things about the emergence of big data (Chapter 2) and Analytics 3.0 (Chapter 1) is that the possibilities for analytics are expansive and go far beyond those of a few years ago. Be sure to take this into account as you build your business plan. The exciting world of big data and operational analytics provides ample opportunity to focus on new differentiators while still adding incremental improvements to existing analytics processes. As we've discussed already, it is rare not to have multiple uses for data once it's captured. This means that even as a case is made with one or two of today's defined business issues, the future benefits that can accrue in other areas should also be mentioned, even if those other areas are still a bit ambiguous and undefined. Some like to call the process of uncovering new value "having a conversation with the data." That conversation can lead to new ideas, insights, and value.

### Differentiators Drive Support

Today, it is often possible to target analytics that differentiate an organization from the start. Even when targeting incremental improvements, look for ways to paint a vision of differentiators that may be possible in the future.

Let's consider an example. Would restaurants or retail stores be interested in knowing how many people walk past their entrances every day and what profiles of those people look like? You can bet that they would, and location data generated by cell phones can tell them that. If a cellular provider is looking to justify storing detailed historical location information for operational purposes, certainly it is possible to explore alternate uses, such as providing foot traffic figures to stores and restaurants. The cellular provider can charge retailers for information about how many people are walking or driving past their doors.

By matching the location data with demographic and usage data, it is also possible to provide information on how many people fitting certain profiles pass by the door. Offering analytics of this nature can be a differentiator for the cellular provider, create a new revenue stream, and can support the costs of capturing the data for the original operational purposes. Note that I am not suggesting that the cellular provider divulge any information on any individual customer. That would be a privacy issue, as we discuss in Chapter 6. Rather, the information provided to the retailers or restaurants should be aggregated. For example, 200 people walk past 124 Main Street on average every day, and 30 percent of them make more than $100,000 per year.

It will take time for an organization to get to the point of offering such services. But discussing the option helps to demonstrate the bigger value that a new source of data can drive over time. This can get people more excited than they would be from just the initial plans that focus only on the value being targeted in the short term. If an organization can at least cross the bar on the return necessary based on initial short-term initiatives, the future potential analytics identified can help get the approval of an investment over the goal line.

## Choosing the Right Decision Criteria

When laying out a business case for operational analytics, it is necessary to decide the criteria that will be the primary drivers of the decision. In other words, what is it that must be maximized or minimized with the investment? It will be necessary to carefully define the criteria to be targeted correctly and to understand the implications of those choices. Many factors come into play when assessing the cost and benefit sides of operational analytics, and some new criteria that have not been widely used in the past will be necessary as well.

The decision criteria for analytics investment cannot be classic IT metrics like price per terabyte, price per hardware node, price per seat license, or seconds to process a specific query. All of those criteria can be examined to ensure that they aren't way out of line, but they can't be the only criteria. One of the key criteria for analytics is to look at the lift in human performance that can be achieved through an investment in one option versus another. For example, consider questions such as:

- How much faster and more efficiently will analytics professionals be able to perform their duties, given each of the investment options?
- How effectively can the organization build, test, and deploy new operational analytics processes with each option?
- How easy will it be to experiment with new analytics techniques?
- Can the environment ingest data rapidly and support rapid change?
- Will new, and possibly expensive, skill sets be needed?

Considerations like these matter for investments in operational analytics and must be assessed for every option.

The faster that an analytics team can produce new insights for an organization and implement what is found into an operational context, the higher the returns will be. Paying a higher cost per terabyte is fine if the team will be able to produce analytics much faster than with a cheaper option. Paying more for an analytics application license is okay if the application is more user friendly and robust. It's all about getting to the results in the most efficient manner possible.

This isn't much different from how you likely make purchases at home. Many people pay extra for a computer that has more memory, or more disk space, or other specific features that are important to them. The cheapest computer may make certain activities that are important to you very difficult; therefore, the extra money for a better computer is worth it. For example, if you don't have enough disk space to store all of your videos, then a computer can't serve as your video editing and archiving platform.

*Paint a Bigger Picture*

Many organizations execute a targeted proof of concept (POC) as a first step. This is a great idea, but it is important not to make the limited scope of the POC the endgame. Solving a single subset of a problem probably won't get a proposal across the finish line for investment, especially when proposing large capital investments and many hours of labor. In other words, a POC might focus on one type of analysis against one set of products. If the endgame is to have the investment support multiple types of models for all products, then that must be made clear. If the returns from the limited POC scope are all that is discussed, then the figures are likely not going to be very impressive. At the same time, the value of the bigger vision may not be obvious from the limited POC either. That is why it is necessary to clearly lay the plan out.

The key is to position a pilot project or POC as but one example of what's possible, not the endgame. Also provide a list of other problems, both similar and dissimilar, that can also be addressed if the plan is approved. Make the point that while the POC didn't specifically quantify the impact possible for the other problems, it is reasonable to assume that analytics to address them will add additional value to the POC findings. If the POC itself had a solid return, having extra upside to add into the mix can only help get the green light.

### Prove a Concept, Not a Specific Case

Design a POC to illustrate the potential of a more general class of approach. Focus on the art of the possible, not just proving the value of the limited scope addressed directly in the POC. While hard figures won't be available outside of the POC's scope, the potential can add enough icing on the cake to get approval.

I had a customer from a large media organization tell me that he had struggled to get one of his analytics initiatives approved. (I won't reveal his company to protect his confidentiality.) His team had executed several successful POCs but had never received approval to make the bigger investment required to scale them out. He suspected that the problem was that the pitches for investment had focused exactly and only on the scope of the POCs. That was the fatal flaw. Focusing only on the return of the exact analytics tested in the POC didn't provide a big enough return. Equally important,

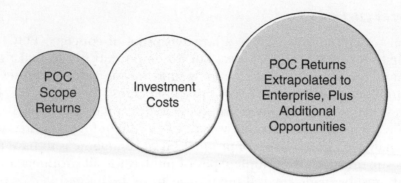

Figure 4.1    Paint a Bigger Picture

that approach didn't paint the bigger vision my customer had for the executives making the decision. Figure 4.1 illustrates the difference.

My customer decided that on his next attempt, he would point to the POC as but one illustrative example of what the investment would enable. He would make clear that the examples executed in the pilot were meant to show how the novel use of a new data source for novel new analytics processes would work in a few relevant scenarios. There were many other similar scenarios that couldn't be tested in the POC but logically would also be successful, given the similarity to the scenarios that had been proven to work. This approach, which some people call showing "the art of the possible," is a much stronger one.

### Time to Insight

When investing to enable the analytics discovery process, I recommend considering a criterion called "time to insight." Time to insight looks at the time to go from a new question to finding the insight desired. This is distinctly different from the criteria required when operationalizing an insight found in a discovery process. As an insight is operationalized, traditional IT metrics, such as how fast the process generating the insight can be executed to support operational decisions, will be important.

The different needs for discovery versus operationalizing are discussed more deeply in Chapter 6. For now, just note that there is going to be a difference between a business case aimed at enabling discovery and one aimed at operationalizing discoveries. The differences are necessary because the two have vastly different goals and priorities. In addition, in today's world, it is no longer acceptable to have discovery cycles measured in weeks or months. Time to insight must be days to just a few weeks.

## Investing for Discovery

The goal of a discovery process is to find new insights rapidly. Doing this requires a different way of looking at investments. Instead of targeting raw processing power or performance, it is better to target a measure like time to insight. Raw performance isn't as critical as the total time required to find an insight. Time to insight balances usability, flexibility, and performance.

Time to insight includes everything from data acquisition, to data preparation, to coding time, to running the analytics process, to identifying the insights hidden within the results, as Figure 4.2 illustrates. Time to insight is literally the total time from start to finish. For example, if one option requires 60 minutes of coding, 30 minutes to execute the code, and 10 minutes to explore the results, then its time to insight is 100 minutes. If another option requires only 20 minutes of coding but 60 minutes to execute and 20 minutes to explore the results, its time to insight also is 100 minutes. Both options lead to a 100-minute total time to insight, though they arrive there via different paths. This means that a business case will need to account for the cost differences between the time components behind the time to insight as well. For example, extra labor time costs a lot more than extra processing time, and labor is often the largest component of time to insight.

Focusing on time to insight helps account for all the factors that impact the time to build an analytics process. Shifting from typical

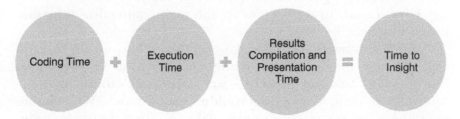

**Figure 4.2    Time to Insight Components**

criteria to something like time to insight makes terrific sense when investing for discovery. After all, new insights are what drive the revenue side of the business case. Minimizing time to insight maximizes the chances of finding the insights that drive revenue. Treating investments in discovery differently isn't something that's typically done today. However, while it will take some getting used to, it must become commonplace.

A time to insight metric will impact not just cost but also employee satisfaction and motivation. Analytics professionals want to develop impactful analytics processes. The faster your analytics professionals can get to a new insight, the faster they can have an impact, and the faster they can move on to the next discovery process. A short average time to insight will keep analytics professionals happy and motivated. Nobody enjoys working in an environment where work takes longer than necessary due to inefficiencies.

### Ability to Operationalize

In the prior section, we discussed how new criteria, such as time to insight, are required for a discovery investment. Let's now look at the different criteria required when investing to make processes operational. Unfortunately, when making analytics operational, it is no longer possible to evaluate analytics tools based on functionality alone. It is also necessary to take into account how well a tool will integrate with the operational environment. A tool can be highly robust in functionality, but if it cannot be easily integrated and cannot provide the level of scale and process simplicity required, then it is not going to work.

When it comes to operational analytics, milliseconds often count. In the long run, it can be better to leverage a tool that is not as user friendly as long as it can be more fully embedded into business processes to handle thousands or millions of analytics decisions every day. It is necessary to assess a tool's ability to operationalize alongside its raw functionality.

This is a different way of looking at things. Historically, organizations found the most user-friendly analytics tools with the most functionality. Analytics processes were executed offline in a distinct environment, so integration didn't matter much. When going operational, an organization must make sure that the integration, scalability, and performance are there too. That can absolutely lead to choosing tools that wouldn't have been chosen in the past. User friendliness is still critical for the discovery process, but the ability to be embedded and scale is more critical for operational processes. It may take more effort to build an operational process initially, but that extra effort gets amortized over millions of faster decisions over time. We discuss these different requirements more in Chapter 6.

### When Going Operational, Functionality Is Not Enough

For operational analytics, functionality and user friendliness can no longer be the primary criteria for tool selection. Tools must integrate effectively with the environment to enable deployment at scale. It can make sense to trade off functionality and user friendliness for scalability and ease of integration.

Not focusing primarily on functionality and user friendliness isn't as unusual as it sounds. When building a single-family home, there are certain products that work just fine. They are easy to install and use and are often chosen for new houses. When it comes to a commercial property, much tougher components are utilized that may be much more expensive to acquire and install. The commercial products might also look worse and be less user friendly, but they are necessary to handle the level of usage that will occur in a commercial environment. Something as simple as a door handle has to be addressed differently. A cheap door handle with standard fittings will work great when a door is opened only three times a day at your home, but it will break in a matter of a weeks if put in a large office building. This same principle is at play when selecting analytics tools to support operational processes.

Given the preceding facts, it may not be possible to have a single analytics tool set from a single vendor that handles all needs. It is entirely possible that different tools will be used for the discovery process than are used when making a discovery operational. Over time, tools will evolve. It is hoped that some will eventually be able to handle both needs with equal effectiveness. As of early 2014, that is not the case.

### Analysis Value versus Technology Value

There are two components to the benefits achieved with an investment in analytics. While unfortunately they are often intertwined, it is very important to separate and distinguish them. The first component is the value of an analysis itself. In other words, regardless of what tools, technologies, or methodologies are used to get to the results, much of the benefit comes from simply getting to the results. Clearly there is a need to have tools and technologies to get to the results, but care must be taken not to associate the benefit of the underlying analytics with any individual tool or platform option.

For example, simple affinity analysis to derive cross-sell offer opportunities is valuable. Regardless of the tools and platforms used to run an affinity analysis, the results have an inherent value. The value of the tools and technologies is in how efficient they make it, compared to other options, to create, test, and execute the analytics process required to get the affinity analysis results. In most cases, as illustrated in Figure 4.3, the inherent value of the analysis will be much larger than the incremental value of a given tool or technology.

The first step should be to determine the benefit of an analysis in the absolute sense, independent of any tool or platform. After that is determined, then determine the effectiveness of the various options for creating that analysis quickly, efficiently, and cost effectively. One trap that people fall into is having a salesperson discuss the huge return on investment (ROI) that analytics created with his or her products can generate. However, those making such a claim often add together the ROI inherent in the analytics with the incremental value offered by his or her company's tools or technologies to get

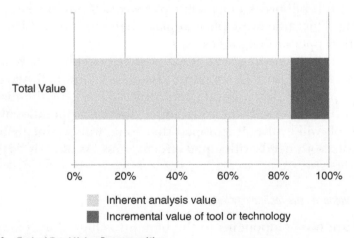

Figure 4.3    Typical Total Value Decomposition

those results. It is necessary to separate the value of the tool from the value of the underlying analysis.

As a side note, if every salesperson for every option you are considering embeds the analysis value with the tool value, then at least it is possible to compare the options on fair footing. Since all estimates include the same inherent value, any differences reflect a difference in incremental tool or technology value.

## Business Case Framework to Consider

Richard Winter from WinterCorp published a terrific study called "Big Data: What Does It Really Cost?"[1] The paper defines a framework for taking into account all types of costs and getting to a measure of what Winter calls "total cost of data" (TCOD) when making hardware and software investments to support analytics. TCOD reflects the total cost across a wide variety of relevant components, such as those we discuss in the next section of the chapter.

Keep in mind that Winter's TCOD framework, as well as much of the discussion in this section of the chapter, focuses primarily on the cost side of the equation. This is purposeful because the components of cost tend to be fairly consistent across organizations whereas the benefits vary widely based on the specific analytics processes being pursued. What is often missed is an accurate assessment of costs when it comes to analytics. Therefore, that is the focus here.

The most important thing about WinterCorp's TCOD framework is that it isn't biased toward one solution or another but simply provides a framework that helps identify and account for the various cost components. For example, two different examples in the paper led to completely opposite conclusions based on the facts. In one case, based on the nature of the data and processing required, a massively parallel relational environment was three to four times more expensive than a Hadoop implementation. In another case, based on the nature of the data and processing required, a Hadoop investment was three to four times more expensive than a relational environment.

Leveraging a framework that's neutral to the tools and technologies being evaluated allows an accounting for all costs in an unbiased fashion. The TCOD framework needs some slight modification for operational analytics, as it was targeted at a slightly different investment. As we discuss shortly, however, combining the TCOD framework with some additional metrics tied specifically to operational analytics is a terrific starting point.

### What Are the Total Costs for Operational Analytics?

It is critical to get to an accurate total cost when assessing options for analytics investment. When considering open source tools, for example, organizations can't get too hung up on the fact that the license for the software is free. It is necessary to look at the full picture of costs over time. It's not that open source tools can't be a tremendous addition to an organization's environment, but it is necessary to look at the total costs and be diligent in looking for cases where perverse incentives are inadvertently driving higher costs over time.

When assessing the costs related to operational analytics, what must be included? The costs include, but are not limited to, these:[2]

- Hardware to support the analytics processing
- Software acquisition (Note that even in the case of open source software, there are costs to install and configure the software.)
- Space the equipment uses and the power consumed
- Fully loaded labor costs to configure and implement security, resource prioritization, and network connectedness
- Acquisition, loading, and preparation of data
- Labor required to develop an analytics process
- Effort to test code logic and accuracy of process output
- Maintenance costs for the platform, software, and analytics processes over time
- Training for staff on how to use all the various components of the analytics environment

All of these costs must be viewed across the typically several-year period of time that represents the life span of the investment.

### Don't Forget Critical Components of Cost

It is easy to miss some of the components behind the total cost of investments in support of analytics. Beyond the initial outlays are ongoing labor and maintenance costs that continue for the life of the investment. The ongoing costs can add up to far more than the initial costs.

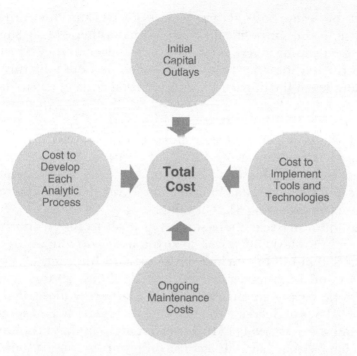

**Figure 4.4    Cost Components of an Analytics Investment**

Obviously, there are many cost components to consider, and the primary categories are shown in Figure 4.4. Some components, such as a hardware purchase, will require large initial expenses but little ongoing expense after that. Other costs will be spread more evenly over time, such as maintenance costs. To compare options appropriately, it is necessary to look at total cost across all of those components over time. The flip side of the equation is that it is also necessary to account for the various returns that will be realized from the investment. Next we discuss some concepts that help create an accurate business case.

### Account for All Costs over Time

Just as with any investment, when making a business case for operational analytics, it is critical to account for all costs, not just key line items, and to account for those costs over the lifetime of the investment. One mistake organizations make is to not fully account for some very real costs that they will face. This is partially driven by the fact that some costs get more attention because they are much more visible and/or politically charged than others. Make sure that people are keeping an eye on all of the costs even as they try to focus on only the few that they're most interested in. Let's walk through a few examples of the impacts of ignoring total costs in day-to-day life.

### Hotel Rates

There was a popular hotel right next to an office that I often traveled to. My employer at the time had a rate of $109 at the hotel, which included breakfast and Internet service. That was a good deal because the breakfast and Internet were priced at $10 apiece. The $109 rate was providing $129 in value.

The following year there was a big push to lower our average nightly room rates. Our travel department set up a new rate for us that was $99 but didn't include breakfast and Internet. By the time breakfast and Internet service was added, almost all travelers were going to be paying an effective rate of $119 every night. The company's goal was to decrease the nightly rate line item, and somebody got a gold star for "saving" $10 per room night at that property. The other charges may have hit against different line items, but at the end of the day, the company was going to be paying more in total.

### Cost per Unit

A client confided that he was struggling with an upcoming hardware investment. His management was focused 100 percent on the cost per server. The performance gap between the more expensive and less expensive servers was at least three times while the costs were only about 25 percent different. His company was heading toward spending nearly three times what was required simply because a lower cost per server was the primary target. He couldn't convince those making the purchase to look at the bigger picture because they were hung up on that one metric. I didn't get an update on how it played out, but I hope that cooler heads prevailed. Focusing on cost per server without taking into account performance is a losing formula.

### Game Show Winnings

*The Price Is Right* was my favorite game show when I was growing up. There are many stories about winners who are shocked to learn that the "free" RV they've won comes with a huge tax bill and a lot of maintenance costs.[3] If contestants want to take a $60,000 RV home today, they better be prepared to pay about $20,000 in income and sales taxes and high gas and maintenance bills. If a contestant is not comfortable with those costs, that free RV isn't really free at all, is it? Contestants had better also look at resale value to ensure that they can sell what will be an officially used RV at a high enough price to net a positive income after taxes and fees. It is a big mistake to look only at the value side without looking into the cost side. As an aside, you don't think that Olympic medals come without taxes, do you? U.S. Olympic athletes face taxes for winning medals because of the cash awards that come with them from the U.S. Olympic committee.[4]

### The Most Overlooked Component of Cost

One of the most often underestimated, if not completely missed, components of a business case for investing in tools and systems supporting analytics is the labor component. It is critical that labor costs are accounted for. There are very real labor costs related to all aspects of building, testing, implementing, and maintaining operational analytics processes. There are also very real labor costs related to implementing and maintaining an analytics platform or a set of analytics tools.

Labor costs can be driven up immensely if an organization doesn't have the right skills on staff and therefore is burdened with inefficiencies during implementation and process creation activities. The costs related to labor can exceed by multiple times the underlying licensing and hardware costs. This can be especially true for analytics processes that are not yet mature and require more care and feeding. Many operational analytics fall into this category today.

A man from a government agency (names withheld for obvious reasons!) confided during a discussion that his organization had reduced a substantial portion of its software licensing fees through a mandate to use open source technologies wherever possible across the agency. However, his team ended up spending millions of dollars on incremental labor and was multiple quarters behind deadlines. This was because a lot of the open source tools the agency migrated to were not ready to replace the commercial tools previously in place. Not only had the organization not saved anything in total, but it had spent millions more and lost a lot of time. Targeting the license fee line item alone led the agency down a path that cost dearly in terms of labor even though the license fee line item was drastically reduced.

### Shine a Light on Labor Costs

Labor costs often are underestimated when assessing the costs of an investment in analytics. Inefficiencies caused by skill or usability gaps may be easiest to overlook. Due to those gaps, one option may require much more labor than another to build the same analytics process.

There's another area where labor comes into play that's very hard to quantify but very real. If it takes extra time to do something on a given platform or with a given tool compared to another option, then that additional time should be associated with that investment choice. Outside of labor costs for implementation and ongoing maintenance, which are easy to identify, if an organization is less efficient with a chosen option, that lack of efficiency can quickly add up and possibly dwarf the other costs.

As you assess potential investments, you must look objectively at all of your costs and all of the skills that you have available. These are summarized in Figure 4.5. Based on available skill sets alone, one organization could be led down a different path than another. As with anything, the right answer is often "It depends." Without going through the process of accounting for your situation, you can't make the right choices.

### Issues that Change the Formula

Realities can lead an organization to deviate from the cheapest cost option, of course. For example, perhaps the capital budget is fully spent this year and everyone has been told that there is absolutely no way that any more capital expenses will be approved . . . period. In that case, any option requiring a capital expense isn't going to

- Installation and configuration
- Ongoing maintenance of both tools and analytic processes
- Analytic process creation
- Analytic process testing and operational implementation
- Incremental effort required to utilize one option over another (often missed!)

Figure 4.5   Labor Costs that Must Be Accounted For

work, and it is necessary to come up with an alternative. That alternative might involve a cloud solution or leasing instead of purchasing equipment, for example. Those options may even be more expensive over time, but a higher long-term cost is the price to be paid for the tight budgets at present.

It's important to understand it's okay to pursue a more expensive option as long as it is being done with a full understanding that more is being paid and an organization understands the reasons for doing it. Knowing and understanding that more will be paid and deciding for practical reasons to do it is okay. That is far different from skipping the exercise of understanding the costs and potentially even fooling yourself into thinking that you aren't paying more when in reality you are.

### Scalability Is Not Just about Storage and Processing

In Chapter 2, we discussed that operational analytics and big data require scale in multiple dimensions. This means not just in terms of storage and processing but also in terms of the number of users, concurrency, security, workload management, and integration with other tools. When making analytics operational, there will be millions of decisions (potentially tens of millions of decisions) being made on an ongoing basis so it is necessary to ensure that the needed scale is available across all the necessary dimensions.

If a chosen investment can't support all the types of scale required for operational analytics, an organization will pay dearly on the back end working around the scale limitations. The cost of those workarounds can really add up. In the worst case, it may not be possible to work around some of the gaps and it may be necessary to start over.

I'll provide an analogy to this concept from my own past. A few years ago, I bought a cheap weed trimmer. I only needed to do a little bit of weed trimming in my yard, so I decided to go with the cheapest trimmer I could find. When I got my purchase home, it didn't work very well, so it took me longer to do the weeding I needed to do. In addition, the string it used was cheap and broke quite frequently. The string was very difficult to change on the spool, and the spool was very difficult to put back on once I did change the string.

In the end, that cheap trimmer cost me a bundle due to the extra time and inefficiency it caused me. After a few weeks of trying to make it work, I abandoned the trimmer and went and bought a more expensive version. If I had really taken into account not just the price of the trimmer but also the total effort it would take me to use it in the ways that I planned, I would have made a different choice from the start. Luckily, a weed trimmer is relatively inexpensive, and I learned my lesson with minimal monetary damage. That won't be the case if similar mistakes are made with investments in operational analytics.

## Tips for Creating a Winning Business Case

Now that we've covered some of the considerations that need to go into a business case for analytics, we turn our attention to concepts that can increase the odds of successfully pitching the case to an executive team. Once a solid business case is created, how can it be positioned most effectively to ensure success in getting it approved? Let's look at a few things to consider.

### Don't Force a Business Case

Don't waste time trying to force a business case where one doesn't exist. If you are trying to make a case and the numbers just aren't working out, then it is time to move onto another problem. When there is a lot of hype around certain approaches, it is easy to buy into all the sizzle and to get sucked into trying to make a business case work. Don't let shiny new technology, data, or tools and the sizzle that surrounds them move a business case past facts and into emotion.

In 2013, people at multiple organizations around the world talked to me about the difficulty they faced justifying substantial investments in the acquisition of social media data and the related analytics of that data. My clients couldn't find use cases that justified increased investment. Each of the organizations had third parties providing high-level sentiment analysis and other trend analyses based on aggregate social media information. However, the organizations couldn't make the case for bringing the raw social media data in-house. The costs for the data and the development of the analytics processes didn't appear to have enough return to make it worthwhile. At each customer, the people I spoke with were stressed over their inability to justify something that they perceived others in the marketplace commonly could justify. They all wanted to know what they were missing.

What I told each of the organizations was that they shouldn't worry. Perhaps investing in detailed social media data didn't make sense for them at the time. Perhaps it never will. If the high-level summaries that the organizations already had access to were sufficient and they weren't able to prove the need for a deeper level of investment, that is okay. After all, even after going to the effort and expense to get the data, matching social media accounts with internal customer accounts can be quite difficult, and the success rate in matching is fairly low. I suggested to each organization that the best path may be to stick with what is already in place for social media and divert energy into finding another higher-value analytics opportunity to pursue.

## Resist the Pressure

Not all business cases will work out, so don't try to force one. Just because a given approach is getting a lot of attention in the marketplace doesn't mean that it will pay off for your organization today. Focus effort on building business cases where you can justify them easily, not where market hype leads you.

Part of the problem my clients faced was that there was substantial hype around social media analytics at the time. It seemed like everyone else was investing and getting a return on social media analytics. I pointed out that I'd had the same conversation with several other organizations just like theirs. Each organization seemed to think that others were doing more than they actually were.

Such scenarios seem a lot like high school, when everyone else seemed to have had a much more exciting life than you did. In fact, most of it was simply rumor, and other kids may have been envying you and what they perceived as your exciting life. In high school, nobody wants to be left out, and that's also true in the business world. Don't give in to the pressure to prove a business case that doesn't exist. Your energy is better spent building cases in areas where you're confident value exists and you're able to prove it.

### To Succeed, Start Small

As mentioned at the beginning of the chapter, the way tools and technologies are used to build analytics processes today make it possible to start with a much smaller investment and then build from there. This point is so important that I've discussed it from different angles in my book *Taming the Big Data Tidal Wave*, and my regular International Institute for Analytics blog and a *Harvard Business Review* blog.[5] I'm going to reinforce some key themes here.

One of the reasons people immediately have concerns when someone suggests starting small is the concept of anchoring, which I first heard about in the book *Predictably Irrational* by Dan Ariely.[6] To illustrate the concept, say that there is a big room full of people. I take half into the hall, tell them that I'm going to have lunch with 10 people today, and have them take their seats again. Then I take the other half of the group into the hall and tell them I am going to be at the airport with 10,000 people that afternoon. We all return to the room, I set a jar of jelly beans on the table in the front of the room, and ask the room how many jelly beans are in the jar. This is where it starts to get interesting.

As it ends up, the half of the people who heard me say the number 10 will on average guess lower than the half of the people who heard me say the number 10,000. This is true even though the jelly beans have nothing to do with the numbers I said. The reason is that the people's minds get anchored on either the number 10 or 10,000. The group that heard 10 starts at 10 and works their way up until they think the number they're guessing is big enough. The group that heard 10,000 works their way down until they think the number is small enough. It is a psychological trick our minds play on us.

### What Do You Really Need to Prove?

Don't go too far in the initial pursuit of a new operational analytics process. The first step is simply to prove that an idea has merit. You don't need the complete, production-ready process from the start. Build just enough to demonstrate the value, then use what is learned to design and create the final process more efficiently.

That's exactly what happens with big data and operational analytics. The phrases sound intimidating. Our minds get focused on big, complex, massive-scale analytics. As we think about how to get started, our minds drift toward highly complex, very difficult paths.

We start aiming for the end state rather than the first steps that lead to the end state.

There is a perspective that is critical here. We don't need all of the data over years of operation for every piece of equipment in a fleet to identify predictive maintenance opportunities. What we do need is enough data over enough time on enough pieces of equipment to establish what trends exist and what the general magnitude of the opportunity is. Instead of starting with a massive project, start with a pilot or proof of concept on a subset of data. That effort can prove that an idea makes sense and can produce a return. Simultaneously build up the final business case as you learn more about both the effort required to create the final operational process and about any data or process issues that will have to be addressed. Feed the results from the pilot into the case for the larger investment. Just make sure that your mind doesn't get tricked into anchoring on something much bigger.

### Accept Some Uncertainty

When entering new areas, like big data and operational analytics, there will be more unknowns than is typical when developing a business case. When pursuing a new initiative of the scale of operational analytics, there will also be a lot of assumptions necessary. These assumptions include the obvious, such as how well the analytics will work and how accurate the data is. There will also be some assumptions about how well the results actually will be implemented and adopted by the organization, once they are available. More or less cultural resistance than expected in an organization can vastly influence the final impact of the operational analytics.

Think back to Chapter 1 and the discussion about drivers being given an optimized daily route based on complex analytics. If the drivers embrace the changes to their usual routes and actually drive the new routes to log fewer miles, there will be a big gain. But if the drivers resist and follow only a small portion of the suggestions, the return will be much less than it could have been. Note that this lack of impact has nothing to do with the power, accuracy, and potential of the analytics process itself. It is purely due to drivers not actually making use of the recommendations. It is a cultural and compliance issue. We discuss these topics more in Chapter 9.

It is critical that an organization understand the assumptions being made and document the risks that either can't be quantified or have a lower degree of precision. When undertaking something new like operational analytics, it might not be possible to specify some of the assumptions as precisely as for other business cases. Many business cases focus on a common situation that has been executed in the past and is understood quite well. For example, imagine a proposal to create a new manufacturing process to produce a fiftieth variation on a product line. In such a situation, it is possible to be very confident in the various assumptions being made about how the equipment will work, how smoothly the line will run, and how the staff will adapt to the new process. After all, something similar has been done 49 times.

### Bracket the Uncertainty

Even if people can't agree on the exact assumptions to make due to uncertainty in the supporting facts, you still can make a business case work. If you demonstrate that the range of assumptions being argued all point to the same decision, it will be possible to move forward without agreement on an exact value but rather a range of values.

However, new and innovative ideas always are going to be a bit more ambiguous. The politics around getting the organization to accept some of the less firm assumptions can be difficult to navigate. Some executives will say they want to assume very low acceptance and adoption of a new process to be safe. Others will want to be aggressive and assume that employees will fully embrace the new process. How do you resolve that gap and get approval?

One way to move past the disagreements is to demonstrate that a wide range of reasonable assumptions all point to the same decision, which is that investing is a smart move. If the uncertainty can't be removed completely, show that the impact of the uncertainty won't be an issue. Whether people want to assume an 80 or a 50 percent compliance rate, if both of those assumptions still point to a positive return, then people can agree to disagree and still feel comfortable proceeding. Over time, the more that an organization embraces analytics, the easier it will be for people to make what might be viewed as a partial leap of faith. It's easier for people to accept some uncertainty when they've seen the same type of uncertainty work out just fine in the past.

### There Are Many Options, So Choose Wisely

As an organization plans where to invest in analytics, it is necessary to weed through all of the possible analytics that *could* be pursued and to decide which of those *should* be given focus. Even if an organization developed a list of 100 compelling operational analytics to implement this year, it wouldn't be possible to implement them all. It is necessary to prioritize and reduce the list to a number that can be handled from a business process change and resource perspective. It just isn't possible to go after everything at once.

Consider creating a quarterly or yearly process of gathering all of the possibilities that the analytics and business teams think they can make a case for. Come to the table with all of the great ideas, and then start to weed through them. Ask:

- Which would have the most internal or external political hurdles?
- Which might be too narrowly focused to have enough upside?
- Which tie to long-term corporate priorities?
- Which are based on data and skills that are readily available?
- Which have been given a high priority by the business team?

Debate the options and then decide which of the options make the most sense to build a business case for. Identify the number that can be handled for the year, but take along a few others just in case the business cases don't work out for some options. By going through the process of starting with all the possibilities and whittling them down, it is possible to be confident that good choices are made.[7]

### Illustration of Doing It Right

A few years ago, a European retail client wanted to capture web browsing history as part of each customer's profile in order to enable better direct marketing and website customization. The effort was projected to cost several million euros, and the team was struggling to get the approval to proceed. In such a situation, many teams would either quit and give up or continue to push the same plan quarter after quarter until the project got approved. In either case, the opportunity would be either missed or severely delayed.

This team had an epiphany. Its members realized that it was true that it would cost several million euros to capture all web browsing history for all customers across all of the organization's multiple websites. However, their executives weren't questioning whether the idea would work as much as they didn't understand to what extent it would work for their organization. The team therefore did something very smart.

Team members identified a couple of popular product lines on one of the company's websites. Then they captured browsing history for customers browsing just those products on that one site for a few months and executed some tests in a pilot. By vastly scaling down the initial scope of the pilot, the amount of data wasn't very big, and the team was able to use existing tools and technologies along with some labor to get it done. The team was able to prove that, for example, sending a follow-up e-mail to someone who browsed an item but didn't buy would produce a big return. In fact, the total return across the tests in the pilot was 800 percent in five months.

Next, the team went back to the executive committee and explained that the 800 percent return on the pilot was achieved in a few months using existing tools, technology, and people. If the team was to build the solution out across all of the company's websites, all products, and all customers, there was a very impressive projected revenue impact to discuss. The team next pointed out that the estimates actually were on the low end because only a few of the fields of the web logs had been used and only a few simple ideas had been tested with the data. Team members had a lot of other ideas about how to use the data that they hadn't tested. While they couldn't quantify the return from the other ideas, the results would only add to the results seen in the pilot. The numbers from the pilot that everyone was excited about represented a floor, not an expected value and certainly not a ceiling, of what could be expected in a full rollout. Team members also discussed that they had now worked with the data, understood it better, and could lower the risk of the rollout because they were much more confident in their work estimates.

With those facts, it was easy to get approval. The executive team was excited to invest in the initiative, knowing that the returns would be there because returns had already been proven. The investment was no longer seen as a risky, huge expense that had unknown benefits months out. Instead, it was seen as a smart investment that everyone knew was going to pay off. In fact, the executives probably would have shoveled the money out the door faster if it had been possible to accelerate implementation.

Notice that the retailer started small and built a business case in stages. However, the endgame was not simply scaling out the exact analytics on the exact products included in the small-scale pilot. The case took into account all costs, including ongoing labor. Team members also pointed out, as suggested earlier in the chapter, the bigger picture they were pursuing. The advantage of starting small and building a business case for analytics is that it shifts focus away from costs and toward the benefits.

## Wrap-Up

The most important lessons to take away from this chapter are:

- Build a case for solving a business problem, not for covering the costs of a project. Also, make it a partnership between business and IT.
- Build a case for analytics with the potential to be a differentiator, not just an incremental improvement to existing analytics processes.
- Prove a concept, not a case. Design a proof of concept to illustrate the potential of a more general class of approach. Don't make it only about proving the value of the limited scope addressed directly in the POC.
- When investing for discovery, use different criteria, like time to insight, that account for the usability and flexibility of options in addition to processing performance.
- If necessary, trade off tool functionality and user friendliness for scalability and ease of integration when making analytics operational.
- Distinguish the inherent value of an analysis from the incremental value that a tool or technology provides to generate the analysis results.
- Identify and account for all costs related to an analytics investment over time within a neutral framework. Don't focus on only certain line items.
- Pay particular attention to ongoing labor costs for both maintenance and to build and test analytics processes. Labor costs often are the most overlooked or underestimated costs.
- Make sure a business case takes into account the various dimensions of scalability required. If not, the gaps will lead to extra costs or even having to start over.

- Don't force a business case where one doesn't exist. A heavily hyped topic isn't going to be right for every organization right now (or ever).
- Start small and leverage targeted pilots to provide tangible results. It isn't necessary to fully implement an analytics process to prove its value.
- Accept that new, innovative initiatives will have more uncertainty than most. If agreement can't be reached on required assumptions, show that all assumptions being argued point to the same decision.

## Notes

1. Richard Winter, *Big Data: What Does It Really Cost?* WinterCorp (August 2013). See www.wintercorp.com/tcod-report.
2. Based on my International Institute for Analytics blog "What Does Taming Big Data Really Cost?" September 12, 2013. See http://iianalytics.com/2013/09/what-does-taming-big-data-really-cost/.
3. "The Price Is Right Winners Reveal Battle with High Taxes," INQUISITR, August 19, 2013, at www.inquisitr.com/912162/the-price-is-right-winners-reveal-battle-with-high-taxes/, or Alan Farnham, "'The Price Is Right'—but the Taxes Are Wrong," ABC News, August 9, 2012, at http://abcnews.go.com/blogs/business/2012/08/the-price-is-right-but-taxes-are-wrong/.
4. See "The Price of Gold: Taking First Place in Olympics Could Cost US Stars as Much as $10G in Taxes," Fox News, February 8, 2014, at www.foxnews.com/politics/2014/02/08/price-gold-taking-first-place-in-olympics-could-cost-us-stars-as-much-as-10g-in/
5. Bill Franks, *Taming the Big Data Tidal Wave* (Hoboken, NJ: John Wiley & Sons, 2012). Franks, "You Don't Have to 'Go Big' to Get Started with Big Data," October 11, 2012; see http://iianalytics.com/2012/10/you-dont-have-to-go-big-to-get-started-with-big-data/. Franks, "To Succeed with Big Data, Start Small," *Harvard Business Review*, October 3, 2012; see http://blogs.hbr.org/2012/10/to-succeed-with-big-data-start/
6. Dan Ariely, *Predictably Irrational* (New York: Harper Collins, 2008).
7. Review the concept of an innovation center from Chapter 10 of *Taming the Big Data Tidal Wave* for more thoughts on one good way to adopt this type of approach.

# 5

# Creating an Analytics Platform

The analytics landscape has become increasingly complex in recent times. In today's world of operational analytics, it is no longer as simple as picking a database and an analytics tool. There are many new tools and technologies to consider adding into a modern analytics environment. These technologies include nonrelational platforms such as Hadoop, discovery platforms that support both relational and nonrelational data and processing, in-memory analytics, graphic processing unit-based analytics, complex event processing, and embedded analytics libraries. We'll talk about each of these.

Over time, further integration will make analytics environments more and more seamless and simple to use. Today, however, it is necessary to deal with a range of components within an analytics platform. The key is to make sure that the platform as a whole is set up so that it can support all analytics needs. This means not just the needs that exist right now but the needs that are anticipated over the next several years.

For operational analytics to succeed, it is necessary to stitch the components together differently and more completely than in the past to create a single, unified analytics environment that can scale to handle any type and volume of data for any kind of analysis. This may sound like an impossible goal, but the market is evolving rapidly today and it is already possible. In this chapter, we discuss how to make sense of all the options and how to put in place an analytics platform that will handle all of the requirements of operational analytics.

Before we begin, note that the marketplace is changing very rapidly. This chapter is being written in early 2014. Although most content in this book isn't highly time sensitive, it is possible that some material in this chapter will have evolved by the time you read it. The general concepts should apply for a long time, but you may have to adapt some of the specifics discussed to take into account the latest tool and technology advances and market offerings.

## Planning

It is no easy task to plan and implement an analytics platform. In this section, we cover a few viewpoints and concepts that should be considered during the planning process.

### Making Analytics Operational Is Not a Technology Issue

Customers are often surprised when I make the claim that the challenge in making analytics operational is really not the technology.[1] However, the fact is that the technology exists today to handle the vast majority of the big data and operational analytics needs of the vast majority of organizations. There are always outlier cases, but chances are that everything your organization needs to succeed today from a technology perspective exists right now. If that's the case, then why does it feel like technology is the root of the challenge to many organizations?

To get to the answer, it is important to understand the difference between technology as a symptom and technology as a cause. In late 2012, I was in a conversation with an employee of a major customer at my company's annual conference. He was from the networking and infrastructure team, an area that I rarely, if ever, deal with. Even though our worlds rarely crossed, he and I were enjoying a chat. When the conversation turned to some of the issues that his company was facing, he challenged me when I claimed that technology was not really his problem.

The customer explained that he understood what I was saying but that his company's network protocols were outdated. With the new volumes of big data and the new analytics requirements coming at the company, the network just couldn't keep up. The network was choking, and he was living a nightmare every day trying to keep it up and running. He wanted to know how I could possibly say that it was not a technology problem.

## Symptom or Cause?

A common symptom of underlying process or policy issues is the impact the issues have on the technologies that they touch. In many cases, what appears to be a technology issue is not. Be sure to distinguish between cases where technology problems are a symptom of larger issues and cases where technology really is the cause of the issues.

I thought about it and asked if it wasn't true that updated networking products were available that, if implemented at his company, would handle the data throughput and analytical requirements that the current network was struggling with. He acknowledged that was true but said he couldn't just go implement an updated network today because he didn't have funding for it. I then pointed out that he had just proved my point. Let me explain why.

In the absolute sense, technology was not his company's problem. He had just acknowledged that the technology to solve his issues was available. Therefore, the technology itself was not the problem. The problem was that his team hadn't convinced upper management of the need to implement that technology. The team hadn't gotten a business case approved and budget allocated. A project team hadn't been mobilized. He was feeling the pain of those issues through his current technology's shortfalls every day. But the technology was not the root problem.

The same concept will be true as organizations pursue operational analytics. There will be times when it feels as if the technology is causing barriers. Be sure to step back and determine if the technology isn't in fact the symptom rather than the problem.

### Components Will Be Added, Not Replaced

It is a common misperception that new analytics technologies are completely replacing mature technologies, but that's not the case at all. As the available technologies evolve and analytics requirements continue to expand, companies are actually adding additional components to an analytics environment as opposed to replacing components.

Perhaps the most common mistaken impression that technologies are being replaced is the idea that Hadoop (or the more general class of nonrelational tools to which Hadoop belongs) is replacing relational database environments. Hadoop is an open source project that allows large files to be split into pieces and processed in parallel. (We better define and discuss Hadoop in more detail later in the chapter.) In reality, Hadoop is augmenting relational environments, and both are going to have a place in the analytics architecture of modern organizations.

A major cause of the confusion stems from the fact that virtually 100 percent of companies today already have relational technology in place. This means that there are many stories in the marketplace of companies supposedly moving to Hadoop. However, the phrase "moving to Hadoop" isn't really accurate. The correct terminology is that companies are "adding Hadoop." Virtually all of the examples that can be found are really about an addition of Hadoop to an existing environment, not a migration of an entire environment over to Hadoop.

Adding to the confusion is the fact that the reverse scenario is very rare. Incredibly few organizations have only Hadoop without a relational environment. The few that exist tend to be in Silicon Valley. Therefore, it is rare to hear of a Hadoop user "moving to relational" or "adding relational" to its environment.

One of the biggest organizations that traditionally used only Hadoop and nonrelational approaches is Facebook. Facebook is known for wanting to build its own technologies and proprietary systems internally. Indeed, Facebook created Hive, an early and popular SQL-like component available to Hadoop users. Yet Facebook announced at The Data Warehousing Institute (TDWI) Conference in May 2013 that it is adding a relational component to its Hadoop environment.[2] Why is Facebook doing this? Because the Facebook team realized that existing relational technology solves some of the problems it faces extremely well. Facebook was spending way too much time trying to make Hadoop do things that it wasn't really designed to do. A mix of technologies made more sense and freed resources to solve other problems.

### Different Platforms, Different Strengths

At first glance, Hadoop sounds similar to parallel relational database platforms. While it is true that they are both a type of parallel processing engine, there are big differences. Perhaps the best description of how Hadoop fits was that of a defense contractor in Washington, DC. (The comments were at a private event under nondisclosure so I can't be more specific.) At the event, a panel was discussing some of the issues their organizations faced due to trying to do too much, too fast with new platforms like Hadoop.

One man on the panel said, "I have realized that Hadoop is phenomenal for solving the exact problems that companies like Google and Yahoo! created it at great expense to solve. If you have those exact problems, such as matching keywords in web searches to websites, then Hadoop is a phenomenal technology. If you have other problems that can be addressed well by the same processing paradigm, then Hadoop is also very helpful. However, there are other types of analytics and processing where Hadoop really isn't efficient or effective at all relative to other options." This isn't a knock on Hadoop. In reality, no processing platform will be ideal for all types of processing and all situations. Every platform has its own strengths and weaknesses. That's why, as we discuss, organizations need to leverage different technology platforms and tools for different types of analytics processes.

If you research how Hadoop works, you'll find that it really is excellent for certain types of computation. One is when scale is primarily required in the processing and storage dimensions we discussed in Chapters 2 and 4. As of this writing, Hadoop doesn't yet provide enterprise-level scale in the other dimensions, such as security, concurrency, and workload management. Hadoop is also terrific for nontraditional data types, such as audio, video, or text that hasn't yet been formatted in an analytics-friendly fashion and may still be in a raw and uncleansed state. This is because data can be stored in Hadoop without any constraints on format.

The sweet spot for a massively parallel relational platform is dealing with high-value data that's already structured and that needs to support a vast pool of users and applications that need to reuse data frequently with performance guarantees included. When making analytics operational, the sweet spot of relational technologies will be encountered frequently.

## Don't Compare Apples to Oranges

Different analytics platforms have different strengths and weaknesses that must be researched and understood when planning an analytics environment. Many people mistakenly think that relational technologies and nonrelational technologies like Hadoop are equivalent, but actually they are complementary, not competitive. Equating them is comparing apples to oranges.

During a webinar called *Total Cost of Data* in November 2013, a vice president from Hortonworks (a company that specializes in Hadoop development, implementation, and related services) made a very important point. He said, "We don't see anybody trying to build an enterprise data warehouse [EDW] with Hadoop. This is a capability issue and not a cost issue. Hadoop is not an EDW. Hadoop is not a database. Comparing these two for an EDW workload is comparing apples to oranges. I don't know anybody who would try to build an EDW in Hadoop." That quote says nothing negative about Hadoop; it simply reinforces that it fits in certain ways. I can easily imagine someone in a similar webinar saying "I don't know anybody trying to use relational technology for image processing."

Organizations pursuing operational analytics will end up using both relational technology and nonrelational technologies at some point in the process. When we talk about the pillars of an analytics architecture later in the chapter, we discuss in more detail how these technologies can fit together. For now, just don't think that they are interchangeable as opposed to complementary.

### Do What's Right Today

Perhaps this holiday season you will decide to buy a new TV and then research to determine the best choice for your purposes. However, you will invariably also learn of the great features that are coming early in the spring in the next generation of TVs. As a result, you can put off buying a TV and wait for the new version in the spring. However, as soon as the new one is available in the spring, you will learn about what's coming in the next generation of TVs due in the fall. This can go on forever. While you put off the purchase again and again, you are stuck with your old TV that does not have any of the new features. At some point, you need to make a decision to move forward. The same is true with analytics platforms and tools. There will always be upcoming releases that promise to improve on the current releases. At some point, it is necessary to move forward with a plan. Otherwise, none of the benefits of current or future releases will be available to the organization.

As a result of the always evolving landscape, it is strongly recommended that unless there is a specific feature that is absolutely

**Don't Be Frozen by Indecision**

It is easy to postpone improvements to an analytics environment by waiting for the next batch of features that are "coming soon." However, there will always be new features coming soon. Make the best decision you can make today and start harvesting value. It will be time to upgrade again before you know it.

critical to the business needs of today, you resist the urge to delay action. Taking no action will lead to highly outdated platforms that will struggle to support current needs. Many tools and technologies allow upgrades to newer versions for either free or a reduced cost. Simply plan out how aggressively your organization wants to implement upgrades and budget for the related time and costs. Also keep in mind that the entire life cycle of technology investments today tends to be only three to five years. This means that you will be evaluating options again before you know it.

If you have a good plan, good requirements, and an approved budget, ask: "Will any of the new features coming in the next several months radically improve results?" If so, alter your schedule to take advantage of the new features. But consider this a risk since new software always has bugs in it, and those releases could be delayed. If new features are more than a few months away, just get going. If you delay based on rumors of what might possibly exist sometime soon, you will never escape the cycle of second-guessing action. Make the best decision possible today and be happy with it.

## Building

Now you're ready to implement an updated analytics environment. This section outlines some of the latest thinking in terms of how to go about the process of updating your environment. We discuss a variety of technologies and how they can be fit together to help your organization make analytics operational. As mentioned at the beginning of the chapter, be sure also to research the latest thinking as of the time you read this.

### Welcome to Fabric-Based Computing

For many years, large organizations focused on trying to incorporate the most valuable data and analytics processes within a single centralized platform called an enterprise data warehouse (EDW). An EDW is a large relational database system that typically uses a parallel database platform for maximum scalability and performance. Parallel systems are comprised of many machines that are all connected together so that data can be presented to users as if the system was a single large machine. In that sense, the data in an EDW is not really in one place; it is spread across many machines that are configured in exactly the same way and are connected in a high-performing fashion.

Making a traditional EDW system seem like a single machine to a user requires lightning-fast connections between the machines that make up the system as well as sophisticated software to manage the processing. The connections allow data movement at scale when necessary (e.g., joining two large tables) while providing incredibly fast performance when data movement isn't needed. From a conceptual level, as opposed to stitching together machines that are identically configured, a fabric-based system connects different types of platforms together. Fabric-based computing stitches together many systems into one big logical system using high-speed networks, to allow any given component to communicate and share data with every other component of the fabric. Many people equate fabric computing with Infiniband[3] technology, which is much faster than traditional network connections. However, the network is merely a foundation for the analytics processes and related process management software. Figure 5.1 illustrates the concept behind fabric-based computing.

In today's fabric-based systems, machines of different configurations and different underlying platforms are able to communicate

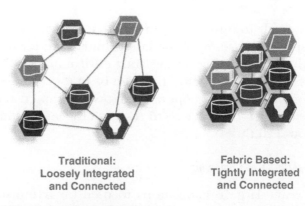

Traditional:
Loosely Integrated
and Connected

Fabric Based:
Tightly Integrated
and Connected

Figure 5.1   Traditional versus Fabric-Based Computing

at blazing fast speeds. Arbitrarily and frequently moving massive amounts of data around the fabric still isn't desirable, but if there is a clear benefit, it is now possible to move data fast enough to support an important requirement without totally destroying performance. Given stringent performance requirements, moving lots of data in a production or operational environment still must be minimized. However, during the discovery process, where performance isn't as big of a consideration, leveraging a fabric provides immense value and flexibility.

## Unified Analytic Environments Are Coming

Fabric-based computing is evolving to support today's need for the analysis of massive amounts of data of different types using a wide variety of analytics techniques. The endgame is to create a unified analytics environment where users don't have to worry about where data sits but can focus simply on how to analyze the data.

Making analytics operational, especially in the era of big data, is going to require embracing the concept of fabric-based computing and the creation of a unified analytics environment. Too many data types and too many different analytics requirements exist to allow a single platform to handle everything with the scale and speed necessary. When users have access to a single unified analytics environment, they will not worry about the specific technologies that comprise it or where in the fabric data physically sits. Instead, users will focus on building the logic of an analytics process. Now let's explore how to put in place the foundation for this future starting today.

### Pillars of a Unified Analytics Environment

There are three main pillars of a unified analytics environment capable of handling operational analytics for an organization. The three pillars are:

1. **The relational database pillar**, which is used to deploy operational analytics at an enterprise scale across the breadth of users and applications that require them. It is the workhorse that embeds operational analytics within business processes.

2. **The discovery pillar**, which is used to easily explore any type of data and test any type of analytics process. It allows an organization to find new insights in data quickly and efficiently.
3. **The nonrelational pillar (usually Hadoop)**, which is valuable for the staging and initial processing of all types of data since it makes no assumptions about data structure. It is also used for the ongoing storage of lower value and/or rarely used data.

To understand how these pillars fit together within a unified analytics environment, as illustrated in Figure 5.2, consider each technology to be a special-purpose brain. Historically, these brains were stand-alone and disconnected. As a result, each brain could take advantage of only its own specialty. Fabric-based computing essentially connects these specialized brains together to create a single brain with multiple specialized components. The components can interact and support each other directly. This is very much how the human brain works. Different parts of our brains handle different things, but the parts are all connected together into a single brain that is much more powerful than the individual components alone. Similarly, a unified analytics environment will enable the whole to be more than the sum of the parts.

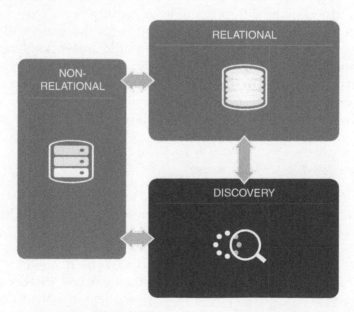

**Figure 5.2    Unified Analytics Environment**

## One Brain with Specialized Components

A fabric-based, unified analytics environment will function like one brain with many specialized subsystems. By connecting different technologies together in this way, the whole can be greater than the sum of the parts, just like a human brain.

Next we next discuss each of the pillars in detail. In addition to the three primary pillars, some optional supporting technologies serve special needs and can be utilized as appropriate. These include in-memory processing, graphic processing units, complex event processing technologies, and embedded analytics libraries. Each of these is defined and discussed.

### Relational Pillar

Virtually every organization today leverages relational database engines to manage the data supporting enterprise applications. Most large organizations have implemented a massively parallel database engine to get the extra scalability such engines provide to analytics processes. Companies with offers in the enterprise, parallel database space include Teradata, IBM, and Oracle, among others. For years, relational technology has been the standard for storing data and enabling the generation of reports and analysis with that data. Since relational technology is the most widely adopted and best understood of the three pillars, we cover it quickly.

A very common misperception is that data must be in a highly structured format and must be fully and formally defined before being loaded into a relational database. Although it is true that many organizations have policies that require a formal data model and structure before loading data, relational technology does not require it. Images or audio are poor fits for a relational system, but web logs and sensor data can be handled, albeit with a little extra effort. Many relational database vendors now even directly support Extensible Markup Language (XML), while some have recently added JavaScript Object Notation (JSON) support. Supporting these formats enables raw data from sensors, for example, to be loaded and queried directly without any further manipulation.

Both XML and JSON formats have a structure, but that structure is not nearly as clean, well defined, and consistent as traditional

```
{ "MFG_Line": {
   "Items" : [

   { "Name" :"Item1",
     "Color":  "Red", "Size": "Large",
     "Prod_ID": 100,        "Barcode": 123458,
     "Create_Time": "2013-08-15 20:07:27" },

   { "Name" :"Item2",
     "Color":  "Brown", "Size": "Medium",
     "Prod_ID": 100,        "Barcode": 123459,
     "Create_Time": "2013-08-16 20:07:27" }  ],

   "Machine": {
     "Temp": 95, "Warning": null,
     "FW_Version": 1.4, "Sensor_Code": 152
   }
}}
```

Figure 5.3    Sample of Semistructured JSON Data

formats, such as fixed-width files or delimited files. XML and JSON often are called semistructured formats. It takes a bit of extra work to extract information from data in these formats, but flexibility is gained. Figure 5.3 shows an example of a JSON file. It is easy to visually comprehend what each piece of data means, but the format is not very friendly when it comes to writing code to parse the data and extract the individual fields.

One big advantage of enterprise-class relational technologies is that they not only scale with respect to data volume and processing power, but they have robust resource management to handle the widely varying demands for data in a large organization. This is important because there will not just be operational analytics occurring at any point in time but also large batch processes, queries to support reporting, and more. Without resource management, these mixed workloads would be a huge problem.

The concept of mixed workloads is easy to visualize as a traffic jam with large trucks, cars, motorcycles, emergency vehicles, vans, and so on all competing for traffic lanes. Instead of different types of vehicles, databases have different requests of different sizes and priorities. Left to the drivers, traffic snarls and everyone slows down. But a robust resource management subsystem will organize everything by priority and amount of resources consumed. Restricted lanes are created for emergency vehicles, toll lanes are created for those who need priority, and so forth. The result is the best possible performance for everyone. A good resource management subsystem allows many users and processes to share the system effectively.

## Backbone for Operational Analytics

The relational pillar is usually the best place to deploy operational analytics. Given its scalability across all of the relevant dimensions as well as its ability to integrate easily with almost any enterprise application, relational technology plays an important role in making analytics operational.

Enterprise-class relational technologies also have sophisticated security capabilities and allow massive concurrency. In other words, the systems can tightly control who sees what data and also can allow many users to access the same data simultaneously. Relational systems also have these additional strengths: availability, reliability, recoverability, and manageability. These features are absolutely critical if hundreds of call center agents plus thousands of field employees plus thousands of headquarters employees all need access to the same information. Most software applications used by large enterprises today are built to work with a relational back end, which further increases relational technologies' appeal and ease of integration.

To summarize, the relational pillar is where organizations usually want to deploy operational analytics processes. Relational technology is the scalable backbone of an organization when it comes to making analytics operational.

### Discovery Pillar

A concept getting a lot of recent attention in the market is that of adding a discovery platform to an enterprise's unified analytics environment. Discovery isn't really a new concept, and most organizations already have a discovery environment of one sort or another. The classic stand-alone environment where analytics professionals have for years developed new analytics is a form of discovery environment. However, the classic analytics environment is rarely well integrated with the other systems an organization has in place, and the environment isn't typically scalable. It is time to evolve past these early discovery architectures. Tools often utilized for discovery processes include SAS, IBM SPSS, and R. Each of these can be utilized within an integrated discovery pillar, not just within a stand-alone environment.

The way in which analytics tools are used has changed recently. Analytics tools have become much more tightly integrated with the scalable platforms that are part of an enterprise's analytics environment. Both relational technologies and Hadoop help make it possible to migrate from distinct, stand-alone discovery environments to a discovery platform that is part of an organization's unified analytics environment.

Discovery platforms go beyond the analytics sandboxes that have long been embedded within other platforms. As a refresher, an analytics sandbox is a logical partition of a large operational system that allows analytics professionals to load and create data in addition to querying data. A sandbox enables rapid exploration and prototyping of analytics processes at scale by leveraging the most scalable platforms an organization owns. Sandboxes recently have been quite popular within relational data warehouse environments. Although a discovery environment can contain analytics sandboxes too, it is more than just a sandbox.

Today's discovery platforms, which are the second pillar of a unified analytics environment, enable the mixing and matching of all kinds of data, both structured and not. A discovery platform should support both relational processing and nonrelational processing. It should also support almost any type of analytics methodology or approach, both traditional and not. This means that it should support not just traditional statistics and forecasting methods but also text analytics (e-mail, documents, etc.), graph analytics (relationships between people, places, or things), geospatial analytics (spatial relationships), and more. Figure 5.4 illustrates how a discovery platform streamlines and combines analytics processing.

One important feature of a discovery environment is that it will have very limited rules and constraints. Discovery platforms like Teradata Aster and Pivotal Greenplum not only provide their own analytics algorithms but also support the use of common analytics tools like SAS, SPSS, or R. Discovery platforms are also perfect for use in an innovation center.[4] A discovery platform may or may not be part of a final and fully deployed operational process. The discovery platform is certainly used to discover and define an analytics process

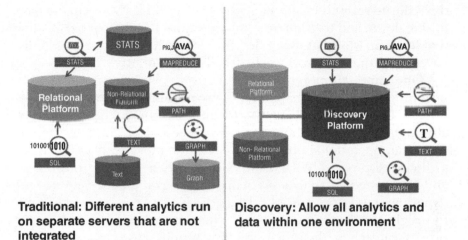

**Traditional: Different analytics run on separate servers that are not integrated**

**Discovery: Allow all analytics and data within one environment**

Figure 5.4   How a Discovery Platform Streamlines Analytics

worthy of deployment. However, once the detailed analytics logic required to implement the discovery is known, it may be possible to place that logic into a production process without the discovery platform being involved. This is because it is often possible to simplify and streamline an analytics process when moving from the discovery phase to the production phase. We cover this in more detail in Chapter 6.

## Target Rapid Insights over Rapid Processing

A discovery platform needs to be flexible and user friendly in order to speed the time required to find new insights. It will be judged by different criteria from operational platforms, such as time to insight. Processing speed and scalability are not nearly as important for a discovery process as flexibility and ease of use.

In some cases, it may be possible to utilize the relational and non-relational pillars to enable discovery without adding another distinct platform. The important point is to have an environment dedicated to discovery. However, regardless of how it is implemented, a discovery platform will have to be configured in a different way from operational systems. Attempting to drive discovery under typical production system constraints is a losing approach. A discovery process needs the flexibility to recast the data, change its layout on a whim, flip the data upside down, and try numerous experiments. It isn't possible to allow that freedom while enforcing the rules of production processes. A discovery environment provides the freedom required.

One important point is that a discovery platform aims to enable new insights to be found as quickly as possible. The platform does not aim to provide the fastest performance or the highest scalability, although these help. Although performance and scalability are important in an operational process, they don't matter nearly as much for a discovery process. What matters most when building prototypes and exploring new analytics is being able to complete an end-to-end experiment as fast as possible. This goes back to the concept of time to insight discussed in Chapter 4. The time to code and test a new process can eclipse the processing time required to execute the code, so having a discovery environment that makes it easy to mix data, run algorithms, and validate a new insight is important. Operational performance and scale can be worried about once something is discovered and is proven to be worth the effort. We discuss this in more detail in Chapter 6.

### Nonrelational Pillar

There is a wide variety of nonrelational platforms available. Hadoop has risen rapidly to become the most popular of the nonrelational platforms and a common component of analytical environments. Nonrelational platforms do not require data to be stored in any specific format and use a variety of programming languages in addition to some basic SQL to interface with the data. Hadoop has gained popularity due to its ability to deal with the unstructured or semistructured data that has become so common in the world of big data. In reality, all data has some structure. However, unstructured data is usually defined as data formatted in a complex way that's not easily converted into an analysis-ready form. Some examples include text, video, and audio files. Another common type of data is semistructured data, which falls in the middle between structured and unstructured data. Examples include many log files like web logs, sensor data, or the JSON data discussed earlier in this chapter. Semistructured data has defined data points, but not necessarily in any consistent order or simple format.

Hadoop handles these types of data particularly well for reasons that are discussed shortly. The fact that Hadoop is open source, and therefore has no license fee, also makes it easy to experiment with at low cost. In addition, there are commercial versions of Hadoop available from vendors such as Cloudera, Hortonworks, and MapR, as well as Hadoop appliances available from vendors such as Teradata, IBM, and Oracle. All of these offerings add value-added features on top of the base open source code.

Hadoop is different from relational technology in some important ways, led by the fact that it requires only that data files be placed on a file system. No specific format or structure of data is required for loading into Hadoop. Since Hadoop doesn't assume anything about the data files it stores, it also doesn't have any special handling for one type of a file over another.

The lack of a required format means it is possible to load text, photos, video, images, log data, sensor data, or any other type of data exactly as it comes in and then process it in parallel. This is in contrast to relational technology, where a row and column structure is assumed by default. While data with a relational structure can be placed in Hadoop, that isn't the sweet spot where Hadoop is differentiated. In fact, Hadoop is both more difficult to work with and slower to execute as compared to enterprise-class relational technology when standard relational operations are desired. This is because databases have all sorts of tools and tricks for dealing with relational data whereas Hadoop does not. Hadoop offers more flexibility with respect to data format, but the specialized functionality to deal with one format as opposed to another is lost.

One of the drivers to use Hadoop is the fact that some data is inherently more valuable than other data. For example, checking account transactions reflect money changing hands whereas a Twitter tweet is merely an opinion. The tweet doesn't have the same value as the financial transaction so it's not worth storing it in a higher-cost system where it probably isn't going to be used that often anyway. Hadoop lets organizations hang on to low-value data so that it is there when needed. It can also store the raw log files from which critical pieces of information are extracted. By archiving raw files in Hadoop, it is possible to go back later and extract additional information as the need develops. Using Hadoop for archival purposes is also similar to having backup files continuously and easily accessible instead of having to go through a painful process of loading tapes. Finally, archiving the raw data can be of great benefit during audits or legal situations.

Think of Hadoop as a refinery of raw iron ore. A refinery dumps dirt and rocks full of iron into a smelter. Hadoop (the smelter) grinds up the mess, heats it, and refines it into iron ingots, throwing away the waste. Gather enough tweets, refine them with text analysis tools, and melt down terabytes of opinions into a much smaller (and more valuable!) set of buyer preferences or trends. The iron ingots (results) then get passed to the manufacturing system (the relational pillar) where they are turned into even higher-value sheet metal, I-beams, or finished goods. Retaining low-value data at a low cost enables more data to be kept than in the past.

Hadoop is becoming the initial storage location for many sources of data. It can be used not only to store data initially but to refine and process the data, as explained, so it can be transformed into something useful for analytics. For example, text data from e-mails, customer reviews, or social media postings isn't very useful in its raw format. To make text data useful requires running text analytics algorithms to extract important facts about the text. Knowing who made a given social media posting, whether the sentiment of the posting was positive, and what products the posting discussed is valuable. Running the processes to extract such information from text is a perfect scenario for Hadoop since it is able to analyze the text in parallel. The structured data extracted from the text is then fed into an analysis process.

One drawback of Hadoop is that care is required when coding in its parallel environment to make sure that a correct answer is generated. Many computations that are simple in a single-threaded environment must be computed in a different fashion when being executed on a parallel system. There are two types of parallelism: node- or worker-level parallelism and system-level parallelism. Node-level parallelism simply executes the same code on each node. The nodes have no knowledge of each other and don't share any information. More complex is system-level parallelism, where the nodes across the entire system coordinate and pass information to get the correct result. Programmers must be careful to create code that matches the level of parallelism required for a given problem.

### Any Data, Any Format, Any Volume

Hadoop's ability to handle any volume of data in any format makes it an important pillar of a unified analytics environment.

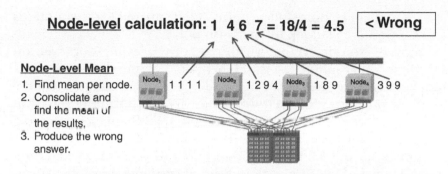

**Node-level calculation: 1  4 6  7 = 18/4 = 4.5**  < Wrong

**Node-Level Mean**
1. Find mean per node.
2. Consolidate and find the mean of the results.
3. Produce the wrong answer.

Node₁ 1 1 1 1    Node₂ 1 2 9 4    Node₃ 1 8 9    Node₄ 3 9 9

Figure 5.5    Incorrect Node-Level Mean Computation

For example, you can't ask for a mean using a node- or worker-level process because each worker will compute the mean of the data on that worker and then report back its own mean. However, you might remember from your Statistics 101 class that you cannot take the mean of means and get the right answer. What you must do is get the overall sum and count to compute the overall mean. (For an illustration, see Figures 5.5 and 5.6.) The programmer must ensure code is at the right level of parallelism to make computations happen correctly within Hadoop. In contrast, a parallel relational environment is constructed so that system-level parallelism is the standard.

Packages coming to market add an SQL-like syntax or even data mining methodologies on top of a Hadoop platform. However, today those options are still not very robust compared to the requirements that large organizations have. This gets back to the need to leverage each platform for what it is good at. As discussed in Chapter 4, there

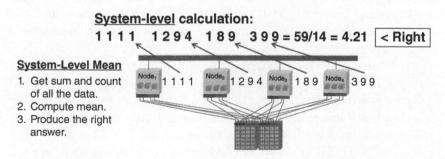

**System-level calculation:**
**1 1 1 1   1 2 9 4   1 8 9   3 9 9 = 59/14 = 4.21**  < Right

**System-Level Mean**
1. Get sum and count of all the data.
2. Compute mean.
3. Produce the right answer.

Node₁ 1 1 1 1    Node₂ 1 2 9 4    Node₃ 1 8 9    Node₄ 3 9 9

Figure 5.6    Correct System-Level Mean Computation

are cases where Hadoop will perform well compared to other options and cases where Hadoop will perform poorly.

How do you determine which type of processing does well on Hadoop? A very simple test is whether your computations can occur independently of each other in a node parallel fashion. If the independent processing of each worker on its own subset of data will get you the same answer as if you processed all the data on one big worker, Hadoop tends to do well. The example of computing a mean in Figures 5.5 and 5.6 is a situation where this isn't true. When finding the mean of sales for each individual customer, it will be true as long as all data for any given customer is stored on the same worker. If information must be passed back and forth between workers to get the same answer as if you processed all the data at once, Hadoop can struggle. This is an oversimplification and there are exceptions, but that single guideline often will point you in the right direction.

Another way to determine if Hadoop is a good place to run an algorithm is whether the algorithm requires sequential or nonsequential processing. In relational systems, SQL gets an answer set and steps through each row in sequence applying functions to each record. SQL doesn't work well if processing needs to bounce around from row to row and from iteration to iteration (often based on the results from the latest iteration). Hadoop uses programming languages like Java, Python, or C++ that accommodate complex handling of the data so that there is no requirement for sequential, row-by-row processing.

One interesting implication of the fact that Hadoop uses C++, Java, or Python is that Hadoop doesn't enable new functionality as much as it enables increased scale of existing functionality. Any program being written today in Java for Hadoop could have been written years ago and submitted to a traditional single-threaded system. The language being used isn't new, but the environment where the language is being executed is new, and it adds tremendous scale to the Java code.

To summarize, Hadoop makes the most sense today as the initial storage location for large data sources and for the initial refinement and processing of that data. Hadoop also makes sense for storing data that has a low value or that will be used only very infrequently. Finally, Hadoop is terrific for archival purposes. It will be rare in the near term for Hadoop to support live operational analytics processes for most organizations.

### Additional Supporting Technologies

Supporting technologies can be added to a unified analytics environment to support the pillars. These supporting technologies address specific types of processing or analytics, are much more specialized, and will be relevant only in certain instances. The technologies discussed next will continue to evolve, and it is likely that over time others will enter into the mix. It is also quite possible that the functionality offered by these supporting technologies eventually will be absorbed into one or more pillars so that additional add-ons are no longer required. Let's go through some of the most common supporting technologies as of early 2014.

### In-Memory Appliances

In-memory analytics appliances load data directly into a large memory pool before running sophisticated algorithms fully within memory. This type of appliance is expensive because of the need for a lot of memory, but the performance is incredible. An in-memory approach is particularly beneficial when it is necessary to continue to build and rebuild a large number of complex models with high frequency. SAS offers an in-memory analytics appliance with several different platforms.

One common use case for an in-memory appliance is in risk models at major financial institutions. A financial institution might need to update risk models for thousands of scenarios or securities on at least a daily basis as it decides how to both hedge and make investments.

### Graphics Processing Unit Appliances

Appliances based on graphics processing units (GPUs) address a different issue from in-memory appliances. An individual GPU supports a massive scale of computational processing, but not necessarily a massive scale of data. Applying GPUs to process analytics is borrowing technology initially developed to generate complex personal computer graphics. GPUs handle PC video displays by applying hundreds, or even thousands, of weak processors to an array of data. Grinding out millions of pixels in a video game requires enormously parallel processing. While not nearly as fast or robust as mainstream microprocessors, GPUs can also be applied to large arrays of mathematical data crunching. Fuzzy Logix is one company that offers a GPU-based appliance.

One use case for GPU processing is a Monte Carlo simulation, which may examine millions or billions of scenarios. People often come across a Monte Carlo simulation (though not at a scale requiring GPUs) during retirement planning. When projecting retirement savings, various levers, such as rate of return and inflation rates, are moved across a wide range of possible values to project how much money will be saved at a given retirement date. After all of the simulations are complete, a summary of how many scenarios led to success and how many led to failure is created.

As each of the different factors is varied across a wide range of possible values, a large number of computations are needed. GPUs are well suited for handling this kind of scenario at an industrial scale. Instead of a simple Monte Carlo for retirement planning, financial institutions run very complex risk simulations on an ongoing basis. You can expect to see GPUs being used for analytics more often in the coming years.

## Additional Support Is Available

Supporting technologies that address specific problems are available to help an organization make analytics operational. Eventually, the functionality of these technologies may be absorbed within the primary pillars. Until that point, specialized appliances or software products will fill the gap.

### Complex Event Processing Technologies

Complex event processing (CEP) is used to analyze streaming data in real time. CEP follows a different approach from historical analytics processes. When looking at a stream of data in real time with CEP, the goal isn't to match it with other enterprise data but rather to look at what's happening right now in the data stream to find signals that require an immediate response. The processing and data handling required for CEP is different from typical analytics processes and necessitates some different technologies to be in place.

One major difference between CEP and other analytics is that CEP is often literally looking at data before the data is even placed in a storage environment. In other words, CEP processes occur on data while it is on its way to one of the pillars to be stored. That way, the fastest possible response is enabled when a signal does show up in the data. Examples of vendors in this space include TIBCO and Informatica.

CEP might be used to identify a fraud pattern on a website as it unfolds without waiting for other fraud identification processes to be executed. It can also be used to monitor data coming off of engine sensors so that any issues can be identified as rapidly as possible. CEP doesn't replace, but augments, typical analytics processes. CEP by its nature is usually applied in highly operational settings.

### Embedded Analytic Libraries

One rising trend is to fully embed analytics algorithms within a relational or nonrelational platform so that the algorithms are easy to add into an analytics process. Unlike just a few years ago, it is now possible to embed even statistical modeling, forecasting, and machine learning algorithms directly within processes and applications.

Embedded analytics libraries help realize the promise of operational analytics by enabling access to analytics functions independent of any user interface or separate application. In other words, there is no need to involve an analysis tool as part of the process because the platform can handle the analytics directly. The downside of embedded functions is that they don't come with a user interface. They are just functions. This means that output will be sent to tables or files instead of a nicely formatted report. Output created in that fashion can be easily accessed by other applications and processes, but it isn't as easy for people to interact with. Fuzzy Logix has a product offering in this space that is available on multiple platforms.

### Is It an Analytics Tool or a Platform?

As analytics functions are more deeply embedded within analytics platforms, the lines between tools and platforms are blurring. When algorithms execute fully within a platform via an embedded function, maximum scale is enabled.

I foresee analytics professionals leveraging traditional analytics tools with graphical user interfaces to discover, develop, and test an analytics process. Once they have defined what needs to be made operational, they will then switch to utilizing embedded algorithmic functions for the purposes of operational deployment. Embedded functions aren't as easy to work with as user interfaces, but once users know exactly what must be built into a final analytics process, the functions won't cause much additional work. This approach allows use of a flexible and user-friendly discovery and development tool set while also allowing the leverage of embedded, native functions for industrial-scale deployment.

## Using

Now that we've defined the components of an enterprise's unified analytics environment, we cover a few important topics around how to maximize the benefits of the environment.

### Any Analysis, Any Data, Any Time

The goal must be to create a unified analytics environment that will enable the analysis of any type or volume of data via any type of analytics method at any time. That means exactly what it says. The capability to analyze text data, generate social graphs, predict response, and then combine those results with customer history and other information is critical. Adding the complexity of multiple pillars makes sense only if an organization plans to use the pillars. Some organizations with minimal analytics requirements may be able to get away with a single pillar for a while. Most large organizations will find it necessary to utilize multiple pillars and supporting technologies, however.

The decision to add components to an analytics environment should be based on a cost-benefit analysis that takes into account how much data has to be replicated to the new platform, how much will it cost to keep the data synchronized, how much will it cost in skills to operate/manage/support/train users, whether the new platform has the necessary characteristics for operational scale, and more. Chasing the newest shiny toy just because it exists makes no sense.

Once the pillars are in place, it is not too hard to optimize their usage and to spread data and analytics processes appropriately across the enterprise's unified analytics environment. The biggest challenge is justifying the addition of a new pillar or supporting technology to an analytics environment for the first time. (See Chapter 4.) This is because the cost to utilize something that is already in place is obviously much lower than the cost to put something new in place.

It is necessary to get the pillars in place first before an organization can achieve the goal of enabling any type of analysis against any data at any time. Performing a periodic review (perhaps yearly) of any primary pillar or supporting technology that an organization does not yet have in place is worthwhile. At that time, it can be assessed whether it is time to build a business case for adding a missing component to the environment. Once there are enough operational analytics requirements to justify bringing in a new pillar, an organization should add it since it will lead to increased flexibility and functionality when building analytics processes.

### End Users Don't Care Where the Data Is Stored

The fact is that end users, whether hardcore analytics professionals or traditional business intelligence users, really couldn't care less where the data they analyze is stored. Users want easy access to data, and they want to be able to create and execute whatever analytics processes they need as easily as possible and with sufficient performance.[5] For example, is a given set of customer facts, such as demographics, a table in a relational environment or a file within a nonrelational environment? Users really don't care as long as they have the access, ease of use, and performance they desire.

### Focus on What Users Want

Users don't care about where data is stored or which pillar analytics are executed on. Users just want the ability to access any data for any analysis at any time. The more users can be removed from the concern of where data is physically stored and analyzed, the more effective they can be.

Vendors are working hard to make the disparate pillars of the unified analytics environment highly integrated, if not transparent, to users. Connectors are being built that allow users to view and access data from one pillar while operating within another pillar. This enables users to focus on the analytics logic required without worrying about where data physically sits. In practice, what this means is that users might see what looks like a table in the relational pillar, but it's actually a view pointing to a file in the nonrelational pillar. When a query is submitted against the view, data is pulled from the nonrelational pillar and passed to the relational pillar in order to process the query. Users won't know this has occurred, nor will they care, as long as performance is acceptable. If performance becomes a problem, system administrators can migrate files stored on the nonrelational pillar into a relational table so that no data movement is needed moving forward. Similarly, data could be moved from a relational table and placed into a nonrelational file if overall processing requirements point to that being the best place for the data. In general, any given piece of data can be placed where it is overall most efficient to be stored so that users won't need to worry about it.

Evaluating both the current capabilities and the long-term plans of any vendors offering products to add into a unified analytics environment is also important. Don't get frozen with indecision by waiting for the next incremental functionality that is coming soon. At the same time, don't ignore the longer-term road maps of the products being considered. Technologies are changing fast, and different vendors are implementing in different ways. You might find two vendors that are equivalent with regard to meeting your needs today, but their road maps show they will diverge so that before long, one vendor may be strongly preferable to the other.

### What about the Cloud?

Readers are certainly familiar with the concept of the cloud and cloud architectures. I will not bother with basic definitions, but I will add some key points in the context of our discussion of operational analytics. I am often asked about using a cloud for analytics processes, both operational and nonoperational. To address that question, it is important to distinguish between cloud architectures and cloud services.

Organizations can implement a cloud architecture behind their firewalls on their own equipment. This is a private cloud, and it can enable effective sharing of resources without any external involvement or loss of control over data. Another possibility is to rent space from an external cloud provider on a public cloud. With a public cloud provider, an organization pays only for equipment and resources that it is using (along with the cloud provider's profit margin).

For a small business or researcher who typically uses the resources of only a fraction of a server, a public cloud can be a very good deal even with the markup that a cloud provider adds. Large organizations pursuing big data and operational analytics usually have so many users using so much data that a public cloud provider can end up costing much more than a private cloud would cost. When utilizing the equivalent of 20 servers virtually 100 percent of the time, an organization will pay a lot more to rent the resources than if it owned them. There are various legal and perception issues related to privacy and security when putting sensitive data out in a public cloud as well. Many consumers are not comfortable with a company storing their personal data on a public cloud, for example.

### To the Cloud or Not to the Cloud?

Private cloud environments are extremely powerful and cost effective, and many organizations will move to this architecture. Public clouds can be quite expensive for large organizations and won't be adopted as widely for operational analytics as market hype suggests. All of the pillars and supporting technologies that we've discussed can operate within a cloud architecture.

Many vendors now offer what are known as analytics as a service packages that sit on top of a public cloud. These applications allow users to build and execute analytics processes with tools that are sold on a subscription or per-use basis. Many, but not all, analytics as a service products can also be brought on premises and attached to a private cloud. Before spending time evaluating a specific analytics as a service offering, ensure that it can fit within your planned environment. For example, if your organization will not allow the use of public clouds, a product that is available only on the public cloud won't be a fit.

Internally owned, secure cloud environments can enable the flexibility required to make analytics operational while also being quite cost effective. Instead of 15 departments all owning a single server that is often idle or underutilized, perhaps 5 servers can more than handle all departments' needs. This will reduce cost and administrative overhead. Internal, private cloud architectures will take hold broadly across the board in the next few years and will support many operational analytics processes.

The public cloud and public analytics as a service offers are going to gain traction mostly with small to midsize businesses or for early-stage research purposes within large companies.

## Wrap-Up

The most important lessons to take away from this chapter are:

- Making analytics operational is not a technology issue for most organizations. Technology issues are the symptoms of underlying policy and culture issues.

- New technologies, such as Hadoop, are not replacing other technologies, such as relational databases, but rather are being added alongside them.
- Analytics environments are evolving to include multiple platforms with different strengths that are each used for different purposes.
- Unless an upcoming piece of functionality is absolutely crucial, don't put off investing today based on what might be available sometime in the future.
- Fabric-based computing is leading to unified analytics environments with multiple interconnected, scalable, and integrated components.
- There are three primary pillars within today's unified analytics environments as well as some supporting technologies. The aim is to allow any type of analysis on any type or volume of data at any time.
- The relational pillar is the backbone for the deployment of operational analytics and provides scalability in all important enterprise dimensions.
- The discovery pillar is used to explore all kinds of data with any type of analytics method and is aimed at finding new insights fast rather than maximizing processing speed.
- The nonrelational/Hadoop pillar is terrific for handling nontraditional data formats and is also a great place to store low-value or infrequently used data. It can also be leveraged for archival purposes.
- Supporting technologies that enable specific types of processing include in-memory appliances, graphics processing units, embedded analytics libraries, and complex event processing technologies.
- Users don't want to worry about where data physically sits or what pillar is processing it. Unified analytics environments are evolving so users will no longer have to worry about these things.
- Cloud architectures can be leveraged within a unified analytics environment. For most large enterprises, however, private clouds will be used instead of public clouds.

# Notes

1. Based on my International Institute for Analytics blog "Taming Big Data Is Not a Technology Issue," November 12, 2012. See http://iianalytics.com/2012/11/taming-big-data-is-not-a-technology-issue/.
2. See Stephen Swoyer, "Inside Facebook's Relational Platform," TWDI, May 6, 2013, at http://tdwi.org/articles/2013/05/06/facebooks-relational-platform.aspx; and Chris Kanaracus, "Hadoop Is Not Enough for 'Big Data,' Says Facebook Analytics Chief," PCWorld, October, 29, 2013, at http://www.pcworld.com/article/2058900/hadoop-is-not-enough-for-big-data-says-facebook-analytics-chief.html.
3. For more information, see http://www.infinibandta.org/.
4. For more information, see Bill Franks, *Taming the Big Data Tidal Wave* (Hoboken, NJ: John Wiley & Sons, 2012), Chapter 10.
5. Based on my International Institute for Analytics blog, "A Unified Environment for Big Data Analytics," April 10, 2013. See http://iianalytics.com/2013/04/a-unified-environment-for-big-data-analytics/.

# CHAPTER 6

# Governance and Privacy

Just as a government can stifle citizens with overzealous creation and enforcement of rules, so can an organization stifle its employees with overzealous governance policies. However, having no rules can lead to a state of anarchy and mayhem that is just as bad as a state of oppressive rules. Governance is an undue burden only when an organization makes it so.

Like many people, I dislike the word "governance" and I cringe when someone tells me they want to discuss it. However, there really isn't a more appropriate word for what we must discuss next. Many readers may be questioning whether to even read this chapter. After all, governance is dry, boring, and tactical, right? Not necessarily. Most people would agree that operational analytics require some sort of ongoing quality assurance and reliability validation. In addition, there must be guidelines in place to send processing to the appropriate place within the unified analytics environment, define security protocols, and establish privacy policies. All of those topics fall under the umbrella of governance.

This chapter focuses on how to govern the unified analytics environment defined in Chapter 5 to allow users and applications the access and resources required to succeed with making analytics operational. We talk about how the governance policies that enable the analysis of big data and making analytics operational are different from traditional approaches. We also lay out some of the implications for privacy because privacy must be a core component of any governance plan.

## Setting the Stage for Governance

We start with a discussion of why governance can be an unpopular topic and then outline a few concepts that need to be applied within a governance framework for operational analytics. Also note that how people interact with and support one another can have as big an impact as the policies that are in place.

### A Lesson from 1984

I reread George Orwell's *1984* recently.[1] One fascinating thread surrounded Newspeak, which is the official language in the book. Big Brother and his associates were purposely evolving the Newspeak language to remove more and more words. The reason for this was tied directly to governmental control. The theory behind the Newspeak plan was that if the words that enabled people to develop new thoughts were taken away, people wouldn't be able to have new thoughts. Big Brother's government wanted to get the Newspeak language to the point where people would not have the ability to conceive of new things or think thoughts that were considered dangerous to governmental control.

In some ways, a production environment at a large organization can be very much like Newspeak. If the analytics environment is locked down too much, it will remove the ability of users to ask new questions of the information it contains and to identify new insights. The difference is that in *1984*, Big Brother and his team actually did want to take away people's ability to come up with new thoughts. In a business organization, usually no one intends to take away people's ability to ask new questions. However, policies often have this effect anyway. These examples get to the heart of why governance has such a bad reputation among users. Many people have never experienced enabling and supportive governance in analytics environments, just stifling and oppressive governance.

### Security Clearance Model

The biggest governance hurdles that many users face are the policies for data access. Data security policies can have a bigger impact on the ability to discover new insights than anything else. After all, if data is not accessible, it can't be analyzed. Luckily, it is possible to adopt a security framework that allows the discovery of new operational analytics while still keeping data safe. Doing so does require some different thinking, however.

I like to draw a parallel between the security protocols in an analytics environment and government security clearance levels. In the government, there are many different levels of security clearance. There is information that virtually everyone can see as well as top secret information that very few people can see. Those with access to the most sensitive information have earned an increasingly higher level of trust over time to be able to view that information. This method should be adopted within an analytics environment.

A core group of analytics professionals tied to discovering new insights and exploring innovative analytics processes must be highly trusted by an organization. These trusted individuals must have access to a broader range of data than most and must be able to mix and match the data in a broader range of ways. They have a top-secret clearance of sorts. For example, trusted analytics professionals should be able, during a discovery exercise, to use data in a way that would not be acceptable in an operational or production setting. Perhaps they are able to combine sensitive customer data from different parts of the organization, for example. It is not that they will be able to violate corporate rules and policies when it is time to migrate a process from the discovery mode to an operational environment, but they need flexibility to discover if there is something worth making operational in the first place.

Note that care should be taken to ensure that while corporate policies are loosened, any applicable laws are closely followed. There are legal limitations on what can be done with medical or credit card data, for example. Provide wiggle room within corporate policies, not legal mandates. At the same time, as we discuss when we talk about privacy, care must be taken not to create analytics that make consumers uncomfortable no matter how legal those analytics may be.

Once a valuable process is found, the trusted analytics professionals can work within the usual security parameters to implement the process in a way that will be acceptable in an operational setting. However, if they are constrained by all production constraints from the start, it will be much harder, if not impossible, for them to find the impactful new insights the organization needs.

## Issue Security Clearances

Just like the government, organizations must allow different individuals to have different levels of security clearance. Trusted individuals operating in the discovery mode must have extreme flexibility, which may include combining data in ways not typically allowed to facilitate new insights.

Working within an environment that handles discovery as well as deployment will make the transition from one mode to the other much easier. This is why the unified analytics environment discussed in Chapter 5 is so critical. Even though people will have a lot more freedom when using the discovery environment, they'll be aware of and understand the constraints within the production environment. If the discovery and production environments are consistent, the process of migrating a discovery to production is far easier than if the environments are different. If analytics professionals know the limits on what is allowed in the production environment, they can account for those limits from the start in one of two ways: Either they can plan a work around for the production implementation from the start, or they can identify what policies need to be changed for implementation. In either case, whatever is put in production will follow the rules.

Another way to view the security clearance concept is like a security system in your house. A security system can have motion detectors, glass breakage detectors, cameras, and more. When you're having a big party, you turn it all off. You know people will be legitimately coming in and out, so you remove the security constraints. It's very easy to turn the security system back on as soon as guests leave. That's how the discovery environment should be viewed. It's not that security principles are being abandoned but rather that some of the features are being purposely disabled for trusted individuals at appropriate times.

### Partnership Is Required

Many organizations have, unfortunately, experienced a long-running feud between the analytics and information technology (IT) departments. I still see many organizations whose analytics and IT teams are far from friendly. If an organization is going to make analytics operational, it's absolutely imperative to get past this issue. Analytics professionals at my company call it "marriage counseling" when we sit down with a client to address this dysfunction. We often have the IT team on one side of the table and the analytics team on the other. Everyone starts with their arms crossed and a scowl on their faces. During pre-meetings, each of the teams has vented about how difficult and unreasonable the other is. Ironically, there is a good reason that the relationships get to this point.

If you take time to look at people's job descriptions, you'll find that everyone is simply doing what they're asked and incented to do. It just happens to be that people's jobs are in conflict. The IT team is tasked with keeping systems stable and running smoothly and keeping users controlled and within bounds. The analytics team is tasked with creating resource-intensive processes and bending rules as needed to find new insights. In order to make analytics operational, it will be necessary to make these teams work together. Bandages cannot be placed over the conflicts.

## A Forced Partnership May Be Necessary

An organization's IT and analytics teams must work together to succeed in making analytics operational. Ideally, the teams will work together voluntarily. If they won't, then senior management will need to force the partnership. Better a forced partnership than no partnership at all.

Operational analytics developed by an analytics team must be embedded within operational production systems, so analytics professionals simply can't stick to the old method of pulling data off into a separate analytics environment. Therefore, the analytics team can't make operational analytics happen without IT involvement and support. At the same time, IT can't develop the analytics processes since that's not its area of expertise. IT is going to need the analytics team's help to build and implement the processes. In addition, the demand from business partners for analytics is strong enough that neither the analytics nor the IT team can ignore it. They are going to be forced to work together to implement operational analytics successfully. Note that even in cases where the analytics team is part of IT, the same conflict often arises, only within teams from the same organization.

Luckily, given how analytics functionality has been integrated with and embedded within operational systems, it's possible for

- Have each individual share his or her job description and objectives
- Let each team explain its concerns about how the other team works
- Allow each team to defend why it does what it does
- Allow each team to suggest how the other team can compromise
- Make everyone offer ways that their team can compromise
- Use executive mandates to resolve issues that teams can't agree on
- Facilitate a strong partnership by tying it to compensation

**Figure 6.1   Creating an IT and Analytics Partnership: Tips for Success**

both IT and analytics organizations to succeed in working together by adjusting traditional governance policies to account for today's technology and requirements. Figure 6.1 has some ideas on how to get started.

If your organization hasn't already done so, it is going to have to force a partnership of necessity between these two important teams. It may be tough at first, but over time they'll learn to be okay with it. In real life, sometimes you don't like someone that you meet. However, quite often after you get to know the person and understand where he or she is coming from, you realize that the person isn't so bad after all. You may not want to vacation with him or her every year, but you are able to get along when necessary. This is the minimum point that IT and analytics teams need to get to. Working together won't be so bad once both teams commit to it and learn what the other has to offer.

### Governing the Internet of Things

The Internet of Things (IOT) was introduced in Chapter 2, and the vast majority of the unimaginable volume of data that it will create is almost completely useless. Let's illustrate with an example. A few years in the future, it will be common to have a smart home with a smart kitchen. There will be sensors in the refrigerator, on the shelves in the pantry, even in individual items. A bottle of ketchup in the refrigerator will be able to report back its status to a food inventory program tasked with generating a current shopping list. The ketchup will, via its sensors, communicate that it is 50 percent full, that it has been at the right temperature continually since being purchased, and that its expiration date is still several months off. Therefore, there is no need to buy new ketchup. Repeat that for the hundreds of products in your kitchen once per second, and it creates a lot of data.

The information created as the kitchen's products communicate is valuable for the centralized inventory application and shopping list generator to collect. However, there is no need for the data in the long term. All we really care about is having a current list of what we need to buy when we go to the store. All of the little conversations that happen between the things in the kitchen to decide what is on the shopping list are irrelevant to us.[2] Ignoring this data is nothing different from what you already do every day. Do couples actually remember every detail of every discussion they have as they create a shopping list before going to the store? No. They remember what's on the final shopping list because that's all that's important to remember.

## Ignore the Incessant Chatter

The IOT will create unfathomable amounts of data. However, most of the data is meaningless beyond the moment. Just as you only remember a few important interactions from your daily conversations, so the vast majority of the communications between things is not necessary to persist.

Our brains are very good at filtering noise out. There are memories that we have seared in our brains from years ago and there are conversations from yesterday that we can barely recall. That's because we are effectively filtering our memories to what's important moving forward. This is exactly what needs to be done with the data from the IOT. While the aggregate amount of data generated by the IOT is unfathomable, any given sensor actually isn't generating much data. Sensor communications are very short bursts of information that are individually very small and manageable. No single sensor on its own poses a data volume issue. The totality of the sensors and their communications is what poses the challenge. For example, an airline may monitor only certain key sensors while a plane is in flight because looking at all sensor data in real time may not be possible or necessary.

Another implication of the IOT is the necessity for global standards and governance policies around the generation and use of the data. Within your home, all of your appliances will need to use the same protocol. If your neighbors use different brands with different protocols, however, it won't impact you. In other cases, we can't afford to have different protocols. Self-driving cars can't be deployed if every brand of car creates its own proprietary method of reporting and collecting data. Crashes would abound as different cars weren't able to communicate effectively. Setting legal and ethical standards for the use of the data is also critical. For example, in what ways and by whom can the driving history of car owners be tracked and analyzed?

The only way self-driving cars will work in real life is if all cars have the same standards. Each car must be able to correctly send and receive information about speed, location, and intention to change trajectory. The need for global standards complicates things initially but is necessary and will be worth it in the long run. Luckily, work is under way to develop these standards. The companies with a stake in the IOT have begun setting up governance standards. Every organization will benefit from these standards when leveraging data from the IOT to drive operational analytics.

## Deciding Where Analytics Happen

One governance issue that comes up often is how to determine which part of a unified analytics environment each step of an analytics process should be executed on. After all, a key component of governance is setting standards for how to utilize the assets that are available. There is no easy answer as to where to direct processing, and it will depend on a wide range of considerations. The factors to consider in this case heavily overlap with the factors considered when building a business case, as outlined in Chapter 4. This makes sense because deciding where to execute a portion of a process is effectively an assessment of the costs and benefits of the different options. It is necessary to ask questions like these:

- Which of the environment's components can handle the processing?
- Which tools have the necessary functionality?
- What skills does the team have in place and available?
- Where is the data required currently stored?
- Are there any prior processes from which code can be borrowed?
- Is the goal discovering a new insight or deploying an insight?
- What are the analytics methods required?

All of those factors, and more, can influence where it makes the most sense for a given process, or portion of a process, to be executed.

Effort is required to determine how best to implement a process within a complex unified analytics environment. Let's talk about a few perspectives to keep in mind.

### Never Say Can't!

One of the lessons I've learned over the years is that if you have an expert user of any given analytics tool or technology, chances are that the expert can build just about anything, given enough time and effort. In the past, I have personally developed analytics processes in what I can't claim was the ideal way. I knew I could hit my deadline using the tools I knew best, so I did. However, saying that I got it done is not the same as saying that there weren't better and more scalable ways to do it. With traditional batch analytics, often it is possible to get away with this. With the time sensitivity and scale required for operational analytics, it is much harder to succeed by hacking together a solution using whatever a person happens to know best.

If top-notch SQL programmers are asked if they can implement a given set of logic, in most cases they will say yes. If SAS or R experts are asked if they can build the logic required, they'll also say yes. If Python or Java programmers are asked if they can build the logic in Hadoop, they're going to say yes as well. What you have to understand is that it likely is true that all the experts can implement the analytics logic. However, it's also true that there are more and less efficient ways to do it.

Don't say that a given analytics process can't be created in a given person's preferred component of a unified analytics environment with his or her preferred toolset. Taking the "can't" approach is picking a fight from the start. When someone is told "You can't build this with your preferred environment and tool," his or her immediate reaction is to say "Oh, yes I can!" and then try and prove it to show that you are wrong. It's counterproductive.

### Don't Pick a Fight that Isn't Needed

Analytics professionals can be stubborn. If told they can't do something, their first goal will be to prove you wrong instead of solving the problem at hand. That's counterproductive. Instead, acknowledge that each person likely can do it his or her way, and then ask the team to find the best way to do it.

The better approach is to have a mature conversation from a slightly different angle. Shift everyone's focus toward finding the *best* way to build the process. What's the most efficient way to build the analytics process and enable it at an operational scale? If phrased in a less threatening manner like that, experts typically will acknowledge that there are some shortcomings within their preferred approaches. Perhaps it takes a lot longer to program with one approach, while another approach may not scale well.

Have each expert assess the total effort required to build the process his or her way. Then the team can compare the results and make an informed decision. When a range of technologies is present within a unified analytics environment, it's much easier to shift processing from one component to another to get maximum performance than with traditional environments. All it takes is going through a condensed version of the business case process.

### Choose What Works Best

The prior topic leaves open one potential problem—namely, it may not be initially clear that one option is more effective than another. Perhaps several choices work well. At a conference a few years ago, there were two talks simultaneously focusing on social network analysis. In Room 1 was a talk about a social network analysis project built in a relational environment; in Room 2 was a talk about a social network analysis built in a nonrelational environment. I attended the nonrelational session and found that a huge part of the discussion focused not on the social network analytics and the value the analytics drove but on the claim that social network analysis just couldn't be done in a relational environment. Ironically, the talk in Room 1 outlined how the same analysis was done in a relational environment and why that was the only place to do it.

Those conference talks proved that there are at least two ways to execute social network analysis. If we dug into the two processes and looked at the amount of effort to code the social network analysis, we would find differences. We would likely also see differences in process performance. It was fair for the speakers in each session to describe the advantages of their own approach. However, both should have steered clear of claims that the analysis couldn't be done another way unless they had proven it. Clearly they hadn't proven it based on the session in the room next door.

### Focus on the Right Mix

To maximize efficiency and effectiveness, it is necessary to get each component of a unified analytics environment doing what it does best and each member of an analytics team building the analytics that he or she is best able to build. Take the time to look at the trade-offs among skills, processing power, and the analytics methods required. To create the optimal process, several components of the unified analytics environment may be involved instead of just a single component. If this sounds obvious, it should. The same principle applies in many situations.

Consider a piece of undeveloped land. If a single-family home developer is approached, he or she will provide the optimal plan for that land when it comes to single-family homes. If a condominium, townhome, or apartment developer is approached, then he or she will provide the optimal way to maximize the value of the land with those structures. If a commercial developer is approached, he or she will provide the optimal way to lay out a strip mall, medical complex, or office park. The important point is that each developer will be correct within the bounds of his or her expertise. This is much like a number of analytics professionals each defining the optimal way to build an analytics process using only their own preferred components of the unified analytics environment and their own preferred analysis tools.

---

### Optimize the Total, Not the Parts

The goal should be to make the best use of the components within a unified analytics environment to optimize the overall effectiveness of an analytics process. Simply choosing one component and optimizing within it alone can lead to approaches that aren't nearly as good as multicomponent options.

---

What the owner of the land should do is to find the best use of the land overall. It very well may be a combination of a cul-de-sac of homes, one or two small apartment buildings, and a small strip mall. Someone must have the vision and skill set to evaluate the bigger picture, not just one perspective. Someone must get the input from each expert and find the best combination of approaches to address the current need. The final answer may contain components of each expert's recommendations. The same approach should be followed for an analytics process. The key is to have people who are able to understand the larger vision and make the trade-offs.

## Governing Operational Analytics

In part because it is not a popular topic, governance is often an afterthought as corporations enter the Analytics 3.0 era discussed in Chapter 1 and start to make analytics operational. It is only after major disconnects that many corporations get serious about the governance of operational analytics. The development and ongoing management of embedded, automated, and highly scaled operational analytics requires different approaches to governance than has traditionally been applied to analytics processes. With batch analytics, a mistake impacts only a single batch, and often there is plenty of time to catch the error before the next batch. With operational analytics, a mistake will continue to propagate rapidly until an intervention is made.

So far, we've covered some of the considerations that come into play when deciding how to go about implementing an operational analytics process. Let's now turn our attention to a couple of real-world scenarios that illustrate the trade-offs that must be made to use the various components of a unified analytics environment effectively.

### Different Requirements

From a governance perspective, one issue that poses a real challenge for operational analytics is that two distinct, and sometimes conflicting, sets of requirements must be met. The first set applies during the discovery process, when an organization is trying to find new insights and determine the analytics processes that will have the highest impact. In this case, maximum agility and limited constraints are required. The second set applies during deployment at an operational level. In this case, the top priority is to ensure speed, reliability, and stability. These two requirements are summarized in Table 6.1. Although they are distinct and seemingly at odds, both are achievable within an appropriately configured analytics environment.

Once an operational analytics process is created and deployed, it will be governed differently from traditional analytics processes. One difference is the governance of the results of each process. Operational analytics are geared toward being good enough and fast enough to meet operational requirements. The aim is to improve, not necessarily perfect, millions and millions of daily decisions. If it

Table 6.1   Discovery versus Production Requirements

| Discovery | Production |
|---|---|
| Ease of use | Processing speed |
| Speed of code development | Process stability |
| Maximum agility | Efficiency of resource usage |
| Limited constraints | Governance standards fully met |
| Find new insights | Operationalize prior insights |

is possible to improve a process further, that's great, but not at the expense of the scale and speed required. Passing by some of the power that is theoretically possible with the analytics can be uncomfortable at first, but it's okay as long as the analytics are demonstrably improving decisions by more than the analytics cost. In a worst-case scenario, a new discovery may have to be abandoned if the effort to make it operational is too large to justify the costs.

Another difference with operational analytics is that the decisions being made must be constantly monitored to see how the process is performing. Operational analytics require the monitoring of decisions that have already happened; in traditional analytics, decisions are validated up front before they happen. Since the decisions in operational analytics will be happening automatically, it will be necessary to identify when something seems off in, say, the last 10,000 decisions that were made. When an anomaly is found, it may be necessary to halt the analytics process and investigate.

## Expect "Oops!" Moments

Just as some products are defective on a real assembly line, so some decisions won't be perfect in an operational analytics process. Big problems can even lead to the need to shut the process off until it can be fixed. As long as the error rate is low enough, it is an acceptable cost of doing business. This can be a difficult fact to accept and often requires a cultural change.

The preceding differences lead to another fact: An organization must be prepared to accept that things sometimes will go wrong with an operational analytics process. Look at the extreme case of the Flash Crash of the stock market in 2010 discussed in Chapter 3.[3] One specific trading algorithm had a flaw that caused it to go haywire. Many other algorithms then fed off what the first algorithm did, and, like lemmings racing off a cliff together, a huge mess was created. The fact is that there will be some glitches when processes are automated and a shift is made from reviewing recommendations before action takes place to monitoring actions after they occur.

This is hard to accept at first, and you may run into cultural resistance within your organization. However, if an organization is diligent in the building, testing, and monitoring of operational analytics processes, problems should be caught before they become significant. It is worth reinforcing here the fact that the discovery process is perpetual. As time passes, adjustments will be required to any analytics process to account for new data, new business realities, or other significant changes.

Experiencing problems here and there is part of the cost of doing business and is something organizations simply need to work through. Even the Flash Crash didn't bankrupt all of the program traders. On a manufacturing line, some products are defective, some food is burned, some bottles break. That's just part of the cost of doing business. As long as errors happen at a low rate and the average quality is high, the manufacturer will be fine in the long run because of the scale achieved. It is the same with operational analytics.

Consider the approaches that credit card companies use to find fraud or that e-mail providers use to identify spam. None of the procedures works perfectly. We still get spam in our inboxes, and credit card fraud still occurs. There are also cases where a valid e-mail gets sent to a spam folder or a bank mistakenly puts a hold on a credit card. However, the situation is far better than it was without analytics.

Organizations can't let people focus on the exceptions and try to invalidate an entire approach because they find one or two examples where an analytics process made an incorrect or suboptimal decision. The question should be whether the analytics *reduce* the overall fraud rate, for example, because no analytics process can eliminate it all. The inevitable errors that slip through cannot be allowed to derail the larger benefit of an operational analytics process.

When people on the front lines identify mistaken decisions, the organization has to be willing to stand behind the process as a whole and help employees understand that a certain error rate is to be expected. People working a physical assembly line reject product regularly if it doesn't meet quality standards, but they don't question the validity of having the assembly line. So, too, some bad decisions will be made with operational analytics, but that can't cause people to call into question the validity of the process as a whole.

### Monitoring Operational Analytics

Though operational analytics are embedded within an organization's business processes to make decisions, people still have to actively monitor the results generated by those decisions. Providing reports, summary statistics, dashboards, and visualizations that allow the stakeholders throughout an organization to monitor how operational analytics are performing on an ongoing basis is as critical as ever. As has been true traditionally, the level of detail or aggregation that anyone sees will depend on the level and role of that stakeholder. This is why, as we soon discuss, classic principles of business intelligence very much apply with operational analytics.

As with traditional analytics, policies will need to be put in place to guide who sees what data. Also, if an anomaly is noticed, who should be alerted and who has authority to shut a process down when something is amiss? Who is responsible for validating that the analytics processes are not degrading over time and in need of a refresh? What is an acceptable error rate? What metrics should be tracked in addition to error rate? Questions like these must be addressed within the context of operational analytics just as with any other analytics process.

Let's consider a manufacturing plant where operational analytics are actively adjusting the assembly line's equipment settings. The plant manager needs to see detailed updates on all the pieces of equipment in the plant. She needs to see the latest data coming off the sensors and whether each machine is performing within specifications. A regional manager, however, might just need to validate that all of the plants in the region look okay in aggregate. Of course, a headquarters executive will care primarily about high-level regional patterns.

### Many Old Rules Still Apply

A critical part of operational analytics is the ongoing effort to monitor the consistency and effectiveness of the decisions that are made automatically. The data itself and the metrics that people want to see may not change from times past. What changes is the way the decisions are being made that lead to the same data and metrics.

The point is that traditional principles about how to filter, aggregate, and provide summaries of data for various stakeholders still fully apply for operational analytics. In fact, in many cases, the standard reports already in place today might not require changes because the data itself and the metrics that people need to see are not necessarily what are changing. Rather, what changes is the method by which the decisions that generate the data and the metrics are being made. An operational analytics process may be making the decisions, but that doesn't mean that the decisions aren't the same ones for the same purposes as in the past. For example, an operational analytics process to suggest offers for call center agents is making the same decisions the agents made on their own in the past. The success of the decisions in producing incremental sales can be tracked in the usual way because the decisions still yield offers that either do or do not generate a response.

### Discovery Platform versus Discovery Environment

I was speaking with a client who had completed a very successful discovery effort. (The effort was also confidential so I cannot reveal who it was.) The client found some compelling new insights that he wanted to put into production and make operational, but there was a catch. The customer's corporate policy was that any component of its infrastructure that became part of even a single production process had to fully comply with all production policies. In other words, if the customer used the discovery platform as a part of any production process, he would effectively lose the flexibility required within the discovery platform to find additional insights. Unfortunately, there was one piece of the new process that really made sense to execute on the discovery platform. The client asked me how this problem could be resolved.

We started by exploring whether it was possible simply to code the final process differently to make it execute in the production platform instead of the discovery platform. Often this is possible once the exact logic required is identified. In this case, it wasn't possible because a proprietary discovery platform algorithm wasn't available elsewhere and would be too expensive to replicate. The client also made the excellent point that even if it had been possible to create the functionality within the production platform, certainly another case would arise in the future where it wasn't possible. Therefore, we needed a more universal approach to solving this type of dilemma.

The key to the solution was recognizing that there is a differ-ence between a physical discovery platform and a logical discovery environment. The discovery hardware and software platform used to find the insight didn't have to be the same physical platform that the production process used. The client had a discovery platform within a discovery environment that was earmarked for innovation and finding new insights. We determined that the fastest and cheap-est solution was to configure a small second instance of the discovery platform within the production environment. The new platform's only role would be to support operationalized processes within the production environment. This solution enabled the discovery pro-cess as well as deployment by following a model not unlike the widely used development, test, and production environments for other platforms. It was just a matter of differentiating a physical discovery platform from a logical discovery environment.

### Time to Insight versus Execution Time

One last topic to address around governance relates to the criteria by which the success of each stage of analytics process development and deployment is judged. Unfortunately, operational analytics can cause extra work compared to traditional analytics approaches. In a classic analytics environment, processes are executed almost exclu-sively in batch mode, and the same environment is used for both development and production. In that case, execution time or pro-cessing speed usually is considered most important. As discussed previously in the chapter, within a unified analytics environment being used for operational analytics, two distinctly different criteria come into play at different points in the process.

The two criteria are the execution time or similar classic perfor-mance metrics and the time to insight concept outlined in Chapter 4. When placed into an operational production environment, analytics processes must be as streamlined and fast as possible. During the dis-covery phase of finding a new insight and determining what needs to be made operational, the fastest time to insight is more important than processing speed. These differing requirements can push orga-nizations in directions different from ones they may have gone in traditionally.

To illustrate, consider the early phases of discovery, where the goal simply is to prove that something is true or not. There is no need to repeat the process on an ongoing basis at that point, so the goal is to get to the answer as fast as possible. If it is possible to code something in an hour that takes three hours to execute, nobody will care. The answer will be known quickly enough to determine whether moving forward makes sense or not. It would be silly to spend 12 hours coding a much more efficient process that executes in a few minutes when there is no evidence that it will be necessary to do it more than once.

---

### Success Measures Differ When Going Operational

When trying to discover new insights, finding them quickly is most important, and it doesn't matter if a process takes a long time to execute. However, when making a new insight operational, maximum speed and scale are needed. Streamlining a discovery process to make it operational can require extra effort.

---

However, once an insight is found that is worthy of being made operational, the process will be run thousands or millions of times per day. In that situation, every second, if not every millisecond, counts. Therefore, spending many extra hours, days, or weeks tuning and optimizing the process to have the maximum speed and shortest execution time makes sense. The extra effort will allow increased performance for millions of executions and is therefore a very small cost when spread out across all of the occasions that the process will be executed. In addition, the extra effort is made only when it is known to be worthwhile.

These facts lead to a potentially disturbing implication to consider. In some scenarios, the process used to discover a new insight may not be one that can be migrated directly into an operational context. During discovery, it is only necessary to get to that insight as fast as possible and prove it is valuable. Sometimes the same code, logic, and process can be applied directly in an operational context, but often it can't. This gap leads to what usually is a two-phase process. First, an insight is proven valuable as rapidly as possible. Second, recoding and rearchitecting of the process used to find the insight is undertaken to make it efficient enough for the operational environment.

In reality, it has been quite common over the years for organizations to recode analytics processes from one platform to another when moving from development to production. For example, analytics processes were often recoded into Cobol for a mainframe. The effort to migrate can be greatly simplified to the extent that analytics are created within a single, unified analytics environment that provides consistency across the discovery and production phases. Instead of having to recode everything completely for a completely different environment, the process can be streamlined within the same set of technologies and tools. This makes deployment easier than in the past.

## Privacy

Privacy is one of the biggest issues surrounding big data and operational analytics, and it is also a critical aspect of governance. Privacy is something that any organization dealing with customer or consumer data in particular will have to take very seriously. However, privacy is an issue with other sensitive information as well. Not only is more and more data about each of us available, but it's becoming easier and easier to combine and link the data.

While all of this data has potential to enable great benefits, it also poses great risks to us as individuals and as a society. After all, if the data is not used appropriately, real damage can be done. Let's explore some considerations about privacy that will be critical when defining governance processes.

### Is Big Data Becoming Big Brother?

Your cellular provider knows everywhere you've been. If you regularly use location services with applications on your smart phone, whoever provides those applications also knows where you've been. Your e-mail provider probably has a copy of every e-mail you've sent. Your cable or satellite provider knows every show you've ever watched, what commercials you skipped, and when you hit pause. Your credit history is on file with multiple organizations, and your health history is increasingly digitized. By now you get the picture. More and more about you is known by more and more third parties than ever before.

In recent years, concerns have been raised about the handling of privacy issues by many well-known companies and many governments. Google, Yahoo!, Facebook, the U.S. government, and many more have experienced backlash over real or perceived privacy violations.[4] The standard privacy policies in place today are all but useless because it's impossible for the average person to read and understand them, there are loopholes throughout, and the policies basically say that the rules are subject to change at any minute. We are essentially forced to trust a company or a government to do the right thing with our data. Unfortunately, what you consider to be the right thing with your data and what an organization considers right may not be in sync. Worse, a lot of data that you think you own is not really yours but rather is owned by the company used to generate the data. Often call detail records, tweets, pictures posted, and more are not owned by the person generating the data but by the owner of the service where it is generated. Generating data does not equate to owning it.

Most people don't have any idea how much their behavior can (and is) being tracked today. This is particularly true when it comes to web activity and connected devices. Even your TV manufacturer may be spying on you in ways that you would never expect.[5] As I write these words, there has been an entire series of revelations about the extent to which the United States National Security Agency (NSA) is collecting data on people. Whether it is tracking our phone calls or capturing our e-mails or spying on the communications of foreign leaders, the NSA is clearly way ahead of where most people thought it was. Unfortunately, that's just what we know about.[6] Few people know what else is going on, and those who do aren't talking. Figure 6.2 summarizes some questions that need to be resolved.

As cameras with facial recognition capabilities are deployed widely in cities across the globe, it is becoming possible to track people as they move around. In fact, camera images already are being used to track down criminals by following them from the crimes to their destinations via a series of video or image captures from different cameras. Although it is becoming increasingly difficult to keep your whereabouts and actions private, many people claim that this isn't anything to worry about. The thinking goes that most people's lives are boring. If you aren't doing anything interesting or illegal, who cares if others have such information?

- Who owns the data that organizations collect?
- Who can access personal data and under what terms?
- Do people have a right to ask for data to be erased and/or provided to them?
- What liability do organizations have for breaches of trust or security?
- What obligation does an organization have to ensure personal data is accurate?

**Figure 6.2   Some Privacy Questions That Need to Be Resolved**

> ## Where Do You Draw the Line?
>
> We all have different lines in the sand that define our comfort zones with respect to privacy. Although we will not all agree on exactly where the lines should be drawn, it is important that clear lines are drawn somewhere. Today the lines are ambiguous at best and nonexistent at worst.

This argument sounds great until somebody in power decides to use your data against you. The U.S. government, for example, was caught red-handed using the Internal Revenue Service to target political groups and individuals whose views the administration in power disagreed with.[7] How will you feel when someone decides to target you for an opinion you hold or a perfectly legal activity that you participate in? Information and data are currency in the modern world, so protect your assets. The money in the vault is no longer all that matters to a bank. The data about the money in the vault also matters.

The laws surrounding privacy are evolving and in flux. Two recent debates are worth specific mention because of their importance and the inconsistency of court rulings tied to them. The first debate relates to whether cellular phone location data or automobile telematics data is private and protected or whether law enforcement can have access to it without a warrant. The second question relates to the NSA spying programs. Let's look at both.

For the first question, the U.S. government claims that phone location data and automobile telematics data are not private. The government argues that when people get in a car or turn on a cell phone, they are aware that all of their activity can be tracked, and they have therefore given up the right to privacy. Part of the government's argument is that the data is actually being collected by a corporation, so it is not really people's data and therefore it is not subject to privacy rules. There were two court cases decided within a month of each other in September 2013. One court ruled that a warrant was required in order to grant access to location information to law enforcement.[8] A second court ruled that a warrant was not required.[9] This question will end up at the Supreme Court, where the final decision will have far-reaching implications.

For the second question, the NSA claims that it has the authority to collect a wide range of information about citizens even if no wrongdoing is suspected. The breadth of the information being captured has been a surprise to most people. Like the cases around warrants for location data, the courts have thus far split on whether the NSA's actions are legal. Within weeks, one court ruled the NSA's activities are legal and another ruled that the activities are illegal.[10] This issue too will end up at the Supreme Court for a momentous ruling.

One last surprising fact is worth mentioning. In the United States, 87 percent of the population can be uniquely identified with only a ZIP code, a name, and a birth date.[11] If just that small amount of information can give away exactly who you are, think how easy it is to identify you with all of the other data being collected. Regardless of whether we would all agree on where to draw the lines in the sand, it should be very clear that we have to draw lines somewhere.

That's enough doom and gloom. Let's move on to a few practical examples of privacy considerations and why they're important. Then we'll dig in on how to ensure that your company keeps itself in balance.

### Setting Privacy Standards

How can an organization define privacy standards in a way that avoids having a privacy scandal end up in the news? I recommend organizations consider three criteria to ensure that they don't violate the trust of their customers and the general public:[12]

1. What is legal?
2. What is ethical?
3. What is acceptable to customers and the general public?

In an ideal world, these three criteria would be completely in sync. However, they are not in sync at all today. Regulations must catch up with all that is now possible, and people must become better educated. Unfortunately, what is legal is often far broader than what is ethical, and what is ethical can go beyond what people find acceptable.

Target, the large retailer, is the poster child for running afoul of the third test while passing the first two. Target has a loyalty program, which is perfectly legal. When people sign up, they acknowledge that they will get targeted offers based on their purchasing patterns.

Since such offers are a clear part of the agreement, it is totally ethical for Target to use customer data to predict customers' behaviors and offer them products. Where Target went amiss was in taking the analytics somewhere that their customers weren't comfortable with, even though it was legal and ethical.

### Apply a Three-Tier Test

When deciding whether an analysis is acceptable from a privacy perspective, ensure it passes three different tests. The analysis must be (1) legal, (2) ethical, and (3) acceptable to customers. The last test is often the strictest.

Target figured out how to predict pregnancy very early—so early, in fact, that it could be before a woman had informed others of the pregnancy. This led to a story in the *New York Times* of a father who received a mailing addressed to his 17-year-old daughter for pregnancy-related products.[13] The father expressed his anger to the local store manager that Target would market such inappropriate items to a teenager. A week later the father came back and apologized to the store manager for being so nasty. It ends up that his daughter was pregnant. Popular opinion was not in Target's favor. The public felt that this analysis crossed the line from helpful to creepy and did not find the analysis to be acceptable.

Always remember that determining what is legal is not enough. Nor is deciding what the ethical and right thing to do is. You must also think through what your customers and the general public will think.

### Privacy Catch-22s

At a private event I attended, the CEO of a hospital chain confidentially discussed a fascinating example of the tight spot an organization can get into with the ambiguity of today's laws and ethics around uses of data.[14] His situation centered on the collection and storage of genetic data and the potential liabilities that collecting such data can bring with it.

Assume that a hospital has your genetic data (DNA data) on file. What happens if three years down the road, a new discovery is made that correlates certain genetic traits to a major disease? Does the hospital have any ethical or legal obligation to retroactively go back and run analysis against all DNA data it has for all patients to identify who is at risk? What will be the costs related to performing such analysis, and how often will such analysis be necessary?

## Ambiguity Leads to Risk

The legal and ethical ambiguity surrounding what is appropriate (or required) and what is not adds risk to the collection of data. It is possible for an organization to get into a situation where it could lose a lawsuit regardless of the decision it made. Watch out for situations than can lead to this catch-22.

It is impossible to predict the costs of performing an unknown amount of future analysis of unknown difficulty against all genetic data in a hospital's possession. The future liability of storing the data can't be fully assessed in the present because there is no way to know how many correlations might be discovered and how difficult it will be to run the analysis to identify those at risk. It is also a catch-22 situation. Some people would sue if the hospital analyzed their data and ran new tests without their permission. They might prefer to be ignorant of the bad news, especially in cases where nothing can be done. Others would sue if the hospital had the opportunity to identify a problem through such analysis but did not do so. It is possible to imagine both cases being decided against the hospital in court. On top of this risk is the potential damage if genetic data is stolen or used inappropriately. The unknowns related to storing genetic data were very concerning to the hospital CEO.

The CEO had a surprising conclusion. He said that his hospital system is considering not storing DNA data beyond the immediate need of the tests requested at the time the DNA is collected. There are so many unknowns about the liability of storing the data from both a cost and legal perspective that the hospital doesn't want to have the data any longer than it needs to. Until the liabilities are clarified, the hospital decided that storing the data isn't worth the risk.

It is unfortunate that current laws can put organizations in a position to have to make such an unexpected decision. Yet I completely understand the CEO's perspective. If it were my company on the line, I would likely make the same decision. Until laws are clarified, there is a lot of risk and liability associated with collecting and storing data that has privacy implications.

## The Future of Privacy Policies

Privacy policies must evolve and improve to deal with today's realities. It is necessary to have a 100-page privacy policy document created by lawyers, but there should also be a much smaller and shorter summary that says in plain language exactly what an organization is going to do with sensitive data and what lines won't be crossed.[15]

Privacy policies must become much more flexible in the way that they allow customers to express their preferences. It's no longer good enough to simply have a simple "Do Not Call" or "Do Not E-mail" list. Perhaps I don't want an organization to call me with offers to sell me completely unrelated products, but I am fine if the organization calls to tell me about updates to a product I already own. For example, my bank is welcome to call about a new type of mortgage plan that may be preferable to my current mortgage, but I don't want a call about a savings account.

Today's realities require entirely new levels of privacy settings. When it comes to location data captured by cellular phones, some people might not want organizations to track where they are for any reason, ever. Other people might be okay with an organization using location information to send offers based on their current locations, as long as the company immediately purges the location information and doesn't keep it for the long term. Others might be fine if an organization keeps all their location information over time for any type of analysis. The point is that organizations must develop an entire suite of detailed settings that customers can manage for an entire range of data types to meet the evolving privacy expectations of consumers moving forward.

### Privacy Policy Flexibility and Transparency Lead to Trust

Although it is harder to administrate, providing customers with the ability to set very detailed privacy constraints will keep organizations out of trouble. Doing this can also be a competitive differentiator, given that few organizations are viewed as highly trustworthy today when it comes to privacy.

A standard practice should be to announce changes that will be made to a privacy policy in plain language well in advance of their enactment. The default action should be the most conservative change for customers. For example, it's perfectly fine to have a pop-up window force me to confirm my knowledge of a new policy the first time I return to a site and to allow me to choose how I'd like to proceed. I can click a choice and be done with it as quickly as possible. However, I must have the ability to make an active and conscious choice rather than having an automated choice made based on an ambiguous notice buried somewhere on the site.

It is certainly harder to administer policies in this fashion, but it's absolutely necessary if organizations are to give customers the control over their information that they want and deserve. The effort to make customers comfortable with how an organization stores, analyzes, and applies data will pay off. Giving people more control of their privacy will not only protect companies from a legal perspective, but it will make customers happy that the organizations respect their wishes. Having robust and flexible privacy policies can be a competitive differentiator compared to a competitor that is in the news with yet another privacy scandal.

## Wrap-Up

The most important lessons to take away from this chapter are:

- Like Newspeak from *1984*, overly restrictive policies can stop new questions from being asked of data. Institute a security clearance policy to allow highly trusted individuals additional flexibility.
- The IT team and analytics team must work together to succeed with operational analytics. If the teams won't partner voluntarily, upper management must force a partnership.
- The IOT will have a large ratio of noise to signal. Although the IOT will create one of the largest pools of raw data, only a small fraction will have value beyond the moment.
- Determining the best way to implement an analytics process can be tough. Don't pick fights by claiming a given approach can't work; rather, focus on finding the best approach from the many that can work.
- Optimize an analytics process across the entire analytics environment, not just within a single component. To maximize value, leverage the full range of capabilities available.
- Operational analytics have two different sets of requirements. During discovery, maximum agility and limited constraints are

required. During deployment, the priority is to ensure speed, reliability, and stability.

- Given the automated nature of operational analytics, things will go wrong, just as with any assembly line. The key is to act quickly to minimize damage so that problems are a minor cost of doing business.
- Operational analytics processes must be monitored and tracked just like any other process. Classic business intelligence standards fully apply.
- Different success metrics, such as time to insight, are required for discovery while traditional metrics, such as process execution time, still apply for production processes.
- Privacy is a huge issue with analytics and big data today. Although there is disagreement on exactly what lines should be drawn, we desperately need lines to be drawn to avoid entering a Big Brother era.
- Any action that impacts privacy must be legal, ethical, and acceptable to the public. Be very careful because these criteria are not always in sync, and it is possible to get into a catch-22 situation.
- Privacy policies and settings must be updated to reflect the robust data and sophisticated requirements of today's world. Doing this not only will minimize legal risks, but it can be a differentiator for an organization.

## Notes

1. George Orwell, *1984* (New York: Signet Classic, 1950).
2. Based on my blog for Cisco titled "When Sensors Act Like Teenagers," September 16, 2013. See http://blogs.cisco.com/ioe/sensors-act-like-teenagers/.
3. See Matt Phillips, "Nasdaq: Here's Our Timeline of the Flash Crash" *Wall Street Journal Market Beat Blog,* May 11, 2010, at http://blogs.wsj.com/marketbeat/2010/05/11/nasdaq-heres-our-timeline-of-the-flash-crash/.
4. See ABC News, "How to Opt Out of Google Policy That Displays Your Photo Beside Ads," October 14, 2013, at http://abcnews.go.com/Technology/google-privacy-terms-conditions-opt/story?id=20563128. See John P. Mello Jr., "Yahoo Mail Redesign Becomes Permanent, Privacy Issues Surface," *TechHive,* June 3, 2013, at www.techhive.com/article/2040642/yahoo-mail-redesign-becomes-permanent-privacy-issues-surface.html. See *Heather Kelly,* "Facebook Home, Privacy and You," *CNN Tech,* April 5, 2013, at http://www.cnn.com/2013/04/05/tech/social-media/facebook-home-privacy/index.html. See Fox News, "Newly Declassified Documents Show Range of Potential Access to NSA Phone Records," July 31, 2013, at http://www.foxnews.com/politics/2013/07/31/newly-declassified-documents-show-range-potential-access-to-nsa-phone-records/.

5. See Pam Baker, "LG Caught Red-Handed Spying on Viewers via Smart TVs," *Fierce Big Data*, November 25, 2013, at www.fiercebigdata.com/story/lg-caught-red-handed-spying-viewers-smart-tvs/2013-11-25.

6. See Associated Press, "NSA Chief Sidesteps Questions on Cell Phone Tracking at Senate Hearing," Fox News, September 2, 2013, at www.foxnews.com/politics/2013/09/26/top-intelligence-official-sidesteps-questions-on-cell-phone-tracking/; Fox News, "NSA Secretly Tapped Google, Yahoo data Centers Worldwide, New Report Claims," October 30, 2013, www.foxnews.com/politics/2013/10/30/nsa-secretly-tapped-google-yahoo-data-centers-worldwide-new-report-claims/.

7. See Jay Sekulow, "Lois Lerner Retires—Courtesy of the American Taxpayer," Fox News, September 23, 2013, at www.foxnews.com/opinion/2013/09/23/lois-lerner-retires-courtesy-american-taxpayer/; Fox News, "Holder Launches Probe into IRS Targeting of Tea Party Groups," May 14, 2013, at www.foxnews.com/politics/2013/05/14/irs-timeline-shows-dc-officials-in-loop-on-tea-party-targeting/.

8. See "Warrant Needed for Metadata Tracking," *Big Data Republic*, July 24, 2013

9. See David Kravets, "Cops Can Track Cellphones Without Warrants, Appeals Court Rules," *Wired*, July 30, 2013, at www.wired.com/threatlevel/2013/07/warrantless-cell-tracking/.

10. See David Kravets, "Judge Rules NSA Bulk Telephone Metadata Spying Is Lawful," *Wired*, December 27, 2013, at www.wired.com/threatlevel/2013/12/judge-upholds-nsa-spying/; and David Kravets, "Court Says NSA Bulk Telephone Spying Is Unconstitutional," *Wired*, December 16, 2013, at www.wired.com/threatlevel/2013/12/bulk-telephone-metada-ruling/.

11. See Nate Anderson, "Anonymized" Data Really Isn't—and Here's Why Not," *Ars Technica*, September 8, 2009, at http://arstechnica.com/tech-policy/2009/09/your-secrets-live-online-in-databases-of-ruin/.

12. Based on my International Institute for Analytics blog "Helpful or Creepy? Avoid Crossing the Line with Big Data," May 7, 2013, at http://iianalytics.com/2013/05/helpful-or-creepy-avoid-crossing-the-line-with-big-data/.

13. See Charles Duhigg, "How Companies Learn Your Secrets," *New York Times*, February 16, 2012, at www.nytimes.com/2012/02/19/magazine/shopping-habits.html?pagewanted=all&_r=2&.

14. Based on my blog for *Big Data Republic* titled "The Legal & Ethical Implications of Big Data," May 24, 2013.

15. Based on my blog for *Big Data Republic* titled "Privacy Implications Matter," November 30, 2012.

# PART

# III

# MAKING ANALYTICS OPERATIONAL

CHAPTER 7

# The Analytics

This chapter focuses specifically on the analytics concepts that will enable an organization to make analytics operational. As we discuss, not everything in the world of operational analytics is new, but there are some new and unique challenges that must be understood and accounted for.

Do not forget that making analytics operational is an evolution, which means that all the lessons and guidelines from the past related to how to build analytics processes still apply, but with a few new twists. Organizations that are already good at building and leveraging analytics and that already have a solid team of analytics professionals on staff are positioned to succeed.

## Creating Operational Analytics Processes

We defined operational analytics in Chapter 1. Let's start here with a few topics surrounding the creation and deployment of operational analytics. It will become apparent that operational analytics have a lot in common with traditional batch analytics, and it isn't necessary to start from scratch. At the same time, as also discussed in Chapter 1, organizations can't leapfrog into operational analytics without first gaining competency in traditional batch analytics.

### Consistency of the Analytics Process

As big data has emerged and people with different backgrounds enter the world of analytics, there are debates about whether a new analytics workflow is required. The answer is no. At a fundamental level, the workflow for developing analytics is very consistent across all data and all types of analytics. The fact that this consistency exists is terrific because we shouldn't need to reinvent the wheel every time we need to apply analytics in a different fashion or use new sources of data.

I have witnessed debates around whether the big data analytics process is something new. I recall a heated debate where I took the position that big data discovery isn't a new process while others took the position that it was. What finally helped settle the argument was when I pulled out the Cross Industry Standard Process for Data Mining (CRISP-DM) model from the 1990s. CRISP-DM describes the fundamental steps in a classic data mining process.

I put a picture of the CRISP-DM process next to the picture of the proposed big data discovery process. I also created a table with the individual steps within each framework next to each other. One of the people who claimed the processes were different said, "Wait a minute, Bill. This is almost the same thing!" Finally he saw my point. Slightly different words or semantics were being used, but fundamentally the "new" process was the same as the "old" process. Table 7.1 shows the similarity of the phases in the two models while Figure 7.1 is an illustrative generic analytics workflow.

Another popular paradigm is the SAS Institute's SEMMA model.[1] "SEMMA" stands for "sample, explore, modify, model, and assess." The SEMMA web page says that SEMMA presumes that a business problem has already been identified up front while deployment is considered an additional step on the back end. Once again, it is very similar to CRISP-DM and big data discovery, as can be seen in Table 7.1.

The fact that different analytics workflow models developed over many years from different perspectives are so consistent

Table 7.1    Phases of CRISP-DM versus Big Data Discovery versus SEMMA

| CRISP-DM | Big Data Discovery | SAS SEMMA |
|---|---|---|
| Business Understanding | Analytics Idea | Business Problem (Assumed) |
| Data Understanding | Data Loading and Integration | Sample and Explore |
| Data Preparation | | Modify |
| Modeling | SQL and Non-SQL Analysis | Model |
| Evaluation | Evaluation of Results | Assess |
| Deployment | Operationalizing | Deployment (Follows) |

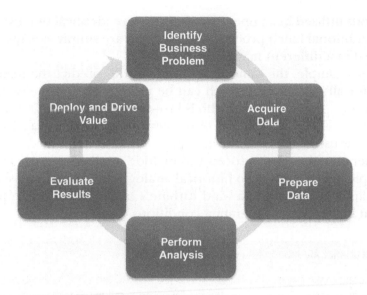

Figure 7.1    Generic Analytics Process Flow

should reassure us that there is a method to the madness of ana-lytics. Moving into big data analytics, operational analytics, or whatever comes next will build on what an organization and its teams already know.

### From Batch Analytics to Operational Analytics

Let's start by reviewing some of the distinctions and similarities between traditional batch analytics and operational analytics. The similarities are high although there are serious challenges found in the differences. First, both operational and batch analytics require significant data preparation and data quality validation. If it is neces-sary to assess the risk of a customer defecting, or the probability of a product selling, or the risk that an engine will fail in the next several minutes of operation, then it is necessary to have the right data, to validate the quality of the data, and to prepare the right metrics to support the required analytics.

Operational analytics focus on real-time or "decision-time" pro-cessing and often are applied to a single customer, product, or engine precisely when needed. This is in contrast to batch analytics, where all engines, all products, or all customers are analyzed at once in a single batch at an arbitrary time. In many cases, the analytics

## Defining Analytics Disciplines

The breadth of analytics required in a modern business environment is increasing. When I started in the field of analytics, most of the analytics processes built by large corporations fell into two core disciplines. First is statistics, which includes anything from analysis of variance, to regression, to tests of significance. Second is forecasting, which includes classic time series and projection techniques. These two analytics disciplines are not enough in today's world, and organizations need proficiency in more than just statistical and forecasting methods. Let's explore a few additional analytics disciplines.

Simulation is an analytics discipline that is becoming more widely utilized. In particular, Monte Carlo simulations are quite popular. The concept behind a Monte Carlo simulation is very simple, and if you've planned your retirement, you may have seen one. There are a lot of assumptions to make when projecting out retirement savings, such as:

- What will be the average annual return on investment?
- How volatile will the returns be over time?
- What will the inflation rate be?

A Monte Carlo simulation explores a vast array of combinations across the ranges provided for each assumption. As different realities unfold, how many of them will lead to a good result and a bad result for a savings goal? After thousands or millions of simulations, a Monte Carlo process provides a distribution of success and failure. The ideal outcome is that a range of reasonable assumptions also lead overwhelmingly to a positive outcome. If that isn't the case, the stated goal may be unrealistic.

The discipline of optimization is also becoming more widespread. Optimization has been used widely for pricing analytics for years, but its reach is starting to expand. Optimization attempts to find the options that best achieve a goal given a variety of factors and constraints. A Monte Carlo simulation explores and quantifies the impact of many options; optimization attempts to find the *best* option. Optimization typically is used when it is possible to control the factors that meaningfully impact the result. With pricing, for example, it is possible to control product prices to achieve the optimal results whereas it is not possible to control inflation rates to support a retirement plan.

Optimization is often built on top of traditional predictive analytics. For example, as a customer visits a website, what is the best offer to display? Even when creating a list of offers for an e-mail blast in batch mode, optimization can help ensure that overall response is optimized, given constraints such as how many of each offer can be distributed and what budget for discounts is available. Two common approaches to optimization are linear programming and nonlinear programming. Information on these techniques is widely available if readers are interested in learning more.

### Expanding Analytics Competencies

Classic statistical and forecasting methods are no longer sufficient to meet organizations' analytics needs. Multiple new analytics disciplines are necessary to handle new data types and new analytics requirements. Be prepared to expand both tool sets and skill sets to incorporate new analytics disciplines.

Streaming data is becoming much more prevalent, especially with the rise of sensors and the Internet of Things. Streaming data is often structured, and, as the name suggests, it is a continuous, rapid, high-volume stream. To handle streaming data, a discipline called complex event processing (CEP) has increased in popularity. CEP looks at a data stream as it flows in and often before the data is stored anywhere. The idea is to analyze the data while it's in transit to make a decision as quickly as possible. The analytics in CEP can include most other analytics disciplines. What makes CEP stand out is that the analytics are applied so quickly and outside of traditional environments. CEP is also highly operational in nature in most situations.

Other analytics disciplines that are becoming prevalent include the following:

- Facial recognition algorithms and other image analytics, which are relevant for applications from social media to security, are becoming common.
- Machine learning algorithms continue to become more and more sophisticated. Companies such as Google are acquiring and applying machine learning technologies behind the scenes.[4]
- Although the theories behind graph analysis were developed years ago, it wasn't until the rise of social networks and the

general desire to look at relationships among people or organizations that it became common.

- Until recently, only large logistics or mapping companies cared about geospatial analysis. Today, smartphones make geospatial analysis something that consumers interact with every day.
- With the ability to capture all text an organization generates and also to convert voice to text, the use of text analytics has exploded. Most large organizations already leverage text analysis.

Moving forward, it will be necessary to add new analytics disciplines into the mix. Be prepared to develop the skills in-house to work with those disciplines and to implement specialized tools to support them.

### The Case for Multidiscipline Analytics

How does an organization incorporate different analytics disciplines, and what will the benefits be? First, let's call the use of different analytics disciplines within the same process "multidiscipline analytics." Next, to illustrate a path to success, let's examine a historical parallel to data warehousing. Data warehousing arose because organizations were collecting more and more data, but it was not being collected in a coordinated fashion. Companies had different data management platforms spread throughout their organizations, and department-focused data marts were everywhere. If someone wanted to perform analysis requiring data from multiple parts of the business, the process of pulling the data together from all of the disparate systems was incredibly difficult and manual.

The concept of an enterprise data warehouse (EDW) is quite simple. An EDW aims, to the extent possible, to get all data required for analysis in one platform. Any given user might have a view of the data that looks exactly like what she saw in a traditional data mart, but because the data is in one place, it is also possible to view the data across data marts. For example, financial data can be combined easily with sales data instead of having to choose one or the other. Over the years, the concept of an EDW has generated immense value for the marketplace, and almost every large company has one in place.

## Mix, Match, and Explore

Having the ability to combine various analytics disciplines is powerful. Just as data sources become more powerful when combined with other data, analytics disciplines become more powerful when combined with other disciplines. A discovery platform enables this combination.

How does the justification for data warehousing tie to multidiscipline analytics? A current challenge with analytics is that even when a centralized EDW exists, every analytics discipline often has its own external environment. A company will have statistics software on one server, text analysis software on another, graph analysis software on another, an optimization suite on another, and so forth. With this proliferation of analytics tools, when combining analytics disciplines, companies run into issues similar to those that existed before data warehousing. It does not make sense to have all these different tool sets supporting different analytics disciplines in different places with limited integration and requiring a lot of data movement.

The solution is to create an environment that can handle all of the analytics requirements in one place. The discovery platform we defined in Chapter 5 is perfect for this, as can be seen in Figure 7.2. An ideal discovery platform will have access to all data repositories

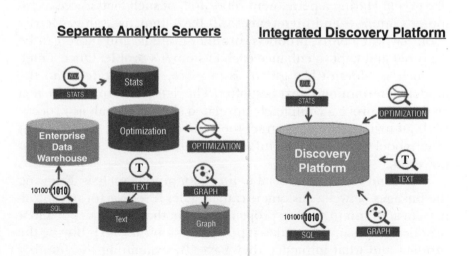

Figure 7.2   A Multidiscipline Discovery Platform

and will enable any analytics discipline. Some people will still choose to focus on a single discipline, just as some users of a data warehouse focus only on data from their department. However, it is now possible to explore how different analytics disciplines can interact and enhance one another.

### Multidiscipline Analytics in Action

Let's walk through some examples that illustrate how applying different analytics disciplines in combination with each other can be more powerful than any single discipline by itself.

When text analytics is used alone, often it is used very tactically and for short-term purposes. Organizations examine social media postings and tag them with a sentiment score to identify if comments are positive or negative. They also identify which products are being talked about. Many times the output is fed into aggregate trending reports that show if sentiment is rising or falling and which products are trending up or down in activity. Often that is the extent of the use of text analytics and the social media data.

However, text analytics can be used in a more strategic fashion. Why can't an organization keep track of every comment that every customer makes about its products? Perhaps a customer said a few years ago that he likes red and a month ago he said that he doesn't like green. Having a permanent repository of such facts about a customer's interests and preferences will have immense value. Metrics about favorite colors, products, product options, and more can be captured and kept to enhance each customer's profile. Once a metric such as "doesn't like green" is in place, it can be fed into the models determining a next best offer. That lets the output of the text analytics improve a completely unrelated statistical analysis process. Without text analytics to extract the color preference, the next best offer model would have less information and would therefore be less powerful.

A second example is social network, or graph, analysis. Knowing the linkages between customers can aid sales forecasts for new products. In addition to making projections from the initial sales of a new product, graph analysis makes it possible to look at who is buying the product and what influence they have. By examining the number and strength of relationships of early adopters, sales forecasts can be enhanced. If many strong influencers are trying the product, they will likely influence others to try it as well. If early sales are skewed toward low influencers, adoption will likely be slower. The additional information that graph analysis makes available can enhance sales forecasts. Better marketing is also possible because key influencers can be identified and then specifically targeted.

A third example involves adding simulation to common modeling efforts. Monte Carlo simulation can help validate the safety of a predicted outcome. A traditional predictive model will provide margins of error that quantify how much noise is in the data as well as the plausible true range of the estimated parameters. Monte Carlo simulation can be used to investigate predictions as all of the parameters vary across their respective margins of error. This will determine the stability of the predictions generated by the model and can reduce risk while increasing confidence in the results.

A final example applies when CEP algorithms are executing against a stream of sensor data. To enhance the CEP processes, machine learning algorithms can be executed against historical data. By looking at the stream over time and applying machine learning to better understand patterns within the data, it is possible to update the event processing algorithms to be more powerful. For example, an algorithm that looks for engine trouble can be updated to account for a previously overlooked trigger found using machine learning analysis to mine the historical data for influencers of engine trouble.

There are myriad ways that analytics disciplines can be combined. Although the examples here focused on pairs, it is quite possible to take the examples further so that many disciplines, not just two, are involved in a single process.

## Focusing Analytics Efforts

When an organization is ready to start making analytics operational, it must begin by focusing effort in the right areas. There are some valuable guidelines to follow to ensure that resources are pointed in the right direction to avoid wasting time and money chasing a flawed premise based on bad assumptions.

### Ask the Right Questions and Make Good Assumptions

The value that can be derived from an analysis is determined by how a problem is defined, what questions are asked, how an analytics solution is designed, and how that solution is implemented once it is built. Choosing the questions to address can have more impact on the value of the resulting analytics process than the details of the process that is developed as a result of those questions.

This makes sense. After all, how can any analysis be accurate and useful if the problem it addresses is poorly framed and the right questions are not asked? It is very easy to perfectly execute a completely inappropriate and incorrectly designed analysis to address the wrong question. Worse, if the wrong question is asked, the mistake may not be identified. If the question seems reasonable and an analysis addresses it well, the initial question may not be challenged again.

### Don't Doom an Analysis from the Start

The way a problem is defined, the way questions are asked, and how an analysis is designed can have a larger impact on the results achieved than any of the hard work that follows. It is easy to develop an analysis that answers the wrong question addressing the wrong problem.

When potentially millions of decisions will be made automatically, being even slightly off base when designing an analytics process can lead to serious consequences. Proper emphasis on the analysis definition and design process is needed more than ever with operational analytics. As always, it is also necessary to take into account the various technical and practical considerations that are present. You can't afford to have an automated operational analytics process executing at scale if you can't trust that it is right.

This brings us to an approach that is not common, but should be. Part of the development process for an analysis should be testing the assumptions being made. A discipline called sensitivity analysis, often used in engineering, can be borrowed to do this.[5]

In any analytics process, specific assumptions will be made. There might be an assumption about the growth rate of sales or the expansion of a competitor's market share or the future costs of raw materials. The output of an analytics process can't be right if the starting assumptions aren't accurate. As actual values become known, they will vary from the precise figure that was assumed (we hope only slightly). The critical question is: As true values deviate to various degrees from our assumptions, what is the impact on the analysis results?

For example, executives may be debating whether inflation will be 3, 4, or 5 percent and may be unable to reach agreement. Sensitivity analysis can come to the rescue by showing how results will be impacted as the inflation rate varies. If, regardless of which executive is most accurate, the analytics results still point to the same answer, then the executives don't have to agree on an exact assumption. Agreeing to a range of assumptions, such as 3 to 5 percent, is fine because the analysis leads to the same decision under any of the executives' assumptions.

I first encountered this need when building marketing mix models that included TV advertising data. The advertising data was at an extremely aggregated level. On top of that, we had to make many assumptions about the data as we prepared it for our models. For example, what decay rate would be used for the advertising impressions? Decay rates are a simple concept. When an advertisement is shown, it can impact sales. However, it can take days for people actually to act on the advertisement by going to a store or hopping online to buy what was advertised. So, an advertising variable that starts high when the TV ad is shown and slowly tapers off over time is created. The speed of the tapering is the decay rate and the decay rate chosen impacts the results. Figure 7.3 shows an illustration of decay rates.

The guidance I was given at the time, which is what many analytics professionals still follow today, is that if a model's parameter estimates are statistically significant and the model has good explanatory power, then the decay rate assumptions are good and the model can be used. However, I stumbled on a huge problem with that approach.

Figure 7.3    Sample Decay Rates

One day I created a good model using a standard decay rate. However, for some reason, I decided to see what would happen if I changed my assumptions about the advertising decay rate and reran the models. I was astonished to see that I still had significant parameters and the model still had a lot of explanatory power. However, the new parameter estimates were different from my original ones by more than the margin of error. Clearly, simply having a good model and significant parameters wasn't enough to prove assumptions valid. In effect, my decay rate assumptions determined the results more than the model itself. The team and I did more work to finalize assumptions we believed were the best possible. However, I am still uncomfortable today with the idea that assumptions can change results so drastically.

### Assumptions Add Risk; Assess the Risk

Many assumptions are made when building an analytics process, and it is highly unlikely that every assumption will be exactly correct. Assessing how results change as actual values vary from the assumptions within a plausible range is worthwhile. Doing this enables you to understand the risks the analysis is exposed to.

It won't always be the case that all reasonable assumptions lead to the same answer. There will be situations where one set of reasonable assumptions produces a result that says "go" and another says "no go." In such cases, it is necessary to reach agreement on a final assumption and document the risk associated with being wrong. When different assumptions lead to different answers, it is wise to use conservative assumptions to be safe. Using sensitivity analysis to assess assumptions won't remove risks, but it will quantify them to ensure that they are understood. A Monte Carlo simulation is a good tool for assessing assumptions in this way.

### Place Your Bets!

We discussed in Chapter 2 that even as the cost of capturing and storing data has gone down, the growth of data and the growth of analytics requirements is increasing at least as fast. There are so many different opportunities for analytics today that it can be overwhelming. Solid judgment must be used when determining where to place bets. In fact, big data and operational analytics are going to require at least as much judgment as in the past. This is because with ever more data to look at in ever more combinations, it is easy to go down paths that don't make sense. Finding spurious correlations that are a distraction more than a reality is also very easy.

For example, one common pitfall when building statistical models relates to the fact that many models provide a measure of confidence in their parameter estimates. A common standard is demanding at least 99 percent confidence that an effect is truly present and that random luck isn't at play. When testing only a few factors, chances are relatively low and acceptable that something completely bogus will be found significant. However, think about the petabytes of sensor data generated by a modern airplane. There will be thousands, maybe even tens of thousands, of metrics available to correlate with events such as an engine overheating. If confidence levels are set to 99 percent when examining 20,000 factors, then it can be expected that 200 completely bogus factors will be found statistically significant.

Judgment is required to decide which metrics should be fed into an analysis so that only reasonable candidates are included. Even after filtering to reasonable candidates, there may be a lot of metrics left, which will lead to spurious effects being identified. After building a model, additional analysis is needed to validate which of the effects found are real. Judgment must permeate the entire process.

### Don't Be Too Quick to Judge

A great example of the themes in this section relates to Boeing and its aircraft, the 787. In 2012, Boeing was in the news because of issues with the batteries on the 787.[6] The issue cost Boeing a lot of money and a lot of brand equity. Someone asked during one of my conference talks if I thought that Boeing had really messed up by not identifying and fixing the battery issue before the plane's release. The person's point was that with all the sensor data available during testing, Boeing should have found the problem. I replied that it was not really fair to view Boeing that way because the answer isn't that simple. I like to consider people or companies innocent until proven guilty. In retrospect, it's easy to think that that battery issue should have been found, but let's consider a few possibilities that would challenge that view.

First, it's possible that Boeing wasn't collecting data that could have identified the specific battery issue that occurred. Second, even if the right data was collected during testing, it's entirely possible that Boeing analyzed it and that there was no troubling pattern to be found. Maybe the issue arose only when the plane was operating in a real-world setting. Moreover, even if the data contained information to identify the problem, that doesn't necessarily mean that Boeing messed up. Let me explain why.

### Don't Fall Victim to Perfect Hindsight

With so much data to analyze from so many different directions, judgment must be used to target the highest-impact opportunities. Document how decisions are made with regard to where focus is (and is not) placed to defend actions against perfect hindsight. A needle in a haystack is almost impossible to find. However, once the needle is spotted, it is almost impossible to miss it.

Given the amount of data generated by a 787 from the myriad sensors it contains, it isn't possible to explore every possible thing that could go wrong. There simply is not enough time in terms of labor or computing power. Boeing engineers and analytics professionals certainly explored the highest-risk areas, but they had to use judgment in determining where the risks were high enough to focus effort. There are components that can't safely fail, such as engines and landing gear. I'm sure Boeing focused immense effort analyzing performance in those areas. However, it doesn't really matter if a flight attendant call button breaks while a plane is in flight. It's easy enough to fix and there's no real risk to crew or passengers. The battery issue falls somewhere in the middle between these two extremes. It is possible that the batteries weren't considered a big enough risk to warrant focus, given resource constraints and past experience.

Of course, it is possible that Boeing did analyze the batteries, that a problem was evident in the data, and that it was missed. Maybe Boeing did mess up. But, without more facts, it is impossible to know.

The lesson to take away is that as an organization acquires more and more data to build more and more analytics processes, analytics professionals need to document their decision processes. This means documenting not only what is analyzed but also what is not analyzed and why it is not. A needle in a haystack is impossible to see until someone points it out to you. Once you know where the needle is, you can't help but see it clearly. Similarly, once there is a problem in an aircraft battery, it's obvious and it's natural to think that it should have been found up front. Documenting why focus was placed where it was can help mitigate the second-guessing that follows an incident. Problems often aren't obvious at all . . . until suddenly they become obvious because they have occurred.

## Comparing Analytics Approaches

There are several different ways to build analytics processes, and distinctions must be recognized between approaches that can, on the surface, seem similar. Some analytics approaches are often misunderstood and considered to be far less logical and scientific than they really are. In this section, we review a few important approaches that will need to be part of any organization's effort to pursue operational analytics.

### Discovery versus Confirmatory Analysis

Historically, most analytics were what we'll call confirmatory analysis. Confirmatory analysis starts with a specific hypothesis or a specific goal. Analysis is then performed either to confirm the hypothesis (or not) or to meet the goal (or not). In other words, analysis begins with a very clear direction and scope. For example, I might be asked to confirm to what extent information on products a customer browsed from a web log increases the lift of the models used to predict the likelihood of purchase. The scope of the task is well defined, I can estimate with confidence the amount of effort it will take me to do it, and the criteria by which success will be judged is clear from the start. This makes such an effort easy to work through typical corporate project justification processes.

The world of big data is focused more frequently on what can be called discovery analytics. Discovery analysis begins not as much with a specific goal or hypothesis in mind but rather to explore whether value can be found within data to address a very broad goal or set of hypotheses. Having very few preconceived ideas doesn't mean analytics professionals have no idea what they will do during the analysis; it simply means that the idea is less formalized, less defined, and less rigid at the outset.

For example, I might be asked to look into whether a new data source can be used in any way to improve the performance of models that predict likelihood of purchase. I am then free to determine the best metrics to generate, the best ways to test those metrics within the analytics process, and the best methodologies to utilize. I may start with a number of ideas, but I'm not sure at the outset which will work, I can't be fully confident in the effort required, and I won't know how to judge success until I know how the analysis has played out. These facts can make people uncomfortable at first. Discovery analysis has been around for quite some time and has always played a role for large organizations. However, there is a new focus on discovery analytics today, and it is getting a bigger portion of resources than in the past. Discovery analysis can also be called exploratory analysis.

## Discovery Is Not Random or Aimless

Discovery analysis is sometimes viewed critically as if analytics professionals are randomly playing with data in hopes of finding something of use. This isn't the case. Discovery analysis does start with a broad goal. However, much leeway is given to analytics professionals to figure out how to achieve that goal.

As organizations increase their use of analytics and, therefore, the analytics talent pool and analytics processing capacity, it is much easier for them to allocate at least a small percentage of resources to discovery analytics. With a small team, it can be difficult to free someone up to perform discovery analytics because there are scarcely enough people to get all the needed confirmatory work completed. When an organization has a large team, it becomes much easier to free up some time for discovery efforts.

A discovery analysis does start with a broad goal, but the best way to reach the goal is unknown when a project is started. There isn't a well-defined analysis plan as there is with a confirmatory analysis project. For example, a detailed analysis plan for building a new recommendation engine in a certain way would be part of a confirmatory analysis. A discovery analysis might start with no more guidance than to find one or more ways to improve the recommendation engine. The analytics professionals are tasked with experimenting to figure out the best way to improve the engine. The team explores various data sources and methodologies until a good option is found. At that point, a more rigid plan can be put in place, and a confirmatory analysis can begin to implement that option.

A real-world analog to the distinction between discovery and confirmatory analysis comes from the energy industry. Oil and gas companies spend a lot of money assessing a broad range of possible drilling locations. That assessment is a discovery process because it aims to explore a range of untested options and determine where to risk drilling. Once a site has been deemed to have potential, it is drilled. This is like confirmatory analysis. The company knows exactly where to drill and what it is looking for. Once the drilling process begins, the company will either find the oil it was hoping for or it won't. In other words, the hypothesis that the location contains oil will be confirmed or rejected.

### Research and Development versus Hacking

People often mistake discovery analysis for mindless hacking and aimless experimentation. That's an absolutely unfair assessment if discovery analytics are being done correctly. Discovery analytics should be considered a research and development (R&D) effort, and there should be intent to eventually monetize any findings. A variety of experiments to find a path to monetization (or to determine that a path doesn't exist) may be necessary, however.

Large restaurant chains and consumer products organizations have test kitchens that experiment with dozens or hundreds of recipes to find the next item to add into the assortment or onto the menu. Similarly, an analytics team may have to try a number of discovery processes before it finds a winner that is worth making operational.

A test kitchen may start with a mission as broad as "create a new chicken sandwich." The cooks will have wide discretion to research what flavors and trends are popular in the market today. For example, what seasonings are on the edge of an emerging trend? A recent example is the proliferation of pretzel bread sandwiches in 2013. Pretzel bread became a hot trend, and many major fast food chains released a pretzel bread sandwich. The point is that the test kitchen was given some direction. Although the cooks knew they needed to create a chicken sandwich, they were given broad discretion to create the final recipe. After determining that pretzel bread was a trend, the focus became finding a tasty pretzel bread recipe and a sandwich recipe that was tasty with pretzel bread. That's how discovery analytics should be as well. Discovery analytics should be viewed as an R&D activity that begins with a general goal.

An organization must ensure that in its culture, discovery analytics are valued as a scientific endeavor and not considered aimless hacking. That slight change in mind-set can accelerate an organization's ability to uncover new analytics that can be made operational. Starting with broad, relevant goals keeps the focus on real business issues rather than on interesting issues that won't have an impact. It is very easy for analytics professionals to get sidetracked chasing interesting, but unimportant, trends if they are just hacking around instead of beginning a formal R&D effort. Validating that an idea has business merit and is more than just interesting is a necessity. An analytics professional should reserve hacking activities for a hobby on weekends.

As discussed in Chapter 6, even during an R&D effort, people must keep in mind the constraints that will be faced if the process is taken into production. For example, a test kitchen isn't going to try a method of cooking that requires an entirely new, expensive piece of equipment without validating that adding that new equipment to every single location to support the new item is feasible. Similarly, accounting for operational constraints during analytics R&D efforts will avoid wasting time on paths that won't be feasible to make operational. For example, the saga of the Netflix Prize is well known.[7] However, much of the winning solution was not implemented because the accuracy gains didn't justify the huge cost required to implement it.[8]

### Hardening a Process for Operational Scale

One aspect of operational analytics can be hard for analytical professionals to accept: namely, it may be necessary to give up some analytics power or sophistication when making analytics operational. What this means is accepting good (not perfect) data and good (not perfect) results as well as altering how success is measured. The theoretical accuracy and lift of an analytics process are not as important as the actual impact the recommendations and decisions drive. For example, if drivers ignore the optimized route they are handed, the analytics behind the suggested routes will have no impact regardless of how good the optimization processes are.

As discussed in Chapter 6, when analytics are being built in a custom or artisanal fashion, the process can be created in a way that makes it somewhat fragile. During an artisanal process, it is possible to add a little bit of elegance and extra sophistication to make the analysis truly unique and optimally valuable because it won't be used enough to expose the lack of scale.

Similarly, you can easily customize the decorations in your home to improve how it looks and make it truly yours. Your décor can include a lot of highly fragile, very beautiful items. However, you wouldn't put those same items in a high-traffic area, such as a shopping mall or office building. In rare cases, such as museums, where fragile and rare items are in public areas, extensive extra security and safety measures, such as thick Plexiglas and vibration-absorbing display cases, are required. Just as it is necessary to have different decorating standards for a house than for a heavily used commercial space, so too must standards for analytics processes be changed to make them operational instead of artisanal.

Producing anything millions of times a day at an industrial scale requires some trade-offs. Manufacturers make trade-offs all the time as they develop product designs. A very pretty design for a wineglass may make it too fragile for the frequent use it would get at a restaurant. The design must be changed to something less pretty but more durable.

Organizations must focus on optimizing the overall impact of an operational analytics process, not optimizing the sophistication or absolute accuracy of the individual decisions within the analytics process. Giving up some sophistication and accuracy can make the difference between having a huge impact in practice and having no impact at all. A little extra accuracy will do no good if the solution cannot be deployed at operational scale.

### Optimize Aggregate Decision Quality

With operational analytics, the goal is not to maximize the quality of each individual decision but rather to maximize the aggregate impact of the process across all decisions. Doing this can require giving up some analytics power in order to make the process hardened enough for industrial scale.

Don't misunderstand me! I am not saying that standards should be abandoned. Rigid quality procedures are wrapped around an industrial manufacturing line even if some concessions have been made in design. If extra accuracy comes at the cost of doubling the time it takes to run a process, it won't work. If a method is highly sensitive to data outliers, it may be too risky to deploy it in a setting where the data can't be validated before it is used. It is hoped that the absolute best solution and the best deployable solution won't be too far apart. However, it is necessary to make the distinction.

Let's return for a moment to the control processes used on a manufacturing line. Manufacturers make use of statistical process control procedures that create ongoing summaries of how the manufacturing process is working. Statistical process control provides insight into whether various metrics are in the expected range and which way they are trending. When any metric moves out of the acceptable range, corrective action is taken. For example, if the temperature of a product as it comes out of an oven moves too high or too low, the production line can be stopped so that the oven can be adjusted.

Applying statistical process control procedures to operational analytics processes is possible. An organization can monitor the decisions that are being made by an analytics process and the data that is feeding the decisions. Are decisions being made in the same proportions as time passes? Is the input data still exhibiting the expected distribution? When one of the measures starts to drift, someone can step in, shut down the process, and investigate, just as would happen for a real assembly line. Traditional business intelligence concepts can be used to monitor operational analytics.

The success of operational analytics is not just about the power and consistency of the analytics but also about how the people and organizational processes actually make use of the recommendations and follow the decisions. Behavior must change as a result of the analytics or the analytics won't have the desired impact. Therefore, cultural change is a key to success with operational analytics, as we discuss in Chapter 9.

## Lessons from the Past

Throughout the book, the point has been made that many old lessons apply in the world of big data and operational analytics. There are classic analytics concepts that must not be abandoned, regardless of the hype suggesting that they should be. Let's take a look at a few areas where hype can get ahead of reality.

### Statistical Methods Are Still Relevant

It has been suggested that classic statistical methods are simply old school, outdated, small data concepts. This is an absolutely false premise. Certainly, as analytics evolves to incorporate new analytics disciplines, disciplines outside of classic statistical methods must be included. Some analytics methods and algorithms, such as search algorithms and natural language processing, aren't based directly on classic statistical methods. That's okay. However, just as adding a nonrelational environment on top of a relational environment does not imply that relational requirements are going to go away, adding additional analytics disciplines on top of statistics does not imply that statistics is going to go away.[9]

No matter how large a data source is, it will still contain inherent variability and uncertainty. The data will never be perfect, and there is natural variability in the populations that we study. No matter how much data we have, it is not possible to perfectly predict what every individual will do or when a given engine will fail, because we will always be missing some information and there will always be factors that have not been accounted for.[10] Statistics can help account for and quantify the risks associated with those gaps. Let's explore an example.

Path analysis is a nonstatistical approach that is becoming very popular. A common use of path analysis is to identify the specific series of actions each customer takes and to correlate paths with outcomes of interest. Actions can include a withdrawal at an ATM, a call to a call center, a deposit into an account, a click on a web page, a tweet, or whatever is of interest to an organization. Dozens of potential actions can be included in a path. Path analysis has been used to analyze traffic on websites for years by looking at how users navigate a site and which paths lead to the most sales. Recently, path analysis has expanded well beyond website traffic.

## Statistics Is Dead . . . Long Live Statistics!

The idea that statistical methods are no longer relevant is misguided. While there is a need to move beyond exclusively using classic statistical methods, statistical methods remain a critical component of operational analytics.

The extraction of key facts about common paths can provide additional power to predictive models through the unique information provided. Consider a scenario where there are four specific interactions: An ATM withdrawal is labeled A, a call center inquiry is labeled B, a branch visit is labeled C, and a complaint is labeled

D. My path happens to be ABCD, which means that I first made a withdrawal, then called the call center, then went into a branch, and then filed a complaint. After identifying each customer's path, it is possible to quickly identify which of the paths were most common and which paths have a positive or negative association with some metric of interest, such as opening a new account or closing an account. Using statistics can make the path data much more relevant and widen its usage. By creating a series of metrics that summarize key traits of each path, it is possible to explore more deeply what aspects of the paths influence the metrics of interest. Summary metrics might include those such as:

- Does calling the call center at any point increase attrition risk?
- Does a complaint matter only if it is the first or last action taken?
- Does a combination of both a branch visit and a complaint matter, but not the presence of either individually?
- Does a complaint matter more when it follows a call center interaction than when it precedes it?
- Does submitting three complaints through any combination of channels greatly increase attrition risk?

These questions can be answered by tagging each customer's path with a series of numeric variables that identify the presence or absence of key characteristics of the path. For example, one variable will contain a 1 if a branch visit and a call center call both occurred, and 0 if not. After creating a wide range of variables, classic correlation or regression analysis can be used to identify which path traits are most associated with a metric of interest. In a scenario like this, a nonstatistical path function is used to provide new information that can be analyzed in a statistically rigorous fashion. Statistics therefore increases the impact of the path analysis. This is another example of the power of multidiscipline analytics discussed earlier in the chapter. Statistics is alive and well.

### Don't Dismiss Sampling

The concept of sampling within analytics processes goes all the way back to the advent of analytics.[11] Historically, often it was necessary to operate on samples of data rather than the entire universe due to processing constraints. In recent years, it has become possible to capture and analyze the whole universe of interest in many cases, so some people have questioned whether the era of sampling is over.

Let's begin by acknowledging that there are cases where sampling just won't work. Finding the top 100 spending customers can't be done with a sample. Every single customer must be examined to identify the top 100. However, such scenarios, while common, aren't the most prevalent type of analytics requirement. In addition, even a model built on a sample will need to be applied to the universe once deployed. So, when it comes time to deploy, sampling isn't an option.

Let's go back to a typical scenario where an average is needed or parameter estimates from a predictive model are desired. Statistically speaking, a sample that is correctly drawn to mimic the population and is of sufficient size will provide essentially the same answer as if all of the data were used. There is no practical difference between the results from a sample and the results from the universe in these common situations. The additional cost of processing a lot of extra data provides no extra return. Even if the universe is used for a model, it isn't appropriate to build a model on literally all the data. Rather, it is necessary to hold back some of the data for validation while using the remainder to build the model. Guess what the validation data and modeling datasets are? They are samples! Sampling can't be avoided in many cases.

Some vehemently argue that if you don't need to sample, then don't. Others argue that using more than the minimal sample required is a waste of time and resources. If someone doing a project for me wants to sample, I'm okay with that as long as the sample is sufficiently large and drawn correctly. If someone wants to use the universe, I'm okay with that too as long as the extra resources required compared to a sample aren't meaningful. I am confident I'll get the same results, so I'm not that concerned about which path is taken. There are plenty of important topics to spend time debating when developing an analytics process. Don't waste time debating sampling.

### Don't Overcomplicate Analytics

One issue worth discussing surprised me when I was first confronted with it: Getting fancy with analytics will sometimes produce a worse result than something simple. This can be true even when theoretically a more sophisticated method should work better. I'm convinced that this is because data always has some uncertainty, is often sparsely populated, and is never fully complete. At some point as analytics get more sophisticated, there is a risk of magnifying the errors or uncertainties in the data rather than controlling and accounting for them. In addition, it is possible to overfit a model, which means that a model is complex enough to start to incorporate the random variation in the data set modeled rather than real effects. Overfit becomes apparent when a model is applied to a validation sample and performs poorly.

A few years ago my team was implementing sales forecasting for products at an individual store level for a large retailer. The scope spanned hundreds of millions of store/product combinations. Many products sold frequently and in a consistent fashion, which matched the assumptions of the most commonly used algorithms for this type of forecast. This client, however, had many products that didn't fit standard sales patterns. My team was hired to develop customized approaches to deal with the patterns that were exceptions. Due to the scale of the organization, the exceptions still represented millions of store/product combinations.

### Don't Get Too Fancy!

When building analytics processes for operational scale, simpler solutions actually can be better than fancy solutions. Operational analytics often operates on a low level of data that can be incomplete and sparse. Getting too fancy can magnify the issues in the data instead of controlling them.

We knew from the start that another consulting firm was also given the same project and that whoever came back with better results would be selected to continue the work moving forward. The other team had more people on the project than we did, so I didn't think we could win with brute force. I also knew from past experience working alongside the other consulting firm that they would try a bunch of fancy algorithms to maximize forecast accuracy for the test cases. However, there was a good chance that the methods wouldn't scale as needed. I asked my team to start with the simplest algorithms and add extra complexity and sophistication until they were convinced that doing more would cause the solution not to scale.

As the project started, I assumed the other team's absolute forecast accuracy would beat ours but that the amount of effort required to scale the other team's solution would be so massive that it wouldn't be feasible. We would win because our slightly less accurate forecasts worked better in practice. I was pleasantly surprised when our forecasts were actually more accurate. Given the incomplete and sparse nature of the data, fancy multistep algorithms amplified the noise instead of controlling it. My team thought we had given up some analytics power to enable operational deployment, a concept we have discussed several times in the book. However, it ended up that the simple approach was better, and we hadn't given up anything at all. Don't assume fancy is always better. Try the simple options too.

### Operational Analytics Must Provide Solutions

With all of our discussion of analytics, it is easy to be fooled into thinking that average people in an organization actually care about analytics. They don't! What most people care about is a solution to whatever problem they have. If analytics is a part of that solution, that's fine with them, but analytics is not what makes them interested. What interests them is that a problem has been solved.

In many situations, my project sponsors actually have had some interest in the analytics. It was safe to discuss both the analytics and the solution they provided with a database marketing executive. The people running such departments understood and embraced the analytics being generated and often came from analytics backgrounds. With operational analytics, many of the consumers and sponsors care only about having a problem solved. The problem might be reducing fraud or increasing supply chain efficiency or decreasing maintenance costs, but they don't care about the analytics outside of the impact that can be made on their problems. In fact, many users of operational analytics will be front-line employees with little or no education relevant to understanding analytics. Such employees must be enabled to leverage the analytics even without understanding the details.

The focus must be on solving problems through analytics. Show that a process works, but don't focus on the analytics directly when showcasing the results. When end users or sponsors have little understanding of or interest in the nuances and complexities that underlie the analytics process, inundating them with details will only overwhelm them. Overwhelming them could cause them to reject the idea of implementing the analytics process. Show that the process works, outline the benefits, and leave it at that unless asked for more.

### Provide Solutions, Not an Analytics Education

Many sponsors and users of operational analytics will have little or no understanding of or interest in analytics. They will care only that a problem is being solved. Convince them that analytics will solve their problem without the technical details. If overwhelmed, they may not implement the solution at all.

Many of us like to be spared the details when we don't understand something. For example, most people don't want to understand how a car engine works or how pressing the gas pedal results in fuel being fed into the fuel injector. The average person simply wants to know that if he or she presses the gas, the car will move forward. Similarly, operational analytics must be communicated in a different way since users may not be people who understand or care about how the analytics work.

Operational analytics should be an embedded part of a solution being provided. If you can demonstrate that the solution provides the required results, sponsors and consumers of the solution will be happy. They won't ever have to understand the details. Whether end users fully understand or appreciate the analytics behind the solution really doesn't matter. Think back to Chapter 1, where we discussed an organization that was able to get drivers to reduce daily mileage. Many of the drivers thought that the computer's suggestions were useless even after rollout since they could find ways to beat the suggestions. Changing the drivers' behavior was the important part. Drivers reduced mileage because the recommendations challenged them to. Whether the drivers understood how the analytics drove that change is not important as long as the change happens.

## Wrap-Up

The most important lessons to take away from this chapter are:

- Operational analytics must start with a solid batch analysis foundation, and the traditional analytics process flow still applies.

- Organizations need the ability to execute and combine multiple analytics disciplines so that they can enhance one another to improve results.
- A discovery platform is an ideal place to apply multiple analytics disciplines to a problem.
- Asking the right questions when designing an analysis can have a larger impact on the results than any of the work that follows.
- Leverage sensitivity analysis to assess the potential impact if observed scenarios differ from initial assumptions.
- It isn't possible to explore all potential analytics. When something is missed, hindsight is always 20/20. Document not only why certain paths are taken but also why others are not.
- Discovery analysis allows a broad goal or hypothesis to be pursued with limited constraints, whereas confirmatory analysis is highly focused and scoped from the start.
- Just like a test kitchen seeks the next big food item, organizations need R&D analytics seeking the next big analytics process. It isn't about mindless hacking but intelligent placing of bets.
- Taking analytics to an operational level can mean giving up analytics power in return for the required scale. Optimize a process's impact across all decisions, not for each individual decision.
- Statistical methods, including sampling, are still relevant and appropriate. The hype that they are outdated will be proven wrong.
- Fancy solutions can magnify rather than control data issues, especially when applied at a low level where data is sparse and incomplete. Simple solutions actually can work better while providing the necessary scale.
- Sponsors and users of operational analytics often won't understand or care about analytics but only about getting a solution to a problem. Going into technical details if not asked risks driving people away.

## Notes

1. See *SAS Enterprise Miner,* "Semma," www.sas.com/offices/europe/uk/technologies/analytics/datamining/miner/semma.html.
2. See BTI Case Study, "Obsession with Quality at Western Digital Corporation," August 2010, at www.teradata.com/t/case-study/Obsession-with-Quality-at-Western-Digital-Corporation-EB-6334.

3. Based on my blog for Big Data Republic titled "Analytics with Big-Data Is . . . Just Analytics," November 1, 2012.
4. See Thomas Claburn, "Google Buys Machine Learning Startup," *Information-Week*, March 13, 2013, at www.informationweek.com/software/information-management/google-buys-machine-learning-startup/d/d-id/1109068.
5. See Joint Research Centre for Sensitivity Analysis at http://ipsc.jrc.ec.europa.eu/?id=752. This discussion is based on my blog for International Institute for Analytics titled "Assumptions Can Be Risky in a Big Data World," June 13, 2012. See http://iianalytics.com/2013/06/assumptions-can-be-risky-in-a-big-data-world
6. See Tim Kelly and Alwyn Scott, "Japan Air Grounds Boeing 787 after Battery Problem," *Reuter's*, January 14, 2012, at www.reuters.com/article/2014/01/14/us-japanairlines-787-battery-idUSBREA0D11820140114.
7. See www.netflixprize.com/
8. See Xavier Amatriain, "Mining Large Streams of User Data for Personalized Recommendations," *SIGKDD Explorations* 14, no. 2 (December 2012), at www.kdd.org/sites/default/files/issues/14-2-2012-12/V14-02-05-Amatriain.pdf.
9. See Kirk Borne, "Statistical Truisms in the Age of Big Data," June 19, 2013, at www.statisticsviews.com/details/feature/4911381/Statistical-Truisms-in-the-Age-of-Big-Data.html; and Marie Davidian, "Aren't We Data Science?" *AMSTATNEWS*, July 1, 2013, at http://magazine.amstat.org/blog/2013/07/01/datascience/.
10. For more thoughts on this concept, see my International Institute for Analytics blog titled "Perfect Information Doesn't Equal Perfect Predictions," December 12, 2013, at http://iianalytics.com/2013/12/perfect-information-doesnt-equal-perfect-predictions/.
11. Based on my blog for International Institute for Analytics "To Sample or Not to Sample . . . Does It Even Matter?" April 5, 2013. See http://iianalytics.com/2012/04/to-sample-or-not-to-sample-does-it-even-matter/.

# The Analytics Organization

If an organization is to generate valuable operational analytics, it needs the right people. More than that, it must organize those people well to enable them to succeed. Except for the rare, highly mature analytics organization, changes to current organizational structures will be necessary over time. I discussed the topics of analytics professionals and analytics organizations in *Taming the Big Data Tidal Wave*. This chapter adds additional perspectives and new information. Let's dive into some of the key considerations you'll need to make as you staff, organize, and successfully operate your analytics organization so that it can succeed with operational analytics.

## A Major Shift Has Occurred

When I see how the career opportunities for analytics professionals have evolved over the years, it's amazing to me. When I first came out of graduate school more than 20 years ago, I fully expected and accepted that I would be a nerd in the corner in the basement. I'd be let out of the basement every now and then, but mostly I would develop cool analytics behind the scenes. That's what the opportunity was for analytics professionals back then, and I was okay with it.

I like to say that in my first job, I talked to someone who talked to someone who might talk to someone who was a decision maker. I was removed from the business decision makers, and I was also removed from information technology (IT). The combination of my team's spot in the organization and how we worked limited our impact. The early attrition (or churn) analysis I developed was executed in batch and targeted a few very specific decision points. The analytics were not an integrated component of what the company was doing any more than I was, and the analytics certainly didn't have an operational aspect at that time.

Today, analytics professionals are regularly seated at the table next to decision makers. In fact, analytics professionals today often are the decision makers. What a huge change from when I started! I got into the analytics field because I liked it. I wish I could claim that I foresaw the future that is now from the start, but I didn't. I got lucky that I chose one of the hottest careers in existence today.

Analytics has not only risen from obscurity, but it's gone to the extreme in the other direction. Legitimate organizations like *Harvard Business Review*, CNNMoney, and *Forbes* talk about analytics professionals being not only necessary but even sexy.[1] After years of trying to come up with a way to explain what I do for a living to people at parties without scaring them off, it's hilarious that suddenly I am considered cool, if not sexy, based on what I do.

As a result of this newfound (and possibly fleeting) popularity, there is an exercise that I like to encourage analytics professionals to do. As you're getting ready for bed at night, stop, look in the mirror for a moment, stare at yourself, and say "I'm an analytics professional and I'm sexy." For the first time in your life, other people might agree with that claim.

As recently as 2012, when organizations talked to me about their analytics strategies, the focus was usually on whether they should hire analytics professionals at all. That was always disheartening to me because as an analytics professional, I would like to think that everyone would find analytics professionals valuable and would not question the need to hire us.

## Analytics Organizations Are Here to Stay

There has been a major shift in recent years. Instead of questioning whether analytics talent is needed, organizations are now concerned about how to organize and expand the talent they have. This shows that the value of analytics professionals is now widely accepted and their roles are expanding.

A notable shift has taken place. Starting in 2013, many organizations started coming to me to talk not about whether they should hire analytics professionals but how they should organize the professionals they have. This points to a big evolution because it reflects two important facts. First, many companies now have enough analytics talent to realize the necessity of thinking about how to organize them. Second, and equally important, is the fact that the new focus on how to organize analytics teams says that they are here to stay. This is a big shift and an exciting development.

Analytics organizations are now mainstream. If your organization doesn't have one, you need one. If it has one, you need to staff, organize, and operate it properly if it is to succeed. That's what the remainder of the chapter is about.

## Staffing

It all starts with staffing. It is impossible to have an organization without the people who belong to it. But who should be on the team, and what are their characteristics? How do you build a well-rounded team? How do you keep them happy in the long term? Let's explore these issues.

### Who Is the Analytics Professional?

Let's first define the term "analytics professional." A lot of names and titles have been used for analytics professionals over the years. Examples include statistician, predictive modeler, analyst, data miner, and, more recently, data scientist. I use the umbrella term "analytics professional" to cover all of these titles as well as other related titles.

The inclusion of the term "data scientist" with the others may surprise due to the hype suggesting that it is a new role. However, if you study what people say data scientists do, why they do it, and how they go about doing it, it's really not much different from what great analytics professionals have been doing for years. The primary distinction found in practice between data scientists and other analytics professionals is that data scientists are likely to come from a computer science background, to use Hadoop, and to code in languages like Python or R. This compares to traditional analytics professionals who are likely to come from a statistics, math, or operations research background; and are likely to use relational and analytics server environments and to code in SAS and SQL. Using different platforms or languages doesn't change the underlying skill set and mind-set required to succeed. All of these professionals pursue the same kind of analytics for the same reasons within large companies that pursue innovative analytics.

There have been benefits from the rise of the term "data scientist." For years, when I hired analytics professionals, I'd say "I need a statistician but who also . . ." The key part of the statement is "but who also . . ." The fact is, there are a lot of people with the title "statistician." Many of them aren't working for big companies and aren't creating innovative analytics. They may be in a research or academic role, for example. Therefore, only a subset of those in a "statistician" or "data miner" role drive innovative analytics into a business process and take part in the activities associated with a data scientist.

However, the term "data scientist" is so new that the small group of people who legitimately claim the title mostly fit the mold of what I have always looked for.[2] The image and thought processes associated with the term "data scientist" capture the essence of the "but who also . . ." traits I have always looked for. I like the fact that we finally have a term that gets to the heart of what we should be looking for when we hire analytics professionals (even if I don't like the term itself).

I worked with Talent Analytics and the International Institute for Analytics to survey a wide number of analytics professionals and assess what makes them unique.[3] The quantitative study aimed to answer two questions:

1. Do analytics professionals have a unique, measurable mind-set and raw talent profile?
2. How do analytics professionals spend their time within the analytics workflow?

Results of the study showed that analytics professionals have a clear, measurable raw talent fingerprint. Curiosity and creativity were highest of 11 characteristics measured. Talent Analytics uses this information to help companies understand their existing analytics bench and assess candidates. The study also showed that analytics professionals' time is heavily loaded toward data preparation and programming with less time spent managing, interpreting, visualizing, and presenting results. This finding is very much in line with perception. It is often claimed that 80 percent or more of effort is spent getting ready for analysis.

### Old School and New School Agree

You might first dismiss me as an "old school statistics guy" when I claim data scientists aren't different from other great analytics professionals. However, "new school data scientists" like Simon Zhang from LinkedIn agree. Simon and I both spoke at the Big Analytics conference in Boston in 2012.[4] During his talk, Simon outlined how his team at LinkedIn recruits candidates and what they look for. I remember getting excited because Simon said virtually everything I planned to say with slightly different semantics. Conceptually, we were in total agreement. He enjoyed my talk for the same reason.

---

### Analytics Professionals as Data Artists

Regardless of the label placed on analytics professionals, success depends on factors outside of technical ability. The most valuable people are as much artists as scientists. Hire data artists with the needed technical skills, and you'll build an organization that can succeed with operational analytics.

---

Simon and I had a very intense conversation afterward and realized that we had both assumed that the other might say something different because that's what the hype in the market suggested about "old school" and "new school" analytics professionals. Instead, we thoroughly confirmed each other's approaches and philosophies. This was an important realization because companies shouldn't have to reinvent the analytics wheel just to account for new data and new technologies. It should be possible to borrow from the past, which is a recurring theme in this book.

I always like to say that the very best analytics professionals are artists as much as scientists.[5] Two painters can paint the same scene using different types of paints and styles. Both paintings can be amazing yet totally distinct and unique. Similarly, two great analytics professionals can use different approaches to address the same problem and each produce compelling results. That's because there is artistry all through the analytics process. The artistry is in how the problem is defined, how the analysis is designed, and how the results are communicated. Note that encouraging artistry doesn't mean accepting totally different answers. There is usually only one best answer. The artistry is in the method by which the answer is found.

Both old school and new school analytics professionals agree that companies don't want someone with only technical skills. They need someone who can paint a compelling picture with data. They need data *artists*.

### Solving the Talent Crunch

The rise of analytics professionals is amazing, but it does have a downside. Namely, there is too much demand for the available supply. It is hard to find and keep analytics talent today. As a result, salaries are getting higher as analytics professionals consider multiple job opportunities.[6] A variety of sources, from McKinsey to the *Wall Street Journal*, have predicted even more of a shortage in the future.[7]

New people are looking to get into the field, but it's going to be a while before they have an impact. Whether it's a new graduate who has to gain experience in the workplace or someone making a midcareer switch, it will take time for these people to gain the experience to become great analytics professionals. Let's look at a few ways to find talent.

### Looking Internally

I am often asked whether it's possible simply to shift people from existing roles into analytics professional roles. For example, is it possible to take business intelligence professionals or "Excel jockey" business users and turn them into analytics professionals? Certainly you should look around your organization because it is inexpensive to do so, but the success rate will be low. Migrating existing employees can be part of a plan, but it can't be the only plan.

### A Square Peg Can't Fit a Round Hole

Many organizations consider turning existing employees into analytics professionals. This can work for a small percentage of employees but not for enough to make it a viable stand-alone plan. Look outside for professionals who have the natural skills and experience required.

The mind-set and skills required to be an analytics professional at a large corporation are hard to find. A lot of the people who fit the profile will already be analytics professionals. If an organization has 20 people to consider shifting into an analytics role, perhaps a few will be able to make the transition. Even for those few, it will take time for them to become productive. Realistically, most of the growth of an analytics organization will come from external hires bringing the right background from the start.

### Analytics Certification

Analytics certifications are now available. The most prominent today is the Certified Analytics Professional (CAP) program sponsored by the Institute for Operations Research and the Management Sciences (INFORMS).[8] The CAP program focuses on five Es:

1. **Exam.** Every certification has an exam. The exam, out of necessity, focuses primarily on technical skills.
2. **Experience.** To be a certified analytics professional, experience is needed. Employers want to know they are hiring a person who has a portfolio of past real-world projects.
3. **Ethics.** Many disciplines, from Certified Public Accountants to medical professionals, have codes of ethics. Analytics professionals need guidelines on how to produce and deliver analytics ethically.
4. **Education.** A relevant educational background has clear benefit.
5. **Effectiveness.** This requirement ties to soft skills and ensures that certified professionals have more than just technical skills and a degree.

The effectiveness criterion is what led me to agree to be a volunteer on the CAP advisory board. As we've already discussed, being a great analytics professional isn't just about technical skills. It's also about soft skills like communication and persuasion. To be certified, candidates have to provide validation that they are able to present and position results effectively. The effectiveness criterion will certainly evolve over time, but the fact that it is a part of the CAP program is terrific. As analytics certification becomes common, it will provide another way for employers to identify solid candidates.

## Analytics Degree Programs

Another recent trend is the establishment of analytics degree programs at both graduate and undergraduate levels at major universities. In 2008 or 2009, I became aware of the first of these programs. As of early 2014, the last list I saw was dozens of universities long, and I know that the list was incomplete. This trend shows that the academic world recognizes the demand for people who understand analytics. Over time, these programs will help address the talent crunch. What differentiates many of today's programs is that they focus on a different mix of skills from traditional statistics, operations research, or business degrees.

In my undergraduate and graduate statistics programs, the focus on technical skills rated 10 on a scale of 10, while the focus on the practical or business applications of statistics rated 0 out of 10. The only time business was ever mentioned in my program was in our textbook examples that had artificially clean data supposedly supporting a business problem. However, our task was to invert a matrix or perform other technical tasks. Business really had nothing to do with it other than a cover story. Similarly, most traditional business degrees have a 10 on a scale of 10 focus on business topics and only perhaps a 1 out of 10 focus on technical topics. An MBA program may require an introductory statistics course, but most traditional business degrees don't focus on the technical skills analytics professionals require at all.

### Balancing Educational Programs

A new type of university degree is rapidly proliferating. Hybrid analytics degrees that focus on both business and technical disciplines are turning out well-prepared graduates with the right mix of skills. Make a point to research the programs near you and start recruiting from them.

What is compelling about these new analytics programs is that they provide enough depth on both technical and business topics to create well-rounded graduates. These degrees yield graduates who have seven out of ten abilities in both the technical and the business arenas. I would much rather hire people who rate seven on technical skills and seven on business skills and try to evolve them into tens in each than to start with people who have all the technical skills but

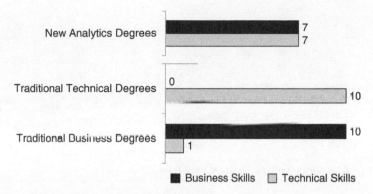

Figure 8.1    Analytics Degrees versus Regular Degrees

none of the business skills required, or the reverse. See Figure 8.1 for an illustration. I started with a ten technical, zero business background and it took a lot of effort and time for me to develop my business skills.

I went to one of the largest and most respected statistics programs in the country at North Carolina State University (NCSU). NCSU also happens to be one of the first schools to offer an MS in analytics. To illustrate how much I support these new programs, I would go first to NCSU's new analytics degree program to look for employees. Although I am loyal to the statistics department, the nature of the analytics program and the way it is targeted to what companies need wins me over. Others must agree with me, because the starting salary for NCSU analytics graduates has rivaled or surpassed top-tier business schools in recent years, according to the program's staff.

### Cover All the Bases

As the demand for different analytics disciplines, different types of data, and different tools rises, it is increasingly difficult for any individual to be proficient at all of it. Today it is necessary to focus on building a team that together covers all the bases, even though the individuals do not. Imagine a pie with multiple slices, as shown in Figure 8.2. One person may cover three or four of the pie slices while another person covers another three or four slices. When the two people are combined on a project team, between them they cover everything needed.

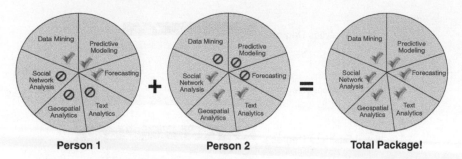

Figure 8.2    Covering All the Bases on an Analytics Team

A real-world example of covering the bases in this manner involves one of the analytics teams at my company. The team began receiving a lot of requests for search optimization support. Nobody on the team had that experience, so when it was time to hire a new person, the primary goal was to get someone with search optimization experience to close that skills gap. The new employee obviously had other skills as well, but the priority was to make sure that the team's search optimization gap was covered.

It isn't necessary to have individuals cover all the bases alone anyway. Study any sports competition from the Super Bowl in American football, to the World Cup in soccer (football to everyone outside the U.S.!), to the NCAA basketball championships. A tournament champion usually has only one or two players selected for the all-star team, and sometimes the champion doesn't have any all-stars. This is because how the team plays together matters more than the individual players. If the 11 best players in the world were actually put on a soccer field together, the team might not do very well because a team can't have 11 captains trying to control the game.

I am not suggesting that standards should be lowered any more than a championship team lowers its standards by not having 100 percent all-stars. Everybody on a championship team is able to play at that level, or they wouldn't be on the team. However, most of the players on the championship team could just as easily have been on a mid-ranked team, and most of the players on a mid-ranked team could just as easily have been on the championship team. Similarly, while an organization needs a team of top-notch analytics professionals, they don't all have to be world renowned all-stars.

### Maximizing Retention

Given how hard it is to find great analytics professionals, an organization certainly wants to retain those it hires. Attrition is a fact of life since analytics professionals are in high demand. The key is to minimize attrition by understanding what motivates and keeps analytics professionals happy.

I've talked to a lot of analytics professionals about what's led them to leave a job, and the Talent Analytics study previously mentioned also looked into the topic.[9] One of the primary reasons analytics professionals leave their jobs is because they get bored and they're not being challenged. I once left a job where I liked the company, I liked the people I worked with, and I really didn't have a problem with anything other than I was getting bored. It is easy to bring in top talent by getting them excited about an interesting upcoming project or two, but there must be more beyond that so people don't leave to find something more interesting once the initial projects are complete. Encouraging analytics professionals to move between business units over time can help keep boredom away by providing the opportunity to work with different parts of the organization on different types of problems.

Developing and communicating career paths is also critically important. One of the biggest advantages of having a formal analytics organization is the critical mass it builds. The bigger the team, the more career path options there will be. Starting with the first interview, ensure that analytics professionals understand the long-term opportunities available to them. Also help them understand the difference that they can make to the organization. Everyone wants to feel like they are contributing more than just a bunch of numbers.

A customer confided in me in late 2013 that his organization was really frustrated about losing three different candidates in the two months before we spoke. When I asked why that had happened, he said it wasn't that the pay was not competitive or that the initial projects they would work on were not exciting. The candidates said his company hadn't effectively given them a longer-term view of how they would fit in the organization and what their career paths would be. If they joined for the good pay to work on the initial great projects, where would they go from there? Other companies painted a better long-term picture and won the battle for the candidates.

> ### Pay Matters, But It Isn't All that Matters
>
> Analytics professionals want to be paid fairly, but pay often isn't their biggest concern. Nothing drives analytics professionals away faster than being bored and not seeing a long-term career path. They also want to be appreciated and feel they are having an impact.

Pay is not the primary motivation for most analytics professionals, but it is important. It isn't possible to pay analytics professionals 30 percent less than the market rate and expect to keep them for too long. A salary study by Burtch Works revealed average pay rates across different levels and different industries.[10] Seek out this type of information before starting the hiring process to make sure you will offer what it takes to win a candidate. Human resource teams must understand that an analytics professional at a given level of experience may require higher pay than the typical employee at that level. Organizations must match the market or they are wasting their time.

## Organizing

Once analytics professionals become part of an organization, it is necessary to organize them in a way that enables optimal impact. Deploying operational analytics throughout a company without an analytics organization to support such initiatives isn't possible. In this section, we walk through some challenges and recommendations related to structuring and organizing analytics teams. Every chance I have to discuss this topic with a customer, I reinforce that focusing on getting the right people in place should be the first priority. The organization won't matter if the right people are not part of it.

### What Standard Structure?

As of 2014, there is no standard structure for analytics organizations. In fact, the way companies organize analytics teams is all over the map. For those who haven't studied this issue, that may be surprising, but it is true. Customers frequently ask me what other organizations have done. I've seen so many different structures that it is hard to recall them all, but that doesn't mean that there aren't more and less effective ways to organize an analytics organization.

There is a logical reason why no standard analytics organizational structure exists. Consider a function like human resources (HR). HR has been an embedded part of virtually every company for decades. Because of that, standard HR structures have evolved. Almost every midsize or large company in any industry will have a vice president of HR. Under that vice president will be a director of benefits, a director of recruiting, and so forth. Similarly, chief financial officers (CFOs) have mostly standardized organizations. Under a CFO will be a team handling compliance, a team handling audit, a team handling accounts payable, and so forth. Given the maturity and ubiquity of HR and CFO organizations, standards have arisen. The problem with analytics is that the discipline hasn't been around as long and so hasn't yet become standardized.

### Recommended Structure

I recommend that organizations evolve over time to have analytics professionals assigned to the company's various business or functional units supported by a centralized team of corporate-level analytics professionals. This represents a mix of centralized and decentralized models and often is referred to as a hybrid or center of excellence model. See Figure 8.3 for an illustration. This approach has a number of advantages and also some disadvantages, but overall this structure will support a company's analytics needs.

Advantages of a hybrid model include the fact that each business or functional unit will have the dedicated resources it needs, as well as additional resources available to handle corporate

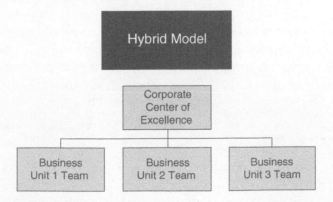

**Figure 8.3   Hybrid Organizational Structure**

initiatives, provide additional business unit support, and ensure consistency of approach. The hybrid model will provide economies of scale both from career development and cost perspectives. Tactically, for example, a company can negotiate for bulk software licenses across all teams rather than having each business unit's team negotiating its own. Disadvantages include the fact that a hybrid structure adds complexity, and there is potential for politics between the central and business unit teams. It is important not to allow analytics professionals within one unit to feel isolated. Everyone needs trusted people to bounce ideas off of and to go to for guidance.

> ### Lack of a Standard Structure Doesn't Mean All Structures Are Equal
>
> Just because there is not yet a standard, widely accepted analytics organizational structure doesn't mean that all choices are equal. A hybrid model is proving to be most effective for a broad range of organizations.

One decision that often concerns people is where the resources assigned to each business unit report within a hybrid structure. They can report directly to the centralized team with a dotted line to their business unit, or they can report directly to their business unit with a dotted line to the centralized team. While some prefer a central reporting structure, I'm not sure that where the unit teams report matters too much.[11] The politics and culture in any given organization can dictate what will work best. The important part is that regardless of who generates official performance appraisals, the business units have to perceive that certain analytics professionals are theirs alone and are part of their teams. Similarly, the analytics professionals who are embedded in a unit have to understand that they're also part of a bigger corporate team that reaches beyond the specific business unit. If those mind-sets are in place, the official reporting relationship won't matter that much.

### Evolving to a Hybrid Model

Although the hybrid model for analytics teams is best for mature organizations, virtually no organization starts there. An organization must have a critical mass of analytics professionals in place before it makes sense, or is even possible, to put a hybrid model in place. Typically, the process starts when one business unit first decides analytics support is needed. As a result, the team hires its first (and the company's first) analytics professional. Over time, that team adds a few more analytics professionals and has some success with analytics. Eventually, other business units hear about all the great things happening with analytics in the first unit, and they want to have their own analytics teams too. So the other units hire some analytics professionals, and this leads to a decentralized structure.

Almost invariably, therefore, organizations start with a decentralized model. Eventually enough analytics professionals are employed across the company that somebody realizes that organizing them differently might be necessary to make the most of the investment. By ensuring that your organization thinks about its analytics structure sooner rather than later, you will force conversation about an analytics strategy and get a solid structure in place more quickly.

## Landing in the Right Spot

Part of deciding how to structure an analytics organization is determining where the central team reports. It is becoming common to place analytics under a leader whose role naturally spans business units, such as a chief strategy officer, chief operating officer (COO), or chief financial officer (CFO).

One last question to address is where the analytics organization's central team reports. I have seen teams report almost everywhere over the years. Eventually, a chief analytics officer (CAO) may report directly to the chief executive officer (CEO). Today, that is not usually the case. One recent line of thought that I've become fond of is the idea of putting analytics under the corporate strategy team because the strategy team is like Switzerland. The strategy team is neutral, naturally works with every business unit, and is an accepted part of every team, just like analytics professionals should be. Equally important is the fact that analytics are strategic and need to be viewed that way. If an organization's major focus is on operational analytics, the COO is also a good spot for the analytics team. The CFO's organization is another neutral location to consider.

> ### Centralize the Costs, Spread the Gains
>
> One advantage of having a corporate component to an analytics organization is the ability to strategically fund projects that would not be affordable to individual business units. By building a process centrally and then deploying it broadly, all business units can reap the benefits.

One benefit of a hybrid model is critically important because it helps drive value. To explain the benefit via illustrative example, let's consider a hotel company with four distinct hotel brands. Any given brand will fund and sponsor only analytics that pay off for that brand. However, there are analytics that can be done across brands that are immensely valuable at a corporate level. There are also analytics that can help each individual brand, but not enough for a single brand to pay to develop the analytics by itself. The corporate-level analytics team can sponsor analytics in these situations. Perhaps the return for any single brand is only half the cost of building a new analytics process. Under those terms, no brand would fund it. However, if the corporate team sponsors the process and deploys it to all four brands, the same cost yields that 50 percent payback four times, and the total benefits make the process a winner.

### Do You Need a Chief Analytics Officer?

If there is going to be an analytics organization, somebody has to be in charge of it. Companies should consider creating a CAO or similar executive position, such as a vice president of analytics.[12] An organization must have an executive-level leader who is the clear owner of all things analytics. Ask people in any company who owns financials, and they'll quickly point to the CFO. Ask who owns marketing, and they'll point to the chief marketing officer. Ask who owns analytics, and they'll either look at you blankly or provide widely varying answers. That is not good.

When I first started in my career, there was debate around whether organizations needed a chief information officer (CIO), but it is now a rare organization that doesn't have a CIO. Clearly, it has been determined that a CIO is both relevant and needed. Today people wonder if there is a need for a CAO. Over the coming years, we're going to see CAOs become much more common. Perhaps in the future CAOs will be as ubiquitous as CIOs. The first event aimed at topics relevant to CAOs that I am aware of was sponsored in summer 2013 by the International Institute for Analytics (IIA). It had over 200 attendees! Not all attendees were CAOs, but all were interested in the concept. The IIA and I were both pleasantly surprised at the strong turnout.

---

### Who Is the Face of Analytics in Your Organization?

If an organization doesn't have a CAO, chances are that nobody is taking ownership of analytics or has the authority to do so. Establishing an executive role for analytics is necessary to formalize analytics as a corporate priority and to establish a champion for the cause.

---

Ideally, analytics managers and executives, regardless of title, will understand analytics and will have a hands-on analytics background. In particular, the first layer or two of management overseeing analytics professionals should be comprised of people who understand how analytics work and how to build analytics processes. Without this background, it's virtually impossible for managers to guide junior members of the team in the right direction. This is especially true when pushing into new areas like operational analytics.

Higher up the chain, it may be possible to have leaders who aren't hardcore analytics professionals by training if they thoroughly understand analytics concepts. Equally important at the executive level is the ability to navigate the politics and corporate culture issues that will certainly be faced as the team focuses on making analytics operational. We address this more in Chapter 9. Having top-down support from not just a CAO but the CEO and executive leadership team is necessary to force the changes that enable analytics to drive value in any organization. The CAO must be the face of analytics for the company and must be a part of the decision process for major initiatives. The position represents the arrival of analytics as a core, strategic part of what a company does.

### What about a Chief Data Officer?

Another title that has been rising in prominence is chief data officer (CDO). I am often asked about the distinction between a CDO and a CAO. Are they the same? No. Based on the job descriptions I've

Table 8.1    Chief Analytics Officer and Chief Data Officer Roles

| Chief Analytics Officer | Chief Data Officer |
| --- | --- |
| Reports to the business | Reports to IT |
| Determines what analysis should be done | Determines what data to acquire |
| Guides deployment of analytics | Governs and makes data available for analytics |
| Documents value driven by analytics | Provides infrastructure in support of analytics |
| Works closely with the CDO | Works closely with the CAO |

seen, however, a lot of companies are inadvertently combining these two roles into one and using one title when they really should be using the other.

As Table 8.1 shows, a CDO is an IT role that typically reports to the CIO. The CDO focuses on the acquisition of data, the governance of data, and making data available for analysis through appropriate tools and infrastructure. The CAO, however, typically reports to the business. Given that data is available for analysis, a CAO is focused on what analysis should be done, how it should be deployed and made operational, and how to derive value for the business through analytics. The CAO and CDO roles meet in the middle at data availability.

Clearly, these two executives must work very closely together, and their fates are highly intertwined. They are the strongest link between the IT and business sides of the organization, and they must have a partnership. It's theoretically possible, particularly for smaller organizations, that one person can play both the CAO and the CDO roles. However, it's important to understand the two distinct roles being played. I have seen various job descriptions that appear to be looking for one of these roles while actually labeling it as the other. Companies need to be clear on what they are looking for because not only are the roles different, but the people with the right experience for the roles are different as well.

### Consider a Cross-Functional Team

Thus far, we've discussed an analytics organization as though it is comprised only of full-time analytics professionals. Having a team of just analytics professionals can be fine, but there are other possibilities to consider. The analytics team may need additional skill sets embedded within it if it's going to be as impactful as possible. Some companies have responded to this consideration by substantially expanding the scope of the analytics organization. For example, I visited with a large cellular company in Europe in 2012. This company realized that it needed a lot of analytics to support its marketing and customer service efforts, including everything from deep analytics to reporting. To address the needs, it created an analytics organization with a larger span than most.

A broad analytics team was formed under an executive leader. The team included not just deep analytics professionals but everyone required to deliver the analytics processes desired. Therefore, the team included business intelligence professionals to build and deploy reports on top of the analytics processes. The team also owned the underlying systems used for the analytics. This meant that database and systems administrators who would usually report to IT were included on the team.

The idea was to give the team control of everything it needed to succeed and to empower the team with authority, not just responsibility. In addition to having responsibility for creating analytics, the team had full authority to do whatever was needed to get things done across the entire span of the analytics cycle. This cut through red tape and political disputes and focused everyone on meeting the analytics needs of the organization.

A broader, cross-functional team is a very interesting model to consider. Over time, such a model may become more common than it is today. However, it's a more mature, more complex model to implement than an organization comprised mostly of analytics professionals. Most companies will start by putting in place the base analytics team before expanding it more broadly.

## Succeeding

Once an analytics organization is in place and staffed, it will need to operate in a fashion that allows it to have maximum impact. Some of the considerations relate to the analytics process, but others are political and organizational in nature. In this section, we dive into several themes that can help an analytics organization operate efficiently and effectively.

### Leverage External Resources Intelligently

Companies often ask me whether analytics should be outsourced if an organization doesn't have an analytics competency. And, if so, how the external resources should be leveraged. Leveraging external resources can add a lot of value because outsiders bring in fresh perspectives and expertise in areas in which an organization does not have strength. However, while external resources can cover gaps in the short term, outsourcing all aspects of analytics should not be a long-term plan.

Outsourcing the execution of analytics in the long run is okay, but an organization must own the strategy, design, and planning around its analytics initiatives. When getting started, it is fine to use external consultants to help develop an initial strategy and build some initial analytics processes. The key to success is that the contract with the consultants should make clear that they will fully transfer all knowledge, analytics logic, and code back to the organization. As the organization ramps up, it must understand everything the consultants did and why, must own whatever analytics processes have been built, and must be able eventually to take the processes over.

> ### You Must Own Your Analytics Strategy
>
> Outsource tactical execution if you must, but under no circumstance should you outsource analytics strategy and design except when first getting started. Manufacturers don't outsource their strategy and design either, only the manufacturing process itself.

Owning the analytics strategy and design is critically important. If analytics is going to be something core and strategic, a company has to know what's happening and why. High-tech manufacturers don't outsource the design and planning of new products because it is too strategic and important to their business. Manufacturers do outsource the manufacturing process itself in many cases, but that is easy to do if you own the strategy and design. You can bet that while Apple has the iPhone manufactured overseas, the design happened within corporate walls at headquarters. In fact, look at an iPhone or iPad and it will say "Designed by Apple in California, assembled in China." Similarly, an organization's analytics must be designed in internally.

Another way to think of the point above is to consider the design and construction of a new home. You will want to be intimately involved in the design of your home. You'll want to know exactly how the rooms are configured and what type of fixtures will be installed. Once all those details are laid out, any reasonably competent contractor can put up the drywall or lay the tile. Similarly, imagine that you've designed an operational analytics process and defined how it will work, how it will be integrated with other applications, and exactly what analytics methods are to be used. You can then hire external resources to go through the process of coding and testing. As long as you understand what they are coding and why, you'll be able to ensure that it is done right.

### To Succeed, Follow Through

As an analytics organization attempts to increase its profile and impact, it must realize that completing an analysis is just one step on the path to success. A billion-dollar opportunity discovered through analytics can be placed on the CEO's desk, but if no action is taken, then no value is added. Analytics professionals tend to want to move onto the next cool project instead of seeing the current project through to the end. A successful analytics organization will set up a process to guide projects all the way to implementation and also set the clear expectation that people will follow through to implementation. Next we discuss several necessary tasks in addition to generating an analytics result.

First is marketing and public relations (PR). A huge component of an analytics organization's job is undertaking marketing and PR efforts to socialize and make people aware of the results that have been found and the implications of those results. The team must let people know that it has found a tremendous opportunity, why it is important to the business, and the impact the analysis can have.

In some cases, the marketing and PR effort will extend beyond the organization's walls and out to the public. Consider popular websites like Amazon or Netflix. Not only do these companies socialize the importance of new recommendation engines internally, but they reach out to the public and invite customers to come back to their sites to see how the updated recommendation engines enhance their experiences. Once analytics are a core component of a business and a competitive differentiator, customers will look forward to hearing what is coming next.

A second area that requires attention is laying out a plan for ongoing process support. With traditional batch analytics of the past, the support for an analytics process was pretty straightforward. If I built it, I owned it. If it broke, I fixed it. If someone had a question, I answered it. Because a process was run in batch on an infrequent basis, that was a feasible, though not ideal, model. With operational analytics, that model won't work since it is about embedding an analytics process deeply within operational systems and having a broad range of front-line employees and applications leveraging that analytics process.

### It Can't All Be Fun and Games

Many analytics professionals dislike activities that take away from doing analysis. Unfortunately, success depends on a number of things that have nothing to do with the quality or value of the analytics. Priority must be given to things like marketing findings and developing support models in order for a discovery to reach its potential. A winning analytics organization understands this.

It is therefore necessary to develop a support model in terms of who will monitor a process and who is going to maintain its code. However, it is also necessary to consider what will happen when people have questions about how to interpret the decisions being driven by the analytics or about other ways to apply the results of the analytics process within the business. Someone must be made available for such inquiries. If the time isn't allocated up front, it can lead to major resource crunches.

A third area that requires follow-through is planning and overseeing the deployment of the analytics process. Once an opportunity has been identified, a lot of work is needed to complete an operational implementation. The analytics organization must help develop a project plan, manage the execution of the plan, and aid in the testing and validation effort to ensure that everything works before the process is turned on in an operational setting.

The implementation process is not something that analytics professionals typically like to do, but they are going to have to do it to succeed with operational analytics. Assigning a professional project manager who is good at managing implementations can be a good idea. However, the analytics organization will have to support the project manager from start to finish.

A final area needing attention is the management of change and adjustment to corporate culture necessitated by analytics. This is covered in Chapter 9. The important takeaway from this section is that without follow-through to ensure that a discovery is implemented, the discovery is worthless.

### Managing Expectations Effectively

Managing expectations effectively is a critical skill that analytics organizations must have. The same point applies to a broad range of disciplines, but it can be especially important with analytics. I had a customer confide in me over dinner that his team had taken a big political hit after completing an analysis. It was not because the results were bad. In fact, the results were very good. The problem was that the team had promised an amazing result but achieved only a very good result. That led the business sponsors to be disappointed.

This example is quite similar to how the stock market works today. If the market is expecting a company to double earnings, but earnings increase only by 80 percent, the stock can experience a large drop in price. It's all about expectations. Making big promises is especially risky when pursuing a new and innovative discovery with analytics. Because success is far from guaranteed, it is necessary to ensure that the sponsors of the effort fully understand the risks and likelihood of success.

When asked to begin a discovery process to explore an idea, an analytics organization shouldn't promise success in proving the idea works. Rather, it should promise a thorough investigation and a clear resolution as to whether the idea will work or not. Guaranteeing that the idea will work isn't possible because the idea hasn't been explored yet. However, it is possible to guarantee resolution. Providing a well-documented summary of why an idea didn't work (in the cases it does not) can add to a growing body of knowledge about what analytics the organization's data can support.

Tied to this theme is the fact that the best thing to do is always to underpromise and overdeliver. Following this guideline has helped me in my career immensely. I try to be very realistic from the start and leave room to delight a project sponsor. If sponsors expect a 100 percent return and only get 90 percent, they are disappointed. If expectations are set at 80 percent and the same 90 percent is delivered, then they are excited. If people will buy in to an effort only if grandiose commitments are made, you must be confident that you can achieve those grandiose commitments or you shouldn't pursue the project at all. There is just too much downside with very little upside. It doesn't do anybody any good to underdeliver so always leave room to delight a project's sponsors.

---

### Don't Satisfy, Delight!

No matter how strong the results from an analytics effort are, success can depend heavily on how results compare to expectations. Always leave room to delight the sponsors of a project. Repeatedly overpromising and underdelivering will undermine an analytics organization's credibility.

---

Let me provide a real example of delighting a project sponsor. A few years ago, my team was hired to build a customer segmentation model for a large customer. When I submitted the statement of work, the project sponsor told me that she needed the project to have a fixed fee instead of an hourly billing structure. Due to budget constraints, she needed to know exactly what her costs would be because she couldn't afford any overruns. I told her that we could charge a fixed fee but that we would have to add 20 percent to our estimates to account for the additional risk that my company would face. She was fine with that, and the project proceeded.

We finished the project right on the original budget because we had scoped it carefully, and we could have walked away with an extra 20 percent profit. However, we sat down as a team and discussed what additional work would truly delight the customer. We decided to spend half of the risk pool to do additional analytics that were not part of our statement of work and that were not expected. We still made an extra 10 percent profit, and the client was absolutely thrilled with what we delivered, which led to more work. We left room to delight our sponsor, and it paid off. It was a win all around.

### Be Consultants, Mentors, and Coaches

If an analytics organization is to be a strategic component of a business the team must have the right mindset. When I started in my career, there was immense pressure at times to be an order taker. I was the nerd in the cube downstairs, and business sponsors sometimes expected to tell me what to do and that I would just go do it. The flaw in this approach is that the people asking me to do things didn't understand how the analytics worked like I did. I found it frustrating to have others tell me how to do my job.

An effective enterprise analytics organization must view itself as a team of consultants, mentors, and coaches, not order takers. When a business partner requests specific actions, the team must think about what has been asked and why. How does the request fit with what is known about the business? How does it match to the data and the tools available? Is the request as submitted the best way to address the underlying question or problem? Some pushback may be necessary. Someone may need to go back and say, "I understand you're asking for A, B, and C. In order to reach your goal, however, we'd recommend doing D, E, and F instead because that is the best path to success. Please let me explain why."

Analytics professionals must take ownership of designing a solution that meets the business team's goals. Consult with the business to understand its needs and explain the proposed solution. Mentor the business to help its leaders understand how to apply the analytics. Coach them on what details to provide in a request to enable the most efficient response. By doing that, the business team will come to trust and value the analytics team's input and over time will stop trying to give orders. Eventually business team members will come to the analytics organization, relay their problem, and leave it to the experts to figure out how to solve it.

### Think Like a Referee

I played soccer for 30 years. As my knees finally gave out, I shifted to being a referee. I learned a tremendous lesson from the senior referee who ran my certification class. Not only did it help me be a better referee, but it also helped me be a better analytics professional.

The instructor told the class that if we were going to make a call, we had to do it quickly and with confidence. Referees have to trust their judgment and be decisive. A good referee should be confident that he will make the right call almost 100 percent of the time. Players, coaches, and spectators will be able to tell very quickly whether a referee is competent and confident. Once the crowd sees that a referee clearly has confidence and has been making the right calls, they will be much more forgiving when a rare mistake is made because it will clearly be the exception. If a referee is seen struggling with what calls to make and delaying the whistles, people will feel justified in protesting. Delaying a call is a sign of weakness and indecision, and it isn't possible to command respect while projecting those traits.

> ### Make the Call!
>
> To be successful, analytics organizations must be willing to take a stand and make calls. Just as referees are expected to make calls in a game, analytics professionals are expected to make calls related to analytics by providing firm recommendations and standing behind results. If you don't have confidence in your findings, then how can anyone else?

This same advice can be utilized by an analytics organization. When asked to solve a problem, the team should be confident and recommend a path. Then, when results are in, the team should confidently present and explain the results and what the results imply. Finally, the team must take a stand and provide specific recommendations for action. The analytics organization will be respected for following this approach, and business sponsors will gain trust in the team.

Project sponsors won't always agree with the recommendations that the analytics organization makes, and sometimes they'll go in a different direction. This is no different from spectators believing that a different call should have been made in a game. However, the analytics team owes it to the business sponsors to take a stand because business sponsors have a lot of other things to worry about. The more the analytics team can enable business sponsors to stop worrying about how to interpret detailed data and analysis results by handling it for them, the better.

### The Wrong Incentives Can Be Costly

Incentives are always important. As an organization makes analytics operational, incentives aligned to the right goals are critical because once analytics are embedded in an operational process, the impact of setting them up incorrectly can be significant. When building an analytics process, is the primary goal to make it easily embeddable? Or is it about the process's performance? Or is it the consistency of the process? Or is it something else?

Setting clear objectives for analytics professionals both annually and on a project level is important. Projects focused on discovery have different goals and different criteria for success than projects aimed at implementing discoveries operationally. People tasked with discovery, for example, should be incented to experiment and look for new things. They should do that efficiently and build prototypes rapidly. People tasked with making a process operational need to do a thorough job of optimizing the speed and efficiency of the process and getting the process fully tested to ensure stability. Naturally, these goals tie to the discussions of governance in Chapter 6.

There are examples where the wrong organizational incentives around analytics have cost a lot of money. For example, tax fraud is a major issue in the United States. One of the biggest types of tax fraud is when fraudsters steal someone's Social Security number, submit a return in the person's name, and receive a big refund.[13] This has become a multibillion-dollar business (if you want to call it a business).[14] Unfortunately, the incentives that the Internal Revenue Service (IRS) has in place perpetuate the problem rather than fix it.[15]

What I am about to explain is public knowledge, so I am not giving away confidential information. When I had some meetings with the IRS, I asked how people could file a totally bogus tax return, given that the IRS has everyone's income and tax payments as reported by their employers, financial institutions, and other income providers. If a tax return's figures don't match what was reported, it can be easily flagged for review, no? That sounds great, but although employer data is received early in the year, it isn't available for analysis until months later, after tax returns are due. Basically, for the entire tax filing season, the IRS can't match employer and taxpayer income and payment information to validate returns before sending out refunds. Sounds crazy, right?

Worse, the IRS is incented and directed to pay refunds as quickly as possible. When someone asks for money, the IRS aims to give it to them fast. This is true even though it is fully understood that billions of dollars in fraud will occur as a result of not performing more basic fraud analysis. The goal is quick customer service, and the IRS hits that goal while costing taxpayers billions.

To make matters even worse, it is possible to do some very solid fraud analysis even if this year's data is not available yet. In my case, I've been with the same company for a number of years earning the same general amount of money while living in the same state. If a tax return is filed in my name from a different state listing a different employer and with an income that differs substantially from what I made in the past, then that should be a red flag. There's plenty of historical data to help the IRS identify potentially fraudulent returns, but little to no analysis is done. Instead, speedy payment of refunds takes precedence.

If the IRS changed incentives to balance speed of payment with time to perform elementary fraud checks, it would save a lot of money. Given that paying a refund typically takes days, the decision time is long enough to do plenty of analysis before money is paid. Instead, analytics end up focused on trying to identify bogus returns *after* the refunds are already paid. Incentives should encourage the intelligent use of analytics, not bypass analytics altogether.

## Wrap-Up

The most important lessons to take away from this chapter are:

- The value of analytics professionals is now widely accepted. Instead of questioning whether analytics talent is needed, organizations are now focused on how to organize and expand the talent they have.
- All analytics professionals, regardless of title, share the same core traits, many of which have nothing to do with technical ability.
- Migrating existing employees to an analytics professional role is generally not a winning strategy. Bringing in external talent with the right background and experience must be a large part of the plan.
- No one person will be proficient in every analytics discipline. A team can cover all needs by hiring individuals who each cover some of the needs.
- Pay is important to analytics professionals, but the key to retaining them is to keep them from getting bored and offer a long-term career paths.
- Although there is not yet a standard structure for analytics organizations, a hybrid model with both centralized and business unit support will win out over time.

- The central component of the team enables the development of analytics processes that have high value at a corporate level but that wouldn't pay off for any individual business unit.
- Both chief analytics officers and chief data officers are becoming more common, and the roles are distinct. It is important to distinguish between the roles even if one person tries to fill them both.
- Outsourcing execution is fine, but in the long run, an organization must own and drive its analytics strategy and the design of analytics processes.
- The job isn't over when an analysis is done. Work such as marketing the results and building a support model for the operational process must also be completed to enable maximum impact.
- Managing expectations effectively by underpromising and overdelivering is crucial. A successful project can be viewed negatively if unrealistic expectations are set and then not met.
- Analytics professionals must be consultants, mentors, and coaches as opposed to order takers, and they must take a stand when needed. They won't be viewed as experts if they don't act like experts.

## Notes

1. See Thomas H. Davenport and D. J. Patil, "Data Scientist: The Sexiest Job of the 21st Century," *Harvard Business Review* (October 2012) at http://hbr.org/2012/10/data-scientist-the-sexiest-job-of-the-21st-century/ar/1; Jessi Hempel, "The Hot Tech Gig of 2022: Data Scientist," *CNNMoney*, January 6, 2012, at http://tech.fortune.cnn.com/2012/01/06/data-scientist-jobs/; Gil Press, "Data Scientists: The Definition of Sexy," *Forbes*, September 27, 2012, at www.forbes.com/sites/gilpress/2012/09/27/data-scientists-the-definition-of-sexy/.
2. I covered the traits that differentiate great analytics professionals in Chapter 8 of *Taming the Big Data Tidal Wave* (Hoboken, NJ: John Wiley & Sons, 2012). Instead of rehashing the details here, I'll refer readers there and move on to some additional information that confirms my points in that book.
3. See Talent Analytics "Four Functional Clusters of Analytics Professionals," July 2013; see also International Institute for Analytics, "Quantifying Analytical Talent" research brief (January 2013).
4. For the agenda, see www.biganalytics2012.com/boston.html.
5. Based on my International Institute for Analytics blog "Keep Your Data Scientist . . . Send Me a Data Artist!" February 6, 2012. See http://iianalytics.com/2012/02/keep-your-data-scientistsend-me-a-data-artist/.
6. See Burtch Works, "The Burtch Works Study: Salaries for Big Data Professionals" (July 2013), at www.burtchworks.com/register_study.php.

7. See McKinsey & Company, "Big Data: The Next Frontier for Competition," at www.mckinsey.com/Features/Big_Data; see also Ben Rooney, "Big Data's Big Problem: Little Talent," *Wall Street Journal*, April 29, 2012, at http://online.wsj.com/news/articles/SB10001424052702304723304577365700368073674.

8. For purposes of full disclosure, I am a member of the advisory board for this program. For information, see https://www.informs.org/Certification-Continuing-Ed/Analytics-Certification.

9. I covered the traits that differentiate great analytics professionals in Chapter 8 of *Taming the Big Data Tidal Wave*. Instead of rehashing the details here, I'll refer readers there and move on to some additional information that confirms my points in that book.

10. See Burtch Works, "The Burtch Works Study."

11. See Tom H. Davenport, "Organizing Analytics and Big Data," International Institute for Analytics, September 23, 2013, at http://iianalytics.com/2013/09/organizing-analytics-and-big-data/.

12. See Brad Brown, David Court, and Paul Willmott, "Mobilizing Your C-Suite for Big Data Analytics," from *McKinsey Quarterly* (November 2012), at www.mckinsey.com/Insights/Business_Technology/Mobilizing_your_C_suite_for_big_data_analytics.

13. See David Adams, "Florida Hit by 'Tsunami' of Tax Identity Fraud," Reuters, February 17, 2013, at http://www.reuters.com/article/2013/02/17/us-usa-tax-fraud-idUSBRE91G05M20130217.

14. See Tax Policy Center, "The Tax Gap: What Is the Tax Gap?" at www.taxpolicycenter.org/briefing-book/background/tax-gap/what-is.cfm.

15. See Scott Zamost and Randi Kaye, "IRS Policies Help Fuel Tax Refund Fraud, Officials Say," CNN, March 20, 2012, at www.cnn.com/2012/03/20/us/tax-refund-scam/index.html.

# The Analytics Culture

Organizations continuously change and evolve their corporate cultures. The use of analytics has already forced a change of culture in many organizations from one of gut-feel decisions to one of fact-based decisions. Shifting to operational analytics will require even more culture change because of the way that operational analytics are more embedded and automated than analytics of the past.

In this chapter, we explore cultural issues that must be considered as an organization attempts to make analytics operational. Many of the themes apply more broadly both within the analytics space and beyond, and most won't be new to readers. However, the themes all apply and are worth reviewing if an organization is going to succeed with operational analytics. To create an analytics culture that embraces operational analytics, four ingredients are required:

1. Proper mind-set
2. Effective policies
3. Facilitation of success
4. Enabling and handling of failure

## Instilling the Proper Mind-Set

The way people within an organization are encouraged to think sets the tone for everything else that happens. Over time, certain mind-sets permeate an organization, and most people fall in line with what is expected and accepted, whether good or bad. Jolting the status quo and forcing new ways of thinking from time to time is necessary so that complacency doesn't set in. Acknowledging this need is an important step, and being prepared for it is the first part of the battle. Let's start by outlining how mind-sets must be aligned as an organization heads toward operational analytics.

### Learn from Fleas

Let's start with a story about fleas that my customers always enjoy. Yes, you read that right, fleas! I promise this story will make sense if you stick with me. I've seen videos of the experiment we'll discuss on YouTube, but I've never been able to validate if the video is a true story about fleas or just an urban legend.[1] Either way, the story helps to illustrate an important point.

Imagine that you are sitting at your kitchen table with your family and you put an empty baby food jar on the table. Next you drop a spoonful of fleas into that jar. I know, I know, why in the world would you ever do this? Just assume that you do. Did you know that fleas can jump very, very high? They can jump the equivalent of a human jumping hundreds of feet into the air from a standstill. Therefore, the fleas dropped into the jar are going to be able to jump right out and scurry around the kitchen table. Of course your family will scream at you and tell you to clean up the fleas. They'll also ask why in the world you have done such a crazy thing. Just blame it on me!

To placate your family, put a lid on top of the jar to keep the fleas from getting out. Once the lid is in place, the fleas will jump, they'll hit their heads, and they'll fall back down. They'll jump, they'll hit their heads, and they'll fall back down. This will happen again and again. However, even fleas are smart enough to realize that it is silly to keep hitting their heads, and eventually they'll begin to jump just below the level of the lid. This is where things start to get interesting.

### Don't Be a Flea!

Fleas get trapped in a lidless jar because they blindly accept that the lid will always be there and fail to notice when it is removed. Foster a culture where analytics professionals are encouraged and expected to avoid being trapped by outdated assumptions by regularly challenging and validating their assumptions.

The amazing thing is that if you wait for a while and remove the lid, the fleas will never jump out again. They have learned where the lid was, and they jump just below that height. The world is wide open for the fleas to explore if they jumped a little bit higher. However, they never again make the effort simply to look up and validate that that lid blocking escape actually still is there. It is also claimed that baby fleas raised in the jar will learn from the adults how high to jump and will also stay in the jar. The fleas get trapped by learned and outdated assumptions.

Corporate culture can make people act a lot like those fleas. We learn where a company's boundaries are and how it does things, and then we tend never to challenge those facts again. Therefore, outdated assumptions can cause us to miss opportunities that are sitting right in front of us. Worse, as new people are hired, they are assimilated into the company's way of thinking. A lot of what is covered during orientation and training is aimed at making sure new employees understand everything they can and can't do. We effectively teach them where the lid is so that they get stuck in the jar with the rest of us just like the baby fleas.

When shifting to a new way of doing things, such as operational analytics, an organization must encourage employees to rethink and revalidate long-standing assumptions. Perhaps a few years ago it wasn't possible to do what is now required, but it may well be possible today. Look up now and then to validate that the limits you learned are still there so you don't end up like a flea trapped in a jar.

### Embrace Analytics from the Top Down

A culture that embraces analytics has to start from the top. This isn't news, and we've talked about it elsewhere in the book, but it is worthwhile to reiterate some important points here.

The fact is that many traditional analytics processes were able to achieve success with only pockets of support. For many years, as long as a marketing department fully embraced analytics, it was entirely possible for marketing to use analytics successfully. This was true even if other parts of the company didn't care. When I was creating batch analytics processes to support direct mail campaigns years ago, we had to update models only once a month and provide a list of customer identifiers. As long as the executive in charge of the mail campaign supported analytics, we could make it happen. Very few others in the organization had to be aware of or support what we were doing.

Operational analytics can't be implemented in a bubble since it is embedded within business processes and influences actions that impact multiple stakeholders across an organization. It is impossible to keep operational analytics under the radar because there will be too many people from too many parts of the organization impacted to operate in a stealth mode.

Therefore, it is first necessary to get all stakeholders comfortable and willing to go along with the plan to use analytics more aggressively. Starting at the chief executive officer (CEO) level, analytics must be embraced or else it will be incredibly difficult to make progress. The corporate culture must embrace analytics as a clear corporate priority.

### Acknowledge the Value of Analytics Professionals

Chapter 8 discussed the importance of analytics professionals viewing themselves not as order takers but as consultants, coaches, and mentors. There is a flip side to that theme, however. An organization must install a culture that values the input of analytics professionals and that encourages and expects them to play the consultant, coach, and mentor roles. An analytics organization can be focused on playing the role of a consultant, but it won't matter if the teams being supported don't listen to the input provided by the analytics team and give the input the consideration that it deserves.

Business leaders can't see analytics and, by extension, analytics professionals as things that undermine their authority and autonomy. Rather, business leaders need to see analytics professionals for what they really are: valuable tools to help them succeed. If analytics professionals help business leaders succeed, then the leaders' authority and autonomy will increase and grow over time because successful people are given more freedom.

### Everybody Needs a Little Love

Establish a culture where analytics, as well as the professionals generating analytics, are valued. Analytics professionals will be more successful in an environment where they feel appreciated and their opinions and suggestions are taken seriously.

It is impossible to provide valuable consulting and coaching to someone who isn't listening and doesn't value the input. If someone isn't listening, advice may as well be an infomercial playing to an empty room. An organization must make clear that analytics are valuable, that analytics professionals are valuable, and that both should be sought out as part of an important decision process.

Decision makers already have a circle of people they trust to help them make decisions. It's a matter of inviting analytics professionals to become part of that circle. Creating a formal organization and appointing a chief analytics officer as discussed in Chapter 8 are two steps that demonstrate commitment to this approach.

### Facilitate Behavior Change

We discussed in Chapter 8 that having the right recommendation isn't enough because if nothing is done with a recommendation, it provides no value. If operational analytics are to succeed, an organization must make sure that people change behavior and follow the recommendations and decisions that the operational analytics generate. If employees are given the chance to ignore or alter the recommendations from operational analytics, the value obtained will start dropping very quickly. When flaws are identified in an analytics process, then certainly the flaws should be fixed. However, individuals can't be allowed to override and change a process's recommendations on their own.

Consider the example in Chapter 1 of the transportation company that spent heavily to improve the quality of its map database. That database was used to execute highly sophisticated route optimization analytics to change how drivers navigate their daily routes. Naturally, there was some resistance from the drivers because they were used to being in control. To overcome this resistance, the company leveraged the concept of gamification with the analytics.[2] In other words, the company turned the route recommendations into a game for the drivers.

Instead of saying "You must drive this route because the computer says so!" the company took a softer approach and created a game that appealed to the ego of each driver. The drivers were asked, "Can you beat the computer?" Initially the drivers were allowed to deviate from the recommendations if they thought they had a better way. The data on how the deviations worked was then incorporated back into the optimization algorithms.

## Resistance to Change? Gamify Your Analytics!

Getting people to change how they do things is hard. One way to facilitate change is to make the adoption of operational analytics into a game. Front-line employees may have little understanding of how analytics work and may feel threatened. Find ways to turn the changes into fun challenges for employees.

My friend confidentially told me of one particular driver who was averaging 150 miles per day when the initial computer recommendation suggested 140 miles per day. The driver claimed the computer didn't know anything, and he was able to get his mileage down to 135 miles per day. Then the computer updated the recommended route to 130 miles per day. The driver again said the computer didn't know anything, and he hit 125 miles per day. In the end, the driver still complained that the computer didn't know anything because he had beaten it each time. However, his mileage had dropped from 150 to 125 miles per day as a result of the challenge.

The company didn't care whether the driver realized the impact the analytics had on him or not. All that mattered was that the driver's behavior changed and mileage was saved. The company let the driver keep his ego intact as long as his behavior changed for the better. By making the analytics process into a game, the company turned strong resistance into a force for good that achieved the change required.

### Overcome Resistance and Pushback

Like the drivers in the previous example, an organization can expect those impacted by operational analytics to be unhappy with the perceived intrusion upon their authority and autonomy. Not everyone will have this reaction, but it is a safe bet that many will because people naturally rebel against anything that implies that we weren't making the right decisions all along. An organization must make it clear that operational analytics aren't needed because people are doing things wrong. Rather, the analytics are needed to help people do things better and more efficiently. This attitude must be made a part of an organization's culture. As the truck driver example illustrates, the right approach, such as leveraging gamification, can turn a negative attitude into a positive outcome.

Let's face it. If a business has been successful, then its people are probably making good decisions far more often than not. Operational analytics handle the exceptions, where what appears to be the right decision may not be correct. If operational analytics can help an organization become incrementally more effective across all employees, all business units, and all products, that will translate into a lot of money.

Redirect employees to consider the fact that as operational analytics processes make some decisions for them, it frees up time to focus on other decisions and activities that are not as easy to automate. Operational analytics can free employees to worry about bigger and more thought-intensive decisions rather than spending time on mundane decisions. This can make jobs less tedious while speeding up many decisions drastically through automated operational processes.

## Provide Help, Not Accusations

Employees will get upset if analytics are used as a stick to show where they go wrong. Don't focus on what employees are doing wrong but on how operational analytics will help them be more successful in achieving their goals.

Let's explore a few examples of pushback being overcome by analytics. The CEO of a regional hospital chain spoke at a private event that I also took part in. He told the story of how his team analyzed the factors that led to an increased chance of a newborn baby being sent to the neonatal intensive care unit (NICU). Being sent to the NICU is not only very expensive, but it means that a baby is at risk. The analysis found that a correlation existed between NICU admission and voluntary labor inducement before a specific week of pregnancy. Voluntary induced labor results from any number of reasons, from discomfort to specific calendar dates, but is voluntary because there is no urgent medical reason to do it. An increased NICU risk was present even when labor was induced at a point in the pregnancy that it was considered safe.

The doctors at the hospital all claimed to agree that inducing labor early had risks and insisted they rarely did it on a voluntary basis. While the doctors felt it was a nonissue, the analytics team was able to produce data that demonstrated early inducement was happening more than the doctors thought and also the link to NICU admission. Several doctors were actually ordering voluntary inducement fairly frequently, and those doctors were surprised at their own data. Doctors see many patients, and although it was true that a low percentage of patients were voluntarily induced, across the year it added up to a substantial number.

Once doctors were made aware of the issue, they changed their behavior, and the hospital was able to lower the percentage of early inducements. This, in turn, led to a lower rate of NICU admission and newborn health issues. Using analytics and data to push back against resistance led to success all around. Luckily, the doctors didn't doubt the analysis itself in this case as much as they doubted that they were guilty of the practice that the analysis found to be risky. That made it fairly easy to overcome their resistance with factual data based on the analysis results.

A long-haul trucking company confidentially told me that it is aiming for a competitive advantage by using telematics data from company trucks to predict which drivers have driving habits most associated with accidents. Accident risk is assessed by studying factors such as a pattern of aggressive acceleration or sudden braking, among others. The company reached out to drivers exhibiting risky patterns and provided coaching on how they might change one or more driving habits to increase safety and productivity.

The company didn't create the analysis to point fingers and tell drivers that they were driving in a dangerous manner. The findings were positioned as helpful suggestions. When the company identified that a driver had behavior associated with more accidents, driver safety was one focal point of the conversation that followed. However, the company also stressed how each driver is paid more when loads are delivered on time and in good condition. By avoiding accidents, drivers achieve a better delivery record. By stressing how the analysis findings could impact driver income, the company was able to overcome resistance and get drivers to change behavior for the better. After all, most people are quite receptive to advice that increases pay.

A major cause of resistance is a feeling of the loss of control. Giving up control of decisions that we currently make every day to algorithms is not a comfortable feeling. A different view, however, can make this loss of control feel less uncomfortable. People shouldn't consider using operational analytics to mean giving up authority but rather as delegating decision-making authority to a trusted algorithm. That's not much different from the regular practice of delegating decisions to other trusted people. Once the framework is in place to allow effective analytics processes to be built, tested, and deployed, trust in the algorithms will grow as they are proven to work. Just as people gain trust in those who make good use of a delegated authority, so too can people gain trust in algorithms.

> ### Delegation Is Not a Loss of Control
>
> Operational analytics should be positioned as a delegation of authority, not a loss of authority. People are comfortable delegating decisions to other people whom they trust. Delegating decisions to a trusted algorithm isn't much different.

## Implementing Effective Policies

The policies that an organization puts in place are a reflection of its culture and of what it values. Having the wrong policies in place can stifle the ability to create and leverage operational analytics. In many cases, slight shifts in mind-set and policy can yield tremendous benefit. Let's look at a few examples.

### Small Shifts in Mind-set Can Yield Big Results

A massive investment in new tools and technology is not usually required to enable operational analytics. Using what is already in place in a slightly different fashion often can do the job. One of my favorite examples of small changes having a huge impact is from the yogurt industry. The story has strongly resonated with many clients. Stick with me through the background. By the end of the story, it will be clear how it ties to operational analytics.

Until about two years ago, there was a frozen yogurt shop approximately a mile from my house. The shop was a classic frozen yogurt shop with a choice of flavors in machines behind a counter. If I requested a medium vanilla, the server would measure out a medium cup of vanilla and then ask if I'd like any toppings. On top of the approximately $3.50 charge for the yogurt, a variety of toppings were available for $0.89 each. At a cost of $0.89 in addition to the $3.50 base price, I never purchased more than one topping.

I thought it was outrageous to pay $0.89 for a spoonful of sprinkles so as a personal protest I often bought no toppings at all. As a result, I wouldn't have a very good yogurt experience, and I didn't visit the shop very often.

Then an interesting thing happened. A little over two years ago, within a six-month period, three new yogurt shops opened within a quarter mile of the initial yogurt shop. Within six months, the original yogurt shop was out of business. Today, all three of the new shops are still in business. There is apparently a lot more demand for yogurt in my area than it appeared, but the original shop was unable to tap the demand. What happened?

The new yogurt shops each have a different business model, which I'll call the modern model. The shops have an entire wall of yogurt machines with different flavors open to the public. Customers can mix and match any amount of yogurt of any flavor mix desired. The shops also have huge topping bars with everything from fruit to sauces to gummy bears to mochi balls from Japan. Customers can add any mix and amount of toppings desired. At the end, the cup is weighed, and customers are charged based on the weight of the cup.

The difference between the two business models is relatively minor and is summarized in Table 9.1. In the classic model, a server prepares the yogurt and charges by the cup and number of toppings. In the modern model, customers prepare their own yogurt and pay by weight. The business models may be almost identical, but at the new shops I always end up with a massive amount of yogurt covered with a huge pile of toppings because I'm so excited to try all the different options. After I weigh my cup, I invariably pay $6.50 or $7.00. Not only do I pay more at a modern shop than I did at the classic shop, but I love the experience, and I can't wait to go back because I get just what I want. I even ask my kids to come with me now instead of the other way around.

## IT Must Begin to Operate Like a Modern Yogurt Shop

A simple change in the way frozen yogurt is served and how customers pay for it has led to a huge boom in the frozen yogurt business. The overall cost model is similar to that of classic yogurt shops, but revenue is higher and customers are happier. Organizations can make similarly minor changes to how information technology (IT) allows data to be accessed and analyzed to enable a boom in analytics.

Table 9.1    Classic versus Modern Yogurt Business Model

| Classic Shop | Modern Shop |
|---|---|
| Server prepares the yogurt | Customer prepares the yogurt |
| Charge is by the cup and number of toppings | Charge is by weight |
| Limited ability to experiment | Unlimited ability to experiment |

Let's examine the business models of the two types of yogurt shops in more detail because it is surprising how similar they are. When investors want to open a yogurt shop, they can choose whether to follow the classic or the modern model. The difference in costs to open either model is trivial. In fact, the modern model is more expensive because it requires additional yogurt machines and a larger number of toppings. Outside of that, there is the same cost for the storefront, the same cost for a cashier, the same cost for a point of sale system, the same heating and cooling bill, and so on. The two models have virtually identical costs, yet the modern model entices customers to pay more per visit and make more visits while also having higher satisfaction. That is a combination that is hard to beat.

Simply changing two small policies totally changed the yogurt business. Instead of a server preparing a customer's cup and the customer paying by the cup and number of toppings, customers prepare their own cups and pay by weight. Those small changes fundamentally shifted the entire experience and the revenue stream. So how does this tie to IT and analytics?

The vast majority of IT organizations follow the classic yogurt shop model. The data is the yogurt. When users need data, IT metes the data to them in preset ways and keeps them distanced from the data. Next, consider the toppings to be like tools. In theory, users can have as many tools as they want to analyze data. In practice, getting a new tool approved by IT typically is so expensive and difficult that users settle for one or two tools. They are never quite happy and always feel they aren't getting their money's worth, just how I felt when visiting the classic yogurt shop.

By shifting how the underlying infrastructure and technologies surrounding a company's data are utilized, it's possible to give people direct access to the data. Just as it is easy to allow access to yogurt machines, so it is easy to allow access to data. Let users mix and match data and create any analysis they want. Let them use any tools they want. Before a discovery is put into production, IT can make sure that the process is hardened as outlined in Chapter 6. It may also be necessary to use only approved tools for production. However, letting users experiment with different tools during the discovery process does no harm and can greatly speed the development of new analytics.

Remember, three modern yogurt shops are successful in my neighborhood, where one classic shop barely survived. Had you asked me if I would have paid more for yogurt, I would have said no. However, once I understood and experienced the alternative, I was happy to pay more since I received more value. Similarly, businesspeople who leverage a more open analytics environment will be happy to pay more for IT support once they find they are getting extra value and experience increased freedom. Some small shifts in policy and culture can open the door for a much healthier and more successful relationship between IT and the business.

### Shifting IT From Serving to Enabling

A blog I wrote for *Harvard Business Review* outlined how IT must make a shift like the modern yogurt shops.[3] IT must enable users to serve themselves data instead of IT serving users the data and getting in the middle of it. Most important, IT must change how users access and pay for data and processing capacity.

Shifting to the modern model doesn't mean ripping out and replacing all the infrastructure and technology that is in place. What is required is deploying the existing resources differently and allowing users more freedom. A classic yogurt shop can become a modern shop simply by moving the store's fixtures around. The concepts of an analytics sandbox and a discovery platform help IT similarly reconfigure the corporate data environment.

When users are given the freedom to make some errors, they also have the freedom to make new discoveries. It's always a trade-off. Over time, children are allowed to explore more on their own and have more freedom. Parents don't try to prevent children from ever making bad decisions. If children are never allowed to make bad decisions, they will become adults totally unprepared for the real world.

## Provide Choice, Not Limits

Give users the freedom to explore data and experiment with new analytics. Some efforts won't turn out well, but many will. Shift your culture to value freedom of use over control of data, and see how positively users respond.

I was once asked a good question about the yogurt shop example. What if someone combines a couple of flavors and it tastes horrible? Put another way, what if users combine data in a way that doesn't work at all? My answer is that the people involved aren't going to hold the yogurt shop or IT responsible in those cases. The people involved know that they chose the mix that turned out poorly. On the upside, they learned that something doesn't work, and they will not make that mistake again. The most important consideration is that if the opportunity for people to create a bad mix of flavors or data is taken away, the opportunity to find an amazing combination that everybody loves is also taken away. Every now and then a flavor mix that warrants being a standard addition to the wall of choices is found.

The fact is, people can make really bad decisions already without using data or analytics. An organization can't be paralyzed by the fear that people might do something wrong if they are given more access to data and more freedom to analyze it (within the bounds of their skills and experience, of course). Users can do something wrong regardless of their level of access to data. It is uncomfortable for many IT organizations to consider this kind of shift. However, small changes in the way a company thinks about data and analytics can yield large dividends.

### Ensure Proper Planning

In Chapter 7, we discussed the need to avoid shortcuts when framing and planning an analysis. Although framing and planning are not the hardest activities in the world, they do take time and effort, and it is easy to take shortcuts or skip the steps entirely. Luckily, all of the common analytics process flows include these steps. Succeeding with operational analytics requires organizations to establish a culture where proper planning and problem framing is not only encouraged but expected. Taking a little bit longer up front to ensure that everything is planned correctly will save time in the long run.

Starting a day later on a month-long project so it can be thought through more thoroughly is preferable to risking the loss of days or weeks later in the process when an issue that hasn't been thought through causes a major problem. I'm not talking about adding months of bureaucracy and red tape. A 100-page detailed project plan that's been approved by 20 people is not needed. What is needed is to make sure that the right people have discussed what analytics are needed, why they are needed, and what the proposed plan of attack will be.

The important thing is to take the time, even when under pressure, to sit back, take a breath, and think things through. If everyone gets in the habit of doing this, it will be much easier to keep it going. Many organizations have a culture where it is okay during a crisis to respond by kicking off work streams as fast as possible to get people busy doing something. If everyone is busy doing something, it must be a good thing, right? That approach places arbitrary action and the appearance of progress over actually ensuring that the results required are obtained.

## Facilitating Success

Although most day-to-day activities rely on individuals, an organization can put in place policies and expectations that facilitate success. In this section, we discuss three specific ways to increase the probability that an organization will succeed in getting operational analytics deployed and adding value.

### Search for Unexpected Value

Organizations should always be on the lookout for ways to find unexpected value in data and new ways to apply analytics. In Chapter 11 of *Taming the Big Data Tidal Wave*, I discussed how one innovation often leads to another that was completely unanticipated at the time of the first innovation but that was dependent on the first. As organizations start using data in more ways and building more analytics processes, they can discover new opportunities that weren't even on the radar when work began. Without pushing the envelope to go after the first idea, it isn't possible to identify the next. The subsequent, unexpected opportunities can be more valuable than the original.

Let's examine a terrific example of this principle from the big data and analytics space. I had a very interesting discussion with

Anthony Goldbloom, the CEO of Kaggle.[4] Kaggle began as a contest site that let organizations provide a data set and a problem and allowed anyone to try and solve the problem. Whoever built the best model (predicting disease as an example) would win the contest and perhaps some money as well. Over time, Kaggle ran many contests and developed a database of over 100,000 contestants. These contestants all have strong analytics backgrounds and interests, as evidenced by the fact that they chose to enter the contests.

Kaggle originally built its contestant database to enable the administration of its contests. Knowing who was participating and where to find them was necessary to distribute the prizes. Over time, Kaggle realized that it had a database not only of basic demographics about analytics professionals but also a lot about contestants' specialties, based on the kinds of contests they enter. The performance of contestants in the contests also provides a very good indication of how skilled each professional is. Recognizing the unique value of the data that Kaggle had captured was an important insight.

### One Analysis Leads to Another

You never know what's around a corner until you walk over and take a look. Similarly, additional applications of data and analytics often aren't visible until after the initial work is complete. Be on the lookout for unexpected value that was never intended or anticipated within your data.

After realizing the value in the database that had evolved, Kaggle has begun to morph itself into a services provider. Kaggle owns a database of over 100,000 analytics professionals at a time when such people are desperately needed in the marketplace. Kaggle realized that it possibly had access to more analytics talent than anyone else in the world and that the information could be monetized. However, without starting the contests, the database would never have been created. It took the first innovative idea to enable the second. In this case, the second idea of matching professionals with employment opportunities could be far more valuable in the long run.

Next, consider again Chapter 1's discussion of the Nike FuelBand and how that product challenges Nike's traditional business model. Over time we can expect personal tracking devices to collect a lot more information than they do today. Pulse rate, blood oxygen level, temperature, and a myriad of other metrics can be collected. This will yield a massive amount of data on users' health and day-to-day body cycles, which can be immensely powerful from a medical perspective. The data initially is intended to enable users to track their daily activities, but it could end up having value for many unanticipated medical purposes (with privacy protected, of course).

Also consider the example of heavy equipment, such as a tractor, using sensors to monitor everything about how it is operating. Say a tractor manufacturer can provide analytics back to a farmer suggesting a specific change in protocol that will increase crop yield. Such guidance will be very valuable to the farmer and can increase product loyalty and cement the customer relationship. However, until a manufacturer starts to collect sensor data for the initial purpose of understanding of how the equipment is operating, the additional analytics attempting to drive better crop yields won't be possible.

### Find the Early Adopters and Influencers

The cultural aspects of succeeding with operational analytics can be harder than the technical aspects. Building an analytics process is only half the battle. As we discussed in Chapter 8, it is also necessary to get people to accept the analytics and make use of them. Current business processes and behaviors must change in response to the analytics. If people think the freedom they have to do their job is threatened, it's even harder to bring them along. One tactic to consider is to identify and leverage early adopters who are also influencers.

Instead of a full rollout of a new process, begin with a limited rollout. Do this not just because it is a safe way to test a new analytics process but to help with cultural issues. Within any organization, it is possible to identify the people who are open to change and are willing to try new ways of doing things. The same people often have influence within the organization. Enlist such people to be the test pilots for a new analytics process and the changes it demands. Once the early adopters make it work, they can help to bring their colleagues along.

Within one multinational corporation I worked with, each country has its own sales organization. As might be expected, different countries have vastly different levels of maturity and success using analytics. The company wanted to roll out a new analytics process to support the sales teams, and my clients knew from experience to expect substantial pushback. To minimize pushback, my clients identified a couple of country managers who were more sophisticated and willing to try new things and recruited them to be in the test group. The limited rollout was a success, and the country managers in the test group were fully supportive of the new analytics process.

---

### Leverage Your Leaders

To gain support for a new analytics process, test it with a group of early adopters who are willing to take the lead when it comes to trying new things. If the early adopters have success, they can then influence those who are more resistant by sharing their stories.

---

My clients next did something very powerful. Once each year, as part of the yearly planning cycle, leaders from around the world get together to discuss what worked and what didn't work in the prior year. At the next annual meeting, the early adopters talked about the success they had with the new analytics process. Everyone heard peers they respected stand up, defend the analytics, and validate that the analytics worked in practice, not just in theory. The political influence of the test group was put to full use. As a result, my clients were able to get many other country managers behind the global rollout.

People are always willing to follow a leader who's had success because they want to mimic that success. Getting operational analytics implemented and, more important, adopted can be easier by starting with a targeted pilot like the one just discussed. This is because key influencers can be leveraged to get other participants behind the new process when it is their turn to get started.

### Prepare a Marketing Campaign

As discussed in Chapter 8, it is necessary to run a marketing and public relations campaign to garner support for a new analytics process. The need for and value of the analytics must be socialized with a range of stakeholders. The case must be made that it is safe to implement the operational analytics and that the analytics will improve results.

The culture within an organization must be one where "fluffy," nonanalytics activity like the marketing process is valued and given priority. Part of an analytics leader's job is to make sure that his or her organization understands the need to develop a marketing plan as part of its role. The process includes answering questions such as:

- Who needs to be influenced within the organization?
- What type of positioning will help to convince them?
- What facts are available to best persuade each person?
- Who should deliver the message to each stakeholder?
- What objections can be anticipated, and how can they be overcome?

A substantial effort may be necessary to get all stakeholders on board, so focusing on the marketing part of an analytics team's culture is important. Also important is instilling in the culture of the broader organization the idea that business leaders must be willing to listen to suggestions of the analytics team and take time to assess the suggestions.

One of my all-time favorite examples of marketing and socializing an analytics approach focuses on how telecommunications companies completely reversed the decisions they were making when customers asked to close their accounts.[5] In the early 2000s, telecommunications companies were excited about the ability to compute accurate profitability at an account level. The carriers could take into account whether a customer made use of high-rent or low-rent cell towers, for example. When an unprofitable customer called to close an account, the carrier often would do nothing to stop them and might even encourage the customer to go look at the competition. The carriers were proud of themselves for "firing" unprofitable customers, and it was the right decision with the data available.

Over time, however, carriers discovered that an account's total influence was more important than its direct profitability. Carriers started to examine the network of individuals each account communicated with. An unprofitable account may interact with very profitable customers who are connected to a lot of other very profitable customers. Social network analysis showed that once one person from a circle closes an account and churns, the probability of others in the circle churning goes up. Once multiple members of a circle churn, the risk that others will also churn goes up dramatically.

Today, most carriers look at the total value that an account influences. When a customer with an unprofitable account calls to cancel and the customer is connected to a very profitable circle, the carrier may purposely lose even more money on the account in order to protect the circle. The goal has shifted from individual account profitability to network profitability.

Let's think about that example in the context of this chapter. Imagine being the first person at the first telecom company to suggest the idea of using social network analysis not only to change but literally to reverse decisions about how to handle customer requests to close an account. Imagine being the first person to suggest purposely losing even more money on an already unprofitable account. There is no way that the first conversation about the idea ended with a decision to implement it right away. Others most likely looked at the analytics professional who suggested the idea like he or she was crazy before dismissing it.

## It's All about Marketing

People won't buy in to a novel idea that challenges the status quo without some convincing. Be prepared to spend a significant amount of time and effort socializing a new idea and helping stakeholders become comfortable with it. Without this effort, the potential of many analytics will not be achieved because the analytics will not be deployed and adopted.

The person who came up with the idea had to keep pushing, showing the evidence, and explaining the business case before someone was finally convinced to do a test. The initial test worked well, and over time the process was rolled out broadly at that carrier. The same pattern of resistance likely was repeated at several carriers that adopted the concept early. Once the analytics were proven successful by the initial carriers and the results went public, other carriers were willing to jump on board quickly. Today, leveraging social network analysis to value an account is widely accepted as a logical business practice, but that wasn't always true. Without an analytics professional willing to execute an extended marketing campaign to get attention for a then-crazy idea, it wouldn't be accepted at all.

Another example involves social media data. It is easy to forget that, as of 2014, most social media platforms aren't even a decade old. Organizations have long been comfortable with scientifically designed surveys and very tightly recruited focus groups because those activities provide solid, controlled feedback on marketing initiatives, products, and brand image.

Imagine being the first person to suggest using social media data to augment surveys and focus groups and to attempt to get a feel for what people are saying about a company. Social media comments are from random people from all over the world, and there is usually no way to know who they are, what their demographic profiles look like, or even whether they have any relevance to a company. Even though a social media sample can be horribly biased, is it possible to identify trends that are important out of social media data?

Once again, people were surely skeptical about the prospects of such an idea working. However, over time, it has been shown that there are situations where the noisy, uncontrolled data from social media can add value. The pioneers in this type of analysis certainly had to undertake a lengthy marketing campaign to garner support for the idea. Every analytics organization needs to commit to doing the same when it uncovers new analytics processes that can have a big impact.

## Enabling and Handling the Right Failures

Not every operational analytics process will work as well as expected. For every needle in the haystack that is found, several searches will prove fruitless. Pushing the envelope to uncover new uses of data and new ways of applying analytics to a business requires taking some risk. Many analytics initiatives, especially during the discovery process, won't yield the desired results. While failure can be expected, the key is to manage the rate of failure and establish a culture that both expects and knows how to handle failure. Let's look at how to do that.

### No Idea Is Bad . . . If It Can Be Tested

There is a popular saying that there are no bad ideas. In reality, there are bad ideas, and we have to try to avoid them. Luckily, analytics make it much easier to validate whether an idea is good or bad. No matter how crazy an idea seems, as long as it can be tested then an organization should test it. Perhaps the idea will work and perhaps it won't, but objective facts based on analytics will provide the answer.

In many cases, tests can be designed and executed quickly and cheaply in today's world. Web-based businesses have taken this to the extreme with the tight embrace of what's known as a test-and-learn environment. On a modern e-commerce site today, there can be dozens, if not hundreds or thousands, of new ideas being tested at any point in time. These tests can range from major experiments, like testing a complete new look for a site, to very small experiments, like changing the font of a product description. The sites randomly allocate the test content and standard content to site visitors, and analytics then measure how the new content changes behavior. Such experimentation should be embraced as part of any corporate culture, not just e-commerce companies.

## Test, Test, Test!

The concepts of testing and experimental design are widely accepted and have been exhaustively proven. With the tools available today, it is easier than ever to utilize these methods. Many modern operational systems make it easy to test new analytics logic. There is no excuse not to do it.

Earlier we discussed the need to get a basic analytics process in place before scaling it to an operational level. Before an analytics production line is turned on, it is necessary to run small-scale tests on subsets of decisions. This will validate how the analytics process will work when it's fully operational. With physical assembly lines, such as those that create consumer electronics, making changes can be quite expensive because a lot of very sensitive and heavy equipment has to be adjusted carefully. With operational analytics, this usually isn't true. Simply inserting and testing new analytics logic within operational systems are all that is required. Changing lines of code for a virtual production line is far easier than rearranging heavy machinery for a physical production line. The ease of testing new logic takes away many of the excuses that can be made for not testing more ideas.

One implication of the prior points is that the funding model for analytics projects will need to change when pursuing discovery. Instead of funding each project based upon a solid ROI estimate for each individual project, projects must be managed as a portfolio. In other words, at the end of the year, the resources focused on discovery must demonstrate that the year's efforts have produced a good return in aggregate. It doesn't matter how many failures were in the portfolio, it only matters that enough successes exist to make up for the failures.

This requires a different approach to budgeting but can have a big impact on productivity. The idea is to have a list of discovery projects to start with. The team must be confident that some of the ideas will work, but just won't be sure which ones will work. Just as a batter in baseball never commits to any given at-bat resulting in a hit, so discovery efforts can't be individually guaranteed. Rather, the goal is to have a good average at the end of the year. This is also the way venture capital works. Even the best venture capitalists lose 100 percent of their investments most of the time. It is the winners in the portfolio that make that risk worth it.

### Don't Take Failure Personally

An organization must accept some failures if it is to truly embrace uncovering and deploying innovative operational analytics processes. Failure is not evil, and failing quickly can be a good thing. However, failing slowly and without making use of analytics is a very bad path to take. Avoiding major failures is easy if an organization plays it totally safe; but playing it totally safe won't move the business ahead either. More likely, the organization will be left behind by competition that has figured out how to use analytics to innovate (and fail) quickly.

Saying that failure is acceptable doesn't mean that people don't have accountability, and it doesn't mean that an organization literally tries to fail. Saying that failure is acceptable means that it has been recognized that attempting truly new and innovative analytics won't yield a 100 percent success rate. In baseball, for example, getting a hit even 30 percent of the time is considered a huge success. As long as the focus is on learning what caused an analytics process to fail and as long as systems enable rapid testing of an idea, the impact of the inevitable failures will be minimized. As a bonus, what is learned from a failure can positively impact future efforts because the factors leading to the failure can be avoided.

An organization must also have a culture that encourages people not to take the results of analytics personally. It is entirely possible for an analysis to prove that an idea you thought was awesome doesn't work at all. That doesn't make you an idiot, and it doesn't mean you don't know what you're doing. The analytics are just making clear that you should look for another idea. Making people comfortable openly suggesting ideas that may not work takes effort. In many organizations, people only suggest ideas that they are highly confident will work because they are afraid they will be perceived negatively if they are associated with a failed idea. An organization's culture has to say this isn't so. It is better to encourage people to take a risk and bring ideas to the table than to allow the organization to safely stagnate.

### Don't Accept Failure through Ignorance

A final cultural point tied to dealing with failure is getting people focused on understanding how to correctly use any analytics being generated. The misinterpretation and misapplication of results can never be acceptable. There is an old saying that a little information is a dangerous thing. A little knowledge of how to use the results of an analytics process is a dangerous thing too.

One of my more popular blog entries discussed a disturbing example of the dangers of using analytics without proper understanding or training.[6] A high school near my home decided to use plagiarism software to assess students' term papers. An advanced placement class full of straight-A students with no history of trouble was flagged for cheating by the software and all students were given no credit for the assignment, which destroyed their grades in the class. The details provided to me made me certain that the software was being used inappropriately. One reason was that any three-word phrases matching between two papers counted as a red flag. In other words, if two students wrote "The author suggests . . .," their papers would each get one red flag. A lot of innocent matches can be expected with criteria this loose. If a paper received enough flags, the author was considered a plagiarist. The teachers, who were inexperienced with this type of analysis, stood by the results of the "expert" software, even when faced with some clearly illogical and unfair flags. It really hurt the students' reputations, their grades in the class, and potentially their ability to get into their colleges of choice.

Just like any other tool, analytics can be powerful and helpful when used in the correct way, but analytics can also do major damage when applied by those who don't understand how to use results correctly. In business, we've all seen cases where statistics or figures are shown to an executive without full context and without explanation of important caveats. After seeing the data without context, the executive orders action that may not be productive or required. It is imperative to ensure that people within an organization are prepared to use analysis correctly in the context of their jobs. As previously discussed, front-line employees don't have to understand how all the math works. Rather, they need to know exactly how to respond to the analysis results they are provided.

### Analytics Used Incorrectly Can Be Worse than No Analytics at All

Make sure that each person in your organization is properly trained to make use of the level of analytics required for his or her job. Using tools, methodologies, or results incorrectly can do more harm than good.

Let's review a few practices that should be standard when producing and using analytics. An organization's culture must require that these standards are followed.

- Someone must fully understand each analysis being done, its strengths, and its weaknesses. Everyone doesn't have to understand the gory details, but somebody must.
- The settings and options utilized in a process must be chosen for good reason. Don't just assume default settings are appropriate in every case.
- When unexpected results are found, investigate further and ask critical questions before jumping to conclusions. No algorithm or software package is omniscient. Unusual results can provide important insights into an analytics process and the data that underlies it.
- When provided with additional facts or data that contradict an initial conclusion, consider them seriously. The goal should be finding the right answer, not defending the initial conclusion.
- Allow people to execute and leverage only the types of analysis they are prepared to execute and leverage correctly. People can get in over their heads and not even realize it.

While the teachers in the plagiarism example should be applauded for their desire to make use of analytics, they went amiss when they proceeded without understanding what they were getting into. They didn't know how to set up the plagiarism algorithms correctly or how to interpret the results. The example illustrates how it is possible to do more harm than good by using analytics out of context or applying analytics beyond the intended scope. Employees must have the training and support needed to use analytics correctly. Failure through ignorance is never acceptable.

## Wrap-Up

The most important lessons to take away from this chapter are:

- Don't get stuck blindly making assumptions like a flea stuck in a jar. Challenge assumptions regularly to ensure that things haven't changed.
- Support for analytics and analytics professionals must exist from the CEO down. Nobody wants to work in an environment where they aren't appreciated for the work they do.
- When people feel threatened and are resistant to operational analytics, leverage their desire to play and win games by making a game where winning is achieved by using the new analytics process effectively.
- Adjustments suggested by analytics aren't accusations of previous improper decision making. Help employees understand how using analytics will enable them to better meet their own goals.
- Operational analytics lead to delegation of authority, not loss of authority. Delegating decisions to a trusted algorithm isn't much different from delegating decisions to trusted people.
- Small changes can transform an organization's analytics productivity. The success of modern yogurt shops results from small but transformational policy changes. Similarly, IT must move from a serving mode to an enabling mode.
- Without the freedom to try some analytics processes that don't work, the freedom won't exist to find those that do. Don't focus on preventing bad ideas; instead, focus on facilitating good ideas.
- Encourage people to be on the lookout for new, unexpected ways to leverage existing data and analytics processes.
- Test a new analytics process with a group of early adopters who are also key influencers. Once the early adopters succeed, they can influence others by sharing their stories of success.

- People need to be convinced to support an idea that challenges the status quo. Prepare to spend significant time socializing a new idea for analytics and helping the organization become comfortable with it.
- With the low cost and effort typically required for testing new analytics processes, it is wise to consider testing even seemingly crazy ideas. As long as an idea can be tested, give it a try.
- Using analytics incorrectly can do more harm than good. All employees must be trained to the level required for their individual jobs.

## Notes

1. For one example, see http://youtu.be/v-Dn2KEjPuc. Or search for "fleas in a jar."
2. For an overview of the concept of gamification, see http://gamification.org/wiki/Gamification.
3. See Bill Franks, "Don't Just Serve—Enable: A New Model for IT Organizations," *Harvard Business Review*, August 28, 2013, at http://blogs.hbr.org/2013/08/dont-just-serveenable-a-new-mo/.
4. See Big Data Republic, "Finding Unexpected Value in Data," July 31, 2013.
5. Also discussed in Bill Franks, *Taming the Big Data Tidal Wave* (Hoboken, NJ: John Wiley & Sons, 2012).
6. See my blog for the International Institute for Analytics, "Analytics Gone Wrong: Dire Consequences for Kids," November 9, 2011, at http://iianalytics.com/2011/11/the-dire-consequences-of-analytics-gone-wrong-ruining-kids%E2%80%99-futures/.

# Join the Revolution!

Yes, the revolution has begun! By now you should understand the importance of the industrial revolution of analytics, and I hope you are ready to join the revolution yourself. Analytics is too important to be relegated to a manual, artisanal process. For an organization to get the full benefits of what is possible with analytics and data, it is time to evolve to operational analytics. Analytics processes are being transformed by industry leaders into embedded, automated, prescriptive, integrated components of both operational systems and the business processes supported by those systems.

This book has covered a lot of ground. Let's summarize one last time some of the most important themes and some recommended actions that you can take to help you and your organization join the revolution:

- Always remember the difference between embedded, automated, prescriptive operational analytics and the operational application of traditional batch analytics. Both add value, but they are not the same.
- Operational analytics requires a strong foundation. Don't expect to jump into operational analytics without having robust analytics capabilities already in place.
- Analytics are now the basis for many purchase decisions, and the demand for analytics is blurring industry lines. Look for opportunities to differentiate and transform your organization's business model with operational analytics.

- The "differentness" of big data can be more challenging than its "bigness," and analyzing big data requires scale in multiple dimensions. However, the power of the new information big data provides is what makes the effort to tame it worthwhile. Embrace big data today.
- Many examples of operational analytics today involve simple algorithms or rules, but that will change. Don't hesitate to start with simple approaches and then make them more sophisticated over time.
- Take the process of building a business case for operational analytics seriously. Be sure to account for all costs, including labor, over time.
- The technology landscape is complex today, and you can expect to have several components within a unified analytic environment capable of supporting operational analytics. The goal is to stop users from worrying about where data is stored and processed.
- The Internet of Things will play a large role in the future of operational analytics. Educate yourself on the IOT now, and start planning for how to incorporate it into your organization's plans.
- Ensure that your organization understands and accounts for the different requirements of a discovery process and an implementation process. Discovery is stifled if attempted under production constraints.
- Don't shortchange governance. An automated analytics process must be carefully monitored. A physical assembly line has problems over time, and so will an operational analytics process. Proper governance keeps errors rare and their impact small enough to be a cost of doing business.
- Privacy is a major issue. Make sure any analytics that your organization implements are legal, ethical, and acceptable to the public. Also develop much more flexible and detailed privacy policies and settings.
- The ability to execute and combine multiple analytics disciplines is required for success. Allow different disciplines to enhance one another.
- Be prepared to trade some analytics power to achieve the operational scale required. Focus on optimizing a process's

impact across all decisions instead of optimizing each individual decision.
- Hiring the right people is paramount. Put a chief analytics officer in charge of an analytics organization with a hybrid structure. Then focus the team on being consultants, mentors, and coaches.
- Support is needed from the CEO down to overcome cultural resistance to change. Focus on the benefits of operational analytics for each stakeholder, and position the analytics as a delegation of authority, not a loss of authority.

With the continuous growth of processing power, increasingly sophisticated algorithms, and an ever larger pool of data, the opportunities for analytics are expanding every day. While operational analytics have not been a large component of the portfolios of most organizations in the past, this is changing rapidly. Now is the time for your organization to enter the world of operational analytics.

If the analytics within your organization are still primarily manual, one-off, artisanal processes, it will be left behind. Just as the Industrial Revolution transformed the manufacturing industry, so operational analytics will transform how analytics are created, deployed, and utilized. The industrial revolution of analytics is already under way. Are you ready to be a part of it?

# About the Author

**Bill Franks** is the chief analytics officer for Teradata, where he provides insight on trends in the analytics and big data space and helps clients understand how Teradata and its analytic partners can support their efforts. Franks also helps determine Teradata's strategies in the areas of analytics and big data. His focus is on translating complex analytics into terms business users can understand and working with organizations to implement their analytics effectively. His work has spanned many industries for companies ranging in size from Fortune 100 companies to small nonprofits.

Franks is the author of the book *Taming the Big Data Tidal Wave* (John Wiley & Sons, 2012). In the book, he applies his two decades of experience working with clients on large-scale analytics initiatives to outline what it takes to succeed in today's world of big data and analytics. The book made Tom Peter's 2014 list of "Must Read" books and also the Top 10 Most Influential Translated Technology Books list from CSDN in China.

Franks is a faculty member of the International Institute for Analytics, founded by leading analytics expert Tom Davenport, and an active speaker who has presented or keynoted at dozens of events in recent years. His blog, *Analytics Matters*, addresses the transformation required to make analytics a core component of business decisions.

Franks earned a bachelor's degree in applied statistics from Virginia Tech and a master's degree in applied statistics from North Carolina State University. More information is available at http://www.bill-franks.com.

# Index